The Gentleviewer's Obsessive Guide to

Second, far more obsessive edition

Kathleen Mattson

The Gentleviewer's Guide to Buffy the Vampire Slayer, Second Edition
ISBN: 978-0-9851600-1-2

Mattson, Kathleen 1964-
      The Gentleviewer's Guide to Buffy the Vampire Slayer, Second Edition
Drama, Broadcast, Television
791.455 — dc19

Paisley Publications
Beaverton, Oregon, USA
www.paisleypubs.com

Images licensed by Deposit Photos at www.depositphotos.com, original image contributors: Old paper by loriklaszlo; Motif by Leonardi; and Drops by Elena Akinina.

Contents

Contents

Contents

Contents

Introduction

Joss Whedon has created some of the most crisply-written and entertaining programs ever to grace our televisions. Not only *Buffy the Vampire Slayer*, but also the remarkable *Firefly* and *Dollhouse*.

To the casual observer, *Buffy's* world is peopled by teenagers, pointy-toothed vampires, and television's best caricature of an English librarian. But when you delve deeper, you see a world where kids grow up fast, where young women have the power to lead, and where the average person can be the biggest hero in the room.

The key that makes *Buffy* delightful to an audience of all ages is the deep care taken to write the characters in a believable way, and the unique language that seems to have leaked into the real world. Beyond the enduring *Buffy*-speak, the writers of the show liberally peppered their characters' dialog with the wittiest cultural references on television. Much of it is geek-esque, with frequent mentions of science fiction classics. But with references to 1980s music, Shakespeare, advertising mainstays, and more, the references in *Buffy* transcend class, stereotype, age, and clique to include everyone in a giant inside joke.

This book should provide hours of fun for Trivial Pursuit enthusiasts as well as fans of Buffy and the other residents of Sunnydale. But be warned that this book is basically comprised entirely of spoilers.

What is a pop culture reference anyway?

This guide began as a mere spreadsheet that charted the characters who appear in each episode, but it quickly grew into a compendium of the show's pop culture references and more.

Capturing the pop culture references was difficult, not just because there are so many, but because until I'd worked on this book I'd never put much thought into defining just what a pop culture reference actually is. When does something stop being *pop* and become *cultural*, and then beyond that to *historic*? A reference to John Wilkes Booth in a play would be considered a pop culture reference in 1868, but what about a mention of him in 1890, or now?

My way around this was to include references to anything that might be unfamiliar to someone from a completely different culture than ours. If you're visiting from the planet Chetziod, you've probably studied enough to get along in our world without being detected. But in all your Earth-101 studies, you might not have come across the word "Shpadoinkle," (an obvious pop culture reference), or have heard about synchronized swimming (a much less obvious one). In short, while many of these references are to the *pop culture*, some are simply to the *culture*.

I must confess that there are some references in here that aren't really cultural references at all as much as just quotes that I loved or that I imagined someone would want to be able to find in the index. Good examples of this are the "feeble banter" reference in episode 1-12, Buffy's pathetic explanation of the Reconstruction as Willow helps prepare her for a history test in episode 1-7, Oz's references to hippos, or the delightfully insane things that Drusilla says. I was tempted to note every mention of puppies, but I had to draw the line somewhere.

Many of the references include a little additional information, such as the year a book was published or when a film was released. For those items where there are multiple references, I cite the one to which the character is most likely to have been referring. For example, in season three when Buffy says: "Gotta stop a crazy from pulling a *Carrie* at the prom," it's more likely that she would refer to the 1976 film than the 1974 novel by Stephen King.

I've set up a web page where I'll post links and additional references if and when I find more. Did I miss something? Let me know at www.paisleypublications.com/btvs.

The never-ending project: About the second edition

Almost immediately after publishing the first book I found more cultural references to include and started compiling notes for the second edition.

New in this edition are the relationship arcs, additional trivia, and indication of the music played in each episode, as well as descriptions and an index of the episode cross references. As this is a book about *Buffy the Vampire Slayer*, not *Angel*, I hunted down *Angel* cross references that appear in *Buffy*, but not the other way around.

There are three different types of notes throughout the book, all denoted by the following icons in the left margin:

 Music in the Episode

 Episode Reference, or *Angel* Episode Cross Reference

 Trivia or other notes of interest

Here's an example of how this looks:

Why 'Mutant Enemy'?

"Mutant Enemy" is the name that Joss gave his first typewriter when he was fifteen years old. It comes from a line in the song "And You and I" by the band Yes. Joss had just 20 minutes to come up with and draw the logo, and he recorded the "Grr Argh" monster voice himself.

Beyond Buffy

Much has been written about the insight and genius of Joss Whedon, so I'm not going to get into that here. What I will say is that even for those who are not great fans of *Buffy the Vampire Slayer*, there are some key episodes which are simply excellent works of art—innovative television, incredible concepts, and moving storytelling. These episodes include:

- *Hush* (4-10), Written and directed by Joss Whedon

- *The Body* (5-16), Written and directed by Joss Whedon

- *Once More With Feeling*, (6-7), Written and directed by Joss Whedon

- *Normal Again* (6-17), Written by Diego Gutierrez, Directed by Rick Rosenthal

- *Selfless* (7-5), Written by Drew Goddard, Directed by David Solomon

- *Storyteller* (7-16), Written by Jane Espenson, Directed by Marita Grabiak

These are the episodes I put on when we want to watch something excellent but don't have time for a film. These are the episodes which undoubtedly are the subject of film and literature classes here and there across the country and beyond.

Come with me now...

In season seven's episode *Storyteller*, Andrew (Tucker's brother) says "Come with me now, if you will, gentleviewers. Join me on a new voyage of the mind—a little tale I like to call *Buffy, the Slayer of the Vampires*."

I extend my own invitation to you, gentleviewers, to enjoy this guide as you watch this great show.

Introduction

Character Arcs

So you finally get someone to agree to sit down and give *Buffy the Vampire Slayer* a fair chance: what episodes should you show? You could cut to your favorites, perhaps *Hush, Once More With Feeling, Selfless,* or *Storyteller*. But since these episodes rely on your knowledge of the characters in order to shine, a recent convert to the show might not get it.

Following are suggested episode-maps of the character arcs for the main characters. Each begins with a narrative of the character's story, then lists the episodes that touch on the high points.

These character arcs and the relationship arcs that follow are ridiculously condensed to tell the critical kernels of these sub-stories in as few episodes as possible. This means that while the story is impacted or touched upon in a great many more episodes, I've pared it down to the ones that matter most.

Buffy Summers   The Slayer, the Hero

Buffy moves to Sunnydale and embarks on her career fighting vampires (1-1), defeating the Master and temporarily losing her life in the process (1-11). When vampire Spike comes to town (2-3), she reveals her ability to lead. The love of her life becomes evil (2-13), and she loses everything (2-22).

Overcome with grief, Buffy runs away to Los Angeles (3-1). Returning after the summer, she gets back into a normal life of school and slaying, and Giles helps the Council test her skills (3-12). Bad-Slayer Faith accidentally kills a human, and spins out of control (3-15). Buffy saves the world yet again on graduation day (3-22).

College is a challenge (4-1), but she perseveres with the support of her friends (4-20). When the Council again tries to assert control over Buffy, she sets them straight (5-12). Buffy's world is turned upside down again when her mother dies (5-16), and she makes the ultimate sacrifice to save her sister and the world (5-22).

Willow and the gang magically bring Buffy back to life (6-1,2). The gang's secrets and personal anxieties are revealed in song (6-7), and Buffy's foreboding and darkness are expressed in her sexually violent relationship with Spike (6-9). Although the forces of the ultimate evil are seemingly insurmountable (7-11), Buffy saves the world—wiping the entire town of Sunnydale off the map (7-22).

Buffy's Character Arc: 20 Episodes

1-1	Welcome to the Hellmouth.	Buffy moves to Sunnydale after being kicked out of school in Los Angeles.
1-11	Prophecy Girl	Buffy is killed by the Master, but is revived by Xander—giving her the chance to defeat the Master at last.
2-3	School Hard	Evil vampire Spike invades Parent Night at school, while Buffy struggles to keep her mom away from Principal Snyder.
2-13	Innocence	Reeling from Angel's return to evil as seemingly triggered by their intimacy, Buffy must take on the Judge.
2-22	Becoming (Pt. 2)	Buffy loses everything.
3-1	Anne	Buffy realizes it's time to return to Sunnydale.
3-12	Helpless	Buffy faces the Watchers' Council's test on her 18th birthday.
3-15	Consequences	During the two Slayers' rebellion streak, Faith accidentally kills a human, leading to drastic consequences.
3-22	Graduation Day	Buffy unites the students of Sunnydale High to stop the Mayor's ascension.
4-1	The Freshman	Buffy is challenged by her new life as a college freshman.
4-20	The Yoko Factor	Buffy's network of friends is falling apart.
5-12	Checkpoint	Buffy stands up to the Council.
5-16	The Body	Buffy comes home to find her mother's body.
5-22	The Gift	Buffy does whatever it takes to save the world.
6-1,2	Bargaining (1, 2)	The gang brings Buffy back from death.
6-7	Once More, With Feeling	Everyone reveals their secrets in song.
6-9	Smashed	Buffy and Spike take things to the next level.
7-11	Showtime	Buffy stages a battle for the Potentials, then rescues Spike.
7-22	Chosen	The end.

Xander Harris

Xander meets Buffy (1-1) and begins to help her fight vampires. He saves Buffy's life so she can save the world (1-11). Due to a Halloween curse, he gains the knowledge and insights of a career Army man (2-6). He experiences the dangers of love spells (2-16). Surrounded by friends with mystical powers, "normal" Xander discovers his own powers (3-13), and finds confidence by seeing both sides of himself (5-3).

Xander helps the gang raise Buffy from the dead (6-1,2), then announces his engagement to his ex-demon girlfriend, Anya (6-6). The gang's secrets and personal anxieties are revealed in song (6-7), Xander leaves Anya at the altar (6-16), and he conquers Evil Willow with his love and a yellow crayon (6-22). Xander battles along with Buffy and the rest of the gang to save the world, losing an eye in battle (7-18) and wiping the entire town of Sunnydale off the map (7-22).

Xander's Character Arc: 14 Episodes

1-1	Welcome to the Hellmouth.	Xander meets Buffy on her first day of 10th grade at Sunnydale High.
1-11	Prophecy Girl	Buffy is killed by the Master, but is revived by Xander—giving her the chance to defeat the Master at last.
2-6	Halloween	The gang is transformed into their Halloween costumes, and Xander picks up military knowledge and experience.
2-16	Bewitched, Bothered, and Bewildered	Heartbroken, Xander asks Amy to cast a spell on Cordelia, but it backfires and makes everyone *except* Cordelia want him.
3-13	The Zeppo	While the gang deals with one of their biggest apocalypses yet, Xander faces his own challenges.
5-3	The Replacement	Xander watches as a duplicate seems to take over his life.
6-1,2	Bargaining (1, 2)	The gang brings Buffy back from death.
6-6	All the Way	Xander and Anya announce their engagement.
6-7	Once More, With Feeling	Everyone reveals their secrets in song.
6-16	Hell's Bells	The wedding that doesn't happen.
6-22	Grave	Xander's love for Willow saves the world.
7-18	Dirty Girls	Xander is badly wounded in a battle.
7-22	Chosen	The end.

Willow Rosenberg The Witch, The Friend

Willow meets Buffy (1-1), begins to help fight vampires, and falls for werewolf Oz (2-15). She experiments with magic (3-11) and learns to assert herself when a vampire version of herself appears (3-16). Her heart is broken when Oz leaves Sunnydale (4-6), and she delves deeper into magic (4-9). She falls in love with Tara, and makes this her choice when Oz returns to town (4-19).

Willow's magic matures as she battles Glory (5-19) and raises Buffy from the dead (6-1,2). The gang's secrets and personal anxieties are revealed in song (6-7). Willow loses Tara because of Willow's magic (6-8), and she hits rock bottom in her magic addiction (6-9,10). After they reunite, Tara is murdered (6-19). Willow gives herself completely to magic, becoming evil as she takes revenge (6-19,20,21,22). Back to normal, she fears her friends will not forgive her (7-3). Willow battles along with Buffy and the rest of the gang to save the world—wiping the town of Sunnydale off the map (7-22).

Willow's Character Arc: 20 Episodes

1-1	Welcome to the Hellmouth.	Willow meets Buffy on her first day of 10th grade at Sunnydale High.
2-15	Phases	Willow and Oz develop a relationship.
3-11	Gingerbread	When Buffy's and Willow's mothers unite to strike back against the supernatural, Willow and Buffy end up tied to stakes.
3-16	Dopplegangland	Evil Willow, brought to peaceful Sunnydale, wants to go back to her own world.
4-6	Wild at Heart	Oz leaves, breaking Willow's heart.
4-9	Something Blue	Willow tries a spell to mend her broken heart, but it instead affects her friends.
4-19	New Moon Rising	When Oz returns to town, Willow must choose between him and Tara.
5-19	Tough Love	When Glory attacks Tara, Willow uses all the magic at her disposal to get back at her.
6-1,2	Bargaining (1, 2)	Willow and the others bring Buffy back to life.
6-7	Once More, With Feeling	Everyone reveals their secrets in song.
6-8	Tabula Rasa	Willow tries a forgetting spell, and loses Tara in the process.
6-9, 10	Smashed, Wrecked	Willow has a magic addiction.
6-19 - 22	Seeing Red, Villains, Two to Go, Grave	When Tara is killed, revenge takes Willow over the edge and threatens the world.
7-3	Same Time, Same Place	Willow can't seem to find her friends.
7-22	Chosen	The end.

Rupert Giles

The Watcher, the Father

Watcher Giles meets his new Slayer, Buffy (1-1). A demon from his mysterious, wild past hunts him (2-8). Angel murders Giles' girlfriend (2-17) and tortures him before Buffy saves him (2-22). Giles shows a darker side when he threatens Snyder (3-2); and after eating candy, he and the other Sunnydale adults revert to their wild teenage ways (3-6).

As part of his Watcher responsibilities, Giles drugs Buffy into helplessness as part of a test (3-12), which ends with his dismissal from the Council. Later, his nemesis Ethan turns him into a demon (4-12). Bored, Giles buys a magic shop (5-2), and he fights by Buffy's side to save the world (5-22).

The gang's secrets and personal anxieties are revealed in song (6-7), and he returns to England. He comes back to confront Willow (6-21), and battles along with Buffy and the gang to save the world—wiping the entire town of Sunnydale off the map (7-22).

Giles' Character Arc: 13 Episodes

1-1	Welcome to the Hellmouth.	Giles meets Buffy on her first day of 10th grade at Sunnydale High.
2-8	The Dark Age	A demon from his past comes to Sunnydale, and we learn about Giles' checkered past.
2-17	Passion	Giles reels from the death of Jenny.
2-22	Becoming, Pt. 2	Angel tortures Giles for information.
3-2	Dead Man's Party	Giles threatens Snyder to help get Buffy back in school.
3-6	Band Candy	Giles reverts to his reckless teenaged self.
3-12	Helpless	Giles administers the Watchers' Council's test to Buffy on her 18th birthday.
4-12	A New Man	Giles awakens to find that he has been transformed into a demon.
5-2	Real Me	Giles buys the Magic Box shop.
5-22	The Gift	Giles and the rest fight by Buffy's side to save the world.
6-7	Once More, With Feeling	Everyone reveals their secrets in song.
6-21	Two to Go	Giles returns from England to stop Willow.
7-22	Chosen	The end.

Angel   The Lover

The enigmatic Angel watches over Buffy, (1-1) and soon a smoldering attraction develops. Passion leads to a kiss, and Buffy learns that he is a vampire (1-7).

Deeply in love, they fight evil side by side. When Angel is captured (2-10), Buffy rescues him. They finally consummate their relationship (2-13), which leads to Angel losing his soul and returning to evil (2-14). Angel revels in his evil, and he kills Jenny to prevent her from returning his soul to him (2-17). We learn about Angel's human past in Glasgow (2-21). Moments after Willow's magic returns his soul, Buffy is forced to kill Angel to save the world (2-22).

Mysteriously returned to the world, Angel turns to Giles for help when he is haunted by those he has killed (3-10). Angel works with the gang to discover the Mayor's plans and the truth about Faith (3-17). After a visit from Joyce, Angel tells Buffy they must stop seeing each other, and that he will leave Sunnydale after the ascension (3-20). Faith tries to kill him (3-21), and Buffy nearly gives her life to save him. He leaves for Los Angeles (3-22). He makes several brief appearances after that, but mainly loves Buffy from afar, returning again briefly to bring her the champion's amulet which Spike will wear to battle into save the world (7-22).

Angel's Character Arc: 14 Episodes

1-1	Welcome to the Hellmouth.	Angel meets Buffy.
1-7	Angel	They kiss, and Buffy learns he is a vampire.
2-10	What's My Line	Angel is kidnapped by Spike and Drusilla.
2-13	Surprise	Angel and Buffy consummate their relationship.
2-14	Innocence	Angel loses his soul and returns to evil.
2-17	Passion	Angel kills Jenny.
2-21,22	Becoming	We learn Angel's backstory. Buffy is forced to kill Angel to save the world.
3-10	Amends	Angel is haunted by his past victims.
3-17	Enemies	Angel helps the gang discover the Mayor's plans and uncover Faith's deceit.
3-20	The Prom	Angel makes plans to leave Sunnydale.
3-21	Graduation Day, Pt. 1	Faith shoots Angel with a poisoned arrow.
3-22	Graduation Day, Pt. 2	Angel drinks from Buffy, helps stop the Mayor, then leaves Sunnydale.
7-22	Chosen	Angel brings to Buffy a special amulet, which must be worn by a champion.

Spike

The Champion

Spike arrives in Sunnydale and vows to take out the Slayer (2-3). He kidnaps Angel in an attempt to heal Drusilla (2-10). Under a spell, Spike and the Slayer plan to marry (4-9). With a chip in his head that prevents him from harming humans, he turns to fighting demons (4-11), and helps Adam fight Buffy by turning her friends against her (4-20). Spike falls in love with Buffy and tells her how he defeated the other Slayers (5-7). He commits to his choice for her over Harmony and Dru (5-14), and stays true to Buffy even in the face of torture (5-18).

He is crushed when Buffy dies (5-22). He sings of his love for her when everyone reveals their secrets in song (6-7), and he and Buffy start a relationship (6-9). Spike nearly rapes Buffy, then leaves town to get a soul (6-19). We learn about Spike's earliest days as a vampire (7-17), and he gives his life to help Buffy save the world (7-22).

Spike's Character Arc: 14 Episodes

2-3	School Hard	Spike arrives in Sunnydale and strikes at the Slayer at Parent Night at Buffy's school.
2-10	What's My Line	Spike kidnaps Angel in order to heal Drusilla.
4-9	Something Blue	When Willow's spell backfires, Spike proposes to Buffy, and we see him when he was human.
4-11	Doomed	Spike learns that he can hurt non-humans.
4-20	The Yoko Factor	In exchange for Adam's help with his chip, Spike works to break up the Scooby gang.
5-7	Fool for Love	Spike tells Buffy the stories of his defeat of the two previous Slayers.
5-14	Crush	Spike professes his love for Buffy.
5-18	Intervention	After Spike gets his BuffyBot, Glory's minions kidnap him.
5-22	The Gift	Spike and the rest fight by Buffy's side to save the world.
6-7	Once More, With Feeling	Everyone reveals their secrets in song.
6-9	Smashed	Buffy and Spike take things to the next level.
6-19	Seeing Red	Spike comes to apologize to Buffy, but ends up trying to rape her and he leaves town.
7-17	Lies My Parents Told Me	Learn about Spike's earliest vampire days and his relationship with his mother.
7-22	Chosen	The end, especially for Spike.

Anya

The Demon

Vengeance demon posing as a high school senior, Anya grants a wish that crosses dimensions and results in her being turned into a human (3-9). After she tries but fails to return to a more evil dimension (3-16), she begins to date Xander, starting with the prom, (3-20), and later they become more involved (4-3).

Anya works with the gang to bring Buffy back to life (6-1,2). Living together, Xander and Anya finally announce their engagement (6-6). The gang's secrets and personal anxieties are revealed in song (6-7). When Xander leaves her at the altar, Anya returns to her vengeance ways (6-16), and seeks solace with Spike (6-18). Her backstory is revealed when Buffy must slay her (7-5), and she perishes while helping the gang save the world (7-22).

Anya's Character Arc: 12 Episodes

3-9	The Wish	When Cordelia wishes Buffy never came to Sunnydale, Anya makes the wish come true.
3-16	Dopplegangland	Anya tries to help Evil Willow get back to her own world.
3-20	The Prom	Anya begins to date Xander.
4-3	Harsh Light of Day	Anya and Xander become more involved.
6-1,2	Bargaining (1, 2)	The gang brings Buffy back from death.
6-6	All the Way	Xander and Anya announce their engagement.
6-7	Once More, With Feeling	Everyone reveals their secrets in song.
6-16	Hell's Bells	The wedding.
6-18	Entropy	Anya seeks solace with Spike.
7-5	Selfless	Anya goes too far, and Buffy has to stop her.
7-22	Chosen	The end, especially for Anya.

Relationship Arcs

The show's relationships provide delightful sidelines that add flavor to the main story arc. Whether they persist over a few episodes or on into the spin-off show, "Angel," here are the episodes with the highlights and milestones of these relationships.

Buffy and Angel: 12 Episodes

1-1	Welcome to the Hellmouth.	Buffy and Angel meet.
1-7	Angel	They kiss, and she learns he is a vampire.
2-7	Lie to Me	Buffy is jealous about Drusilla.
2-13	Surprise	Angel gives Buffy a claddagh ring, and they consummate their relationship.
2-14	Innocence	Angel loses his soul and returns to evil.
2-21,22	Becoming	Buffy returns Angel's soul, then is forced to kill him and send him to hell.
3-4	Beauty and the Beasts	Angel returns from a hell dimension.
3-20	The Prom	Angel makes plans to leave Sunnydale.
3-22	Graduation Day, Pt. 2	Angel leaves Sunnydale.
1-8 of "Angel," I Will Remember You		The couple shares one last beautiful day which only Angel will remember.
5-17	Intervention	Buffy is comforted by a visit from Angel.

Buffy and Riley: 10 Episodes

4-1	The Freshmen	Buffy and Riley meet.
4-7	The Initiative	Riley realizes that he is attracted to Buffy.
4-10, 11	Hush, Doomed	The pair learn each other's secrets and work together to avert an apocalypse.
4-12	A New Man	Buffy introduces Riley to Giles.
4-14	Goodbye Iowa	Suffering from withdrawal, Riley's behavior affects their relationship.
4-14	Who Are You?	Buffy is upset that Riley slept with Faith, albeit in Buffy's body.
5-2	Real Me	Riley is starting to tire of taking second place to Buffy's Slayer duties

| 5-10 | Into the Woods | Riley's insecurities drive him to the arms, and teeth, of a vampire; he leaves Sunnydale to fight other demons. |
| 6-15 | As You Were | Buffy's head is turned when Riley and his wife come to town. |

Buffy and Spike: 26 Episodes

4-9	Something Blue	Spellbound, Buffy and Spike plan to wed.
5-4	Out Of My Mind	Spike has an erotic dream about Buffy.
5-5	No place Like Home	Spike starts hanging out in front of Buffy's house.
5-7	Fool for Love	Spike is rebuked when he tries to kiss Buffy.
5-14	Crush	Spike reveals his feelings to Buffy, who is repulsed.
5-18	Intervention	Spike plays with his BuffyBot. Buffy learns the depth of Spike's faithfulness.
6-3, 4	After Life, Flooded	Buffy finds some consolationconfides in telling Spike the truth of her despair.
6-5	Life Serial	Buffy drinks with Spike.
6-7	Once More With Feeling	Spike sings of his love for Buffy, and they end the episode with a kiss.
6-8	Tabula Rasa	Buffy tells Spike they will never kiss again, but they do.
6-9,10	Smashed, Wrecked	The pair's relationship progresses to a violently sexual level.
6-13	Dead Things	Still having sex, Spike calls it love while Buffy says she doesn't trust him. Buffy is convinced something is wrong with her that she lets Spike do what he does.
6-15	As You Were	Buffy is humiliated and Spike is amused when Riley catches them in bed. Buffy tells Spike that their relationship is over.
6-18	Entropy	Spike still loves Buffy, and the gang finds out about the affair.
6-19	Seeing Red	Spike comes to apologize to Buffy, but ends up trying to rape her and he leaves town.

7-2	Beneath You	Buffy realizes that Spike has a soul and that he feels real remorse over the rape.
7-8, 9	Sleeper, Never Leave Me	Spike tells Buffy what she means to him, and she wants to help him.
7-10, 11	Bring On the Night, Showtime	Spike is sustained by his faith in Buffy, and Buffy rescues him from The First.
7-13	The Killer in Me	Buffy has Spike's chip removed.
7-20, 21	Touched, End of Days	Spike comforts Buffy, and they tell each other that they care about each other.
7-22	Chosen	Buffy tells Spike that she loves him, and he gives his life as her Champion.

Xander and Cordelia: 9 Episodes

2-10	What's My Line	Cordelia and Xander kiss in the basement.
2-11, 12	Ted, Bad Eggs	Cordelia and Xander carry on a relationship in secret.
2-13	Surprise	Xander suggests they admit they are dating.
2-14	Innocence	Xander and Cordelia's secret is discovered.
2-16	Bewitched, Bothered, and Bewildered	Xander tries a love spell when Cordelia breaks up with him on Valentines Day
2-20	Go Fish	Cordelia is proud of Xander's new position on the swim team.
3-3	Faith, Hope, and Trick	Xander and Cordelia are a secure couple.
3-8	Lover's Walk	Cordelia ends the relationship when she sees Xander with Willow.

Xander and Anya: 17 Episodes

3-20	The Prom	Anya asks Xander to the prom.
4-3	The Harsh Light of Day	Anya asks Xander where their relationship is going, then takes him to bed.
4-12	A New Man	Xander and Anya are dating.
4-18	Where the Wild Things Are	Anya is adjusting to what it means to be in a relationship.

5-3	The Replacement	Xander gets an apartment for him and Anya to share.
5-10	Into the Woods	Xander tells Anya that he loves her.
5-22	The Gift	Xander asks Anya to marry him right before they go into battle.
6-4	Flooded	Xander explains why they need to wait to get married.
6-6	All the Way	Xander announces his engagement to Anya; Xander starts get nervous about marriage.
6-7	Once More With Feeling	Xander and Anya sing of their fears about their upcoming marriage.
6-15	As You Were	Wedding planning is fraying their nerves, and Xander explains the difference between marriage and a wedding.
6-16	Hell's Bells	Xander leaves Anya at the altar.
6-18	Entropy	Anya returns, wanting her vengeance, which she gets when Xander sees her with Spike.
7-5	Selfless	Xander can't bear to let Buffy kill Anya.
7-14	First Date	Anya is worried about Xander.
7-16	Storyteller	The pair talks about the wedding and that they are still in love, ending up in bed.
7-20	Touched	The pair seek comfort together in bed, or more accurately, on the floor.
7-22	Chosen	Xander is proud that Anya went out fighting.

Willow and Oz: 11 Episodes

2-4	Inca Mummy Girl	Oz sees Willow dressed as an Eskimo and is intrigued.
2-6	Halloween	Oz sees Willow crossing the street.
2-9	What's My Line	Willow and Oz finally meet when they are both selected for a special career.
2-13	Surprise	Oz asks Willow on a date, and she later asks if he'd like to make out with her.

2-15	Phases	Willow feels ignored by Oz, learning his secret when she confronts him.
3-3	Faith, Hope, and Trick	Willow and Oz are a secure couple.
3-8	Lover's Walk	Oz puts a time-out on the relationship when he sees Willow with Xander.
3-10	Amends	Oz tells Willow he'd like them to get back together, and she attempts a seduction.
3-21	Graduation Day, Pt. 1	Oz and Willow consummate their relationship.
4-6	Wild at Heart	Oz meets another werewolf, resulting in infidelity and him leaving Sunnydale.
4-19	New Moon Rising	Oz returns, but Willow loves another.

Willow and Tara: 11 Episodes

4-10	Hush	Willow and Tara meet and form a bond.
4-12	A New Man	The girls work together on magic, deepening their relationship.
4-14	Who Are You?	When Willow introduces Tara to Buffy, Tara realizes that it's not really Buffy.
4-19	New Moon Rising	Willow chooses Tara over Oz, and comes out to Buffy.
5-2	Real Me	Willow and Tara move in together, and Willow strives to include Tara in the gang.
5-6	Family	Willow makes it known that Tara is part of her family.
5-19	Tough Love	Tara is gravely hurt and Willow goes on the attack in revenge.
6-6	All the Way	Tara is concerned about Willow's use of magic, unaware that Willow has been using magic on her.
6-8	Tabula Rasa	Tara leaves when Willow's magic goes too far.
6-18	Entropy	Tara and Willow get back together.
6-19	Seeing Red	Willow loses Tara forever.

Willow and Kennedy: 6 Episodes

7-10	Bring On the Night	Kennedy meets Willow, and immediately starts flirting.
7-11	Showtime	Willow and Kennedy get to know each other, but Kennedy misunderstands magic.
7-13	The Killer in Me	Willow and Kennedy kiss, just as a spell wreaks havoc on Willow.
7-15	Get It Done	Kennedy is amazed by Willow's power.
7-20	Touched	Kennedy and Willow take their relationship further.
7-22	Chosen	Kennedy and Willow deepen their bond on the eve of battle.

Giles and Jenny: 6 Episodes

2-2	Some Assembly Required	Giles nervously asks Jenny on a date.
2-7	Lie to Me	Giles and Jenny continue to date, and she takes him to a Monster Truck Rally.
2-8	The Dark Age	Jenny calls for a break in the relationship when she is hurt by a demon.
2-11	Ted	Giles and Jenny rekindle their relationship.
2-14	Innocence	Giles learns of Jenny's role in Angel's curse and scorns her.
2-17	Passion	After tentative steps to get back together, Jenny is killed by Angel.

Cordelia and Wesley: 5 Episodes

3-15	Consequences	They meet and are attracted to each other.
3-17	Enemies	Cordelia asks Wesley on a date.
3-20	Prom	They go to the prom.
3-22	Graduation Day	They kiss—the worst of their lives, curing them of their attraction to each other.
1-10 of "Angel," Parting Gifts		They kiss again and while they do a better job, they don't get back together.

Spike and Drusilla: 7 Episodes

5-7	Fool For Love	Spike and Drusilla meet (told as backstory).
2-3	School Hard	Spike is devoted to the frail Drusilla.
2-7	Lie to Me	Spike is jealous about Angel.
2-10	What's My Line	Spike restores Drusilla's health, and in the end she saves him.
2-13	Surprise	Spike plans a party for Drusilla.
3-8	Lover's Walk	Spike returns to Sunnydale after Drusilla has left him. (See their breakup in episode 5-7.)
5-14	The Crush	Spike chooses Buffy over Drusilla.

Character Arcs

Season Zero: the Pitch Pilot

Aired: Never

Thanks to YouTube we can see the earliest attempt to bring Buffy and her Sunnydale gang to television. The company that produced the show, 20th Century Fox, produced a short "pitch pilot" to send to the television networks. Written and directed by series creator Joss Whedon, this pilot has the same general story line as the actual series pilot which was reshot and then aired in March 1997.

There are several notable differences in the pitch pilot from the pilot which aired. The school that is situated above the Hellmouth is not Sunnydale High, but rather is Berryman High. Also the key character Willow is played by Riff Regan, and the role of Principal Flutie is played by well-known character actor Stephen Tobolowsky.

You can learn more about this pitch pilot on Wikipedia, which includes a link to a video on YouTube, at the following URL:
http://en.wikipedia.org/wiki/Unaired_Buffy_the_Vampire_Slayer_pilot

While some of the cultural references in the aired pilot are also in the pitch pilot, following are additional references that didn't make the final cut.

Pitch Pilot Pop Culture References

❖ *What kind of name is Aphrodesia?*

In the released pilot, two girls in the locker room say, "What kind of name is Buffy anyway." In the unaired pilot it is easier to hear that right after the girl says that, another girl says, "Hi Aphrodesia."

❖ *Sunnydale High: Typical American high school*

Joss said: "Sunnydale high is based on every high school in America, because so many kids feel like their school is built on a hellmouth."

Dingoes Ate My Baby

When asked by Cordelia who is playing at the Bronze, one of the girls in the posse says, "Dingoes Ate My Baby—they rock!"

Laura Ashley (Fashion designer), Home Depot, Martha Stewart

"Laura Ashley is definitely back. She's back, and this time it's personal. See, they mated her with the Home Depot guy, and that's how we got Martha Stewart." (Buffy complimenting Willow on her dress.)

Freud, Existentialism, The Muppets Take Manhattan (1984 film)

XANDER: (Talking about the kids from the school film club) "They spend their time deciding that every movie is an existential meditation on Freudian sexuality."

BUFFY: "Even *The Muppets Take Manhattan*?"

Bambi, Betty Rubble, Wilma Flintstone

PRINCIPAL FLUTIE: "Bambi. Betty. Uh. Wilma?"

BUFFY: "Buffy."

Cindy Lou Who, The Grinch Who Stole Christmas

"You don't know anything about it. I was happy. I was Cindy Lou Who just coasting through my life, when vampires, which are only supposed to be in cheesy movies, start killing people—people I know." (Buffy to Giles about what it was like to become the Slayer.)

Lionel Ritchie

"It was pretty striking. You know, sleeves rolled up, collar. Very Lionel Ritchie. I mean, who's still sporting that look?" (Willow to Buffy, describing the clothes worn by a guy at the Bronze.)

Nosefrato (1922 film)

At the end of the episode, Buffy throws a stake which impales a poster for the classic vampire film, *Nosefrato*.

Season One:
Buffy Meets the Master

Aired: 1996-1997
Big-bad: The Master
(Episode Table is on page 237)

*"Why couldn't Xander be possessed by a puppy,
or some ducks?"*

   – Willow

*"Things involved with the computer fill me with
a child-like terror. Now if it were a nice ogre or
some such I would be more in my element."*

   – Giles

"To read makes our speaking English good."

   – Xander

*"I may be dead, but I'm still pretty,
which is more than I can say for you."*

   – Buffy

Season One:
Buffy Meets the Master

Buffy Summers had a rough time in her freshman year at Hemery High in Los Angeles. She just wanted to shop, flirt with boys, and be a cheerleader. But instead she discovered that she was the Slayer—the one girl in all the world chosen to battle the forces of evil. And battle she did, resulting in the school gym burning down, her expulsion from school, and her parents seriously freaking out about her new obsession with vampires. Add a divorce to the mix, and Buffy's mother, Joyce, decided it was time to hit the road.

Buffy and her mother arrive in Sunnydale just before the start of the new school year. Joyce is looking forward to starting over in her new life as the manager of an art gallery in a new town. Buffy is ready to leave slaying behind and insert herself into a new social scene far away from the Los Angeles vampires. But being the Chosen One doesn't change just because you have a new zip code. Buffy is soon back in the biz: fighting vampires and training with her new Watcher, Giles.

While her life as a popular girl seems permanently behind her, she makes fast friends with Willow and Xander, who readily partner with her in her fight against evil. She also falls in love with Angel, a vampire with a soul who has loved her since before they met. Drawing strength from her friends, Buffy learns not to care that the world doesn't thank her or even notice that she is keeping evil at bay.

Season one shows us the horrors of the high school social life, which is harder for Buffy to navigate than the mortal danger of slaying vampires. It also shows us that beneath the veneer of cliques and high school stereotypes are real people with individual strengths that are unseen unless you look.

The Master comes to represent all that Buffy must overcome: her fears, her resistance to her role as the Slayer, and her childhood. When Buffy finally defeats the Master, we see that when you grab hold of fate and take control of your life, it'll turn out okay—or at least it won't kill you... for long.

Season One Episodes and Pop Culture References

1-1   Welcome to the Hellmouth (Part 1)

Written by Joss Whedon, Directed by Charles Martin Smith

Buffy Summers moves to Sunnydale with her mother, only to learn that the town is situated above a Hellmouth and she must stop the Master from escaping from where he has been trapped below. Meet Watcher Giles, sidekicks Xander and Willow, and popular girl Cordelia.

 Music in this Episode

> "Saturated," "Believe," "Swirl," and "Things Are Changing" by Sprung Monkey

 Multiple Roles: Luke

> *The actor who plays Luke also plays The Judge in season 2.*

John Tesh, James Spader, Frappuccinos

CORDELIA: "If you hang with me and mine, you'll be accepted in no time. Of course, we do have to test your coolness factor. You're from L.A., so you can skip the written. But let's see: vamp nail polish?"

BUFFY: "Over?"

CORDELIA: "So over. James Spader."

BUFFY: "He needs to call me."

CORDELIA: "Frappuccinos."

BUFFY: "Trendy, but tasty."

CORDELIA: "John Tesh."

BUFFY: "The devil."

CORDELIA: "That was pretty much a gimme, but you passed!"

Sears

"Willow, nice dress! Good to know you've seen the softer side of Sears." (Cordelia being mean to Willow.)

The Slayer Intro

GILES: "To each generation a Slayer is born, one girl in all the world, the chosen one, one born–"

BUFFY: "With the strength and skill to hunt the vampires, to stop their evil blah blah blah."

Pepper spray

"It's for self defense. Everybody has them in L.A. Pepper spray is so passé." (Buffy to Xander when he gives her the stake that she dropped in the hall at school.)

Starbucks

"Not much goes down in a one-Starbucks town like Sunnydale. You're big news." (Xander when Buffy comments that everyone seems to want to know about her.)

Neiman Marcus

GILES: "What do you know about this town?"

BUFFY: "It's two hours on the freeway from Neiman Marcus."

Time-Life Books

"What, did you send away for the whole Time-Life series? Did you get the free phone?" (Buffy commenting on Giles' book collection.)

Watchtower

"Hi, I'm an enormous slut." "Hello, would you like a copy of the Watchtower?" (Buffy to herself as she looks at two different dresses in the mirror.)

Turtle Wax

"Sorry that's incorrect. But you do win this lovely watch and a year's supply of Turtle Wax." (Buffy responding to Angel by reciting a stereotypical game show consolation-prize patter.)

Box of Raisins

This is what Willow is snacking on as she sits alone at the bar in the Bronze.

Barbie

"No, we're friends. We used to go out, but we broke up... He stole my Barbie. Oh, we were five." (Willow when Buffy asks about her relationship with Xander.)

Seize the Moment

"My philosophy– do you want to hear my philosophy? Life is short. Not original, I'll grant you, but it's true, you know? Why waste time being all shy and worried about some guy and if he's going to laugh at you. Seize the moment, 'cuz tomorrow you might be dead." (Buffy when Willow points out that Buffy seems not to be shy around boys.)

❧ *Jesse asks Cordelia to dance*

Joss Whedon says that the dialog in the scene where Jesse asks Cordelia to dance was based verbatim from his personal experience in school.

Bovril

"I'd much rather be home with a cup of Bovril and a book." (Giles when Buffy teases him about partying with the teenagers at the Bronze.)

❧ *What is Bovril?*

Similar in concept to bouillon, Bovril is a meat extract common in England which can be made into a broth or beverage by adding water, or used to flavor soups or other foods.

Epstein-Barr, Hepatitis, Chronic Fatigue Syndrome

"My mom doesn't even get out of bed any more. And the doctor says she has Epstein-Barr. I'm like, Please! It's chronic hepatitis. Or at least Chronic Fatigue Syndrome. I mean, nobody cool has Epstein-Barr anymore." (Cordelia to her posse at the Bronze.)

DeBarge ('80s Motown band)

"Okay, first of all: what's with the outfit? Live in the now, okay? You look like DeBarge." (Buffy to a vampire dressed in long out-of-style clothes.)

TV ratings

"Now, we can do this the hard way, or... well, there's actually just the hard way. This is not going to be pretty. We're talking violence, strong language, adult content." (Buffy taunting a vampire before a fight.)

1-2   The Harvest (Part 2)

Written by Joss Whedon, Directed by John T. Kretchmer

Buffy's Slayer identity is revealed to Willow and Xander when she saves them and many of Sunnydale's other young people from being harvested by the Master's minions as part of his plan to rise into the world.

 Music in this Episode

"Right My Wrong" by Sprung Monkey
"Wearing Me Down" and "Ballad For Dead Friends" by Dashboard Prophets

 The Master's batty makeup

The makeup artist designed the Master's look based on that of a bat, with the intention of showing that the Master was devolving into another creature.

Computer hacking

GILES: "So all the city plans are just open to the public?"

WILLOW: "Um, well, in a way. I sort of stumbled onto them when I accidentally decrypted the city council's security system."

British

"I'm researching this Harvest affair. It seems to be some sort of preordained massacre: rivers of blood, hell on earth. Quite charmless. I'm a bit fuzzy however on the details. It may be you can wrest some details from that dread machine.... That was a bit, um, British, wasn't it?" (Giles when Willow says she wants to help find Jessie and stop the Harvest.)

Royal family

"Well, maybe that's how they do things in Britain. They've got that royal family and all kinds of problems." (Principal Flutie when Buffy tells him that Giles asked her to go off-campus to get him a book.)

Exacto knife

"There was this time I was pinned down by this guy who played left tackle for varsity, well at least he used to before he was a vampire. He had a really thick neck and all I had was this little Exacto knife..." (Buffy when Xander asked if she had experience with beheading.)

The Wild Bunch (1969 film)

"Don't go *Wild Bunch* on me." (Buffy to the gang telling them not to be heroes.)

 ### *"... in nine hours, moron."*

The scene in when Buffy tricks the vampire into thinking the light is sunlight ("...is in nine hours, moron"), is one which Joss actually wrote for the Buffy *movie. This was how Kristy Swanson's Buffy was supposed to have killed the Paul Rubens vampire character: by outwitting her foe instead of, as Joss puts it, just being a bimbo with powers.*

1-3   Witch

Written by Dana Reston, Directed by Stephen Cragg

Buffy tries out for cheerleading, but the competition turns into a battle for her life when one of the girls turns out to be a witch who is hell-bent to get on the team at any cost.

Cheerleading, Pom poms

"This is madness. What can you have been thinking. You are the Slayer. Lives depend upon you. I make allowances for your youth but I expect a certain amount of responsibility, instead of which you enslave yourself to this cult. You have a sacred birthright, Buffy. You have been chosen to destroy vampires, not wave pom-poms at people." (Giles, aghast, when Buffy tells him she plans to try out for the cheerleading squad.)

L.A. Lakers, Laker Girl

CORDELIA: "Just look at that Amber. Who does she think she is, a Laker Girl?"

WILLOW: "I heard she turned them down."

Glass half full

"That's the thrill of living on the Hellmouth. There's a veritable cornucopia of fiends and devils and ghouls to engage. Pardon me for finding the glass half full." (Giles when Xander comments that they don't know what caused the cheerleader to catch fire.)

Mommy Dearest (1981 film)

"So mommy dearest is *Mommy Dearest*?" (Buffy asking about a friend's mother possibly being abusively controlling.)

Farrah Fawcett, Gidget ('60s TV show)

BUFFY: "Mom, I've accepted that you've had sex. I am not ready to know that you had Farrah hair." (Looking at Joyce's old high school yearbook.)

JOYCE: "This is Gidget hair. Don't they teach anything in history?"

Gymnastics

"Great parenting form. A little shaky on the dismount." (Joyce to herself about her parenting skills.)

Invisible Man

XANDER: "Cordelia, you haven't been mean to me all day. Is it something I've done?" (Cordelia walks away.)

XANDER: (To Willow). "Okay, see how she has no idea I'm a man much less a human being? This is the 'invisible man' syndrome: a blessing in Coredelia's case, a curse in Buffy's."

Sabrina the Teenage Witch (Comic, '90s TV show)

"The test was positive—she's our Sabrina. I just don't think she realizes what she's doing." (Buffy to Xander and Willow that their test proves that Amy is the witch.)

Macho Man (1978 song), Village People

"Macho, macho man. I want to be a macho man!" (Buffy showing much more than her usual enthusiasm, singing the song as she leaves for school.)

Sour Grapes

CORDELIA: "Hey I'm really sorry you guys got bumped back to alternate. Hold it, wait. No I'm not."

AMY: "I know I'll miss the intellectual thrill of spelling out words with my arms."

CORDELIA: "Oh, these grapes are sour."

1-4   Teacher's Pet

Written by David Greenwalt, Directed by Bruce Seth Green

Xander is attracted to a sexy substitute teacher who turns out to actually be an insect demon who killed their science teacher. This is the first in Xander's long string of unfortunate attractions.

 Music in this Episode

"Already Met You" and *"Stoner Love"* by Superfine

Hotdogs

BUFFY: "Oh, Hotdog Surprise. Be still my heart."

WILLOW: "Call me old fashioned, I don't want more surprise in my hotdogs."

Monster Island (Location in '60s-era Japanese Godzilla films)

"Oh, this is fun. We're on Monster Island." (Xander on how there are so many different types of evil things in Sunnydale.)

Wrong Touching

"You have to see the counselor. Everyone who saw the body has to see a crisis counselor... We all need help with our feelings, otherwise we bottle them up and before you know it powerful laxatives are involved. I really believe that if we reach out to one another we can beat this thing. I'm always here if you need a hug, but not a real hug, because there's no touching in this school. We're very sensitive to wrong touching." (Principal Flutie to the students in an attempt to correctly deal with a dead teacher having been found in the school.)

Mercedes Benz

"I'm just saying, when tragedy strikes, we have to look on the bright side, you know? Like, how even used Mercedes' still have leather seats." (Cordelia on how she is seeing the positive side of finding a dead teacher's body.)

Computer hacking

GILES: "This computer invasion that Willow is performing on the coroner's office—one assumes that it is entirely legal?"

BUFFY: "Entirely. Of course."

GILES: "Right. Wasn't here. Didn't see it. Couldn't have stopped you."

The Exorcist (1973 film)

"We are talking full-on *Exorcist* twist." (Buffy about Ms. French, who turned her head completely around.)

Predator (1987 film), Shoulder pads

BUFFY: "Her fashion sense screams *Predator*."

WILLOW: "It's the shoulder pads!"

BUFFY: "Exactly."

National Enquirer (Advertising slogan)

"Enquiring minds want to know." (Willow on where the boy is who worked with Ms. French after school yesterday.)

911

"Buffy, 911! Blayne's mom called the school. He never came home last night." (Willow when she sees an alert on her computer.)

Cucumbers, Yogurt, Shawarma, Greek food

"I like cucumbers, like in that Greek salad thing with yogurt. Do you like Greek food? I'm excepting shawarma of course. I mean what's that all about, it's a big meat hive." (Xander, nervously babbling at Ms. French's house.)

 Shawarma: the connection to another Joss Whedon project

Shawarma provides a connection to another Joss Whedon project: the 2012 blockbuster film "The Avengers." In the film, watch through the end of the credits to see the superheroes enjoying a quiet post-battle shawarma-fest.

Pekingese

"Yes Carlisle, you were right about everything. Well no, you weren't right about your mother coming back as a Pekingese." (Giles, on the phone with a former colleague, about the insect-demon.)

Eeny-meeny-miney-moe

XANDER: "What is she doing?"

BLAYNE: "I think it's eeny-meeny-miney-moe."

1-5 Never Kill a Boy on the First Date

Written by Dean Batali, Directed by David Semel

Trying to be a normal teen on a normal date becomes impossible for Buffy when she must slay vampires and defeat the Master's plan to bring in the Anointed—all while keeping her Slayer identity a secret from her date.

 Music in this Episode

"Strong" and "Treason" by Velvet Chain
"Let the Sun Fall Down" by Kim Richey
"Rotten Apple" by Three Day Wheely

Emily Dickinson, Security blanket

OWEN: "I lost my Emily… Dickinson. It's dumb, but I like her around."

BUFFY: "Kind of a security blanket. I have something like that. Well, it's an actual blanket. And I don't really carry it around anymore. So, Emily Dickens, huh? She's great."

OWEN: "Dickinson."

BUFFY: "She's good also."

Soylent Green (1973 film)

"At least you don't have to eat your Soylent Green." (Owen to Buffy, pointing out the positive side of her having spilled her food.)

Emily Dickinson, American

GILES: "Oh. Emily Dickinson."

BUFFY: "We're both fans."

GILES: "Yes. She's quite a good poet. I mean, for a–"

BUFFY: "For a girl?"

GILES: "For an American."

Cereal Boxes

"Yeah, yeah, I read the back of the box." (Buffy assuring Giles she knows to keep her identity a secret from Owen.)

Time Machine

GILES: "A violent and disturbing prophecy is about to be fulfilled...."

BUFFY: "We'll be ready, whenever it is."

GILES: "Which is tonight."

BUFFY: "Tonight, okay– Wait, not okay. It can't be tonight."

GILES: "My calculations are precise."

BUFFY: "No. They're bad calculations. Bad!"

WILLOW: "Buffy has a really important date—Owen."

GILES: "All right. I'll just jump into my time machine go back to the twelfth century and ask the vampires to postpone their ancient prophecy for a few days while you take in a dinner and a show."

BUFFY: "Okay, at this point you're abusing sarcasm."

Tourist dollars

XANDER: "So Buffy, how did the slaying go last night?"

BUFFY: "Xander!"

XANDER: "I mean, how did the *laying* go. No, I didn't mean that either."

BUFFY: "It went fine, thank you. There's some new hoity-toity vampire sect in town."

XANDER: "Well hey, they bring in the much-needed tourist dollars."

Tweetie Bird

After seeing Owen's fancy watch, Xander looks at his Tweetie Bird watch.

Chess club

BUFFY: "Tonight? You and me?"

OWEN: "Well, we could invite the chess club, but they drink and they start fights...."

Clark Kent, Superman

"This is the '90s, and the 1990s in point of fact—and I can do both. Clark Kent has a job. I just want to go on a date. And look, I won't go far, okay? If the apocalypse comes, beep me." (Buffy convincing Giles to let her go out on a date with Owen.)

911

"Pick up the phone. Call 911. That boy is going to need some serious oxygen after I'm done with him." (Cordelia when she sees Angel enter the Bronze.)

Ben and Jerry's

BUFFY: "I'm sure this isn't exactly what you had in mind for our first date."

OWEN: "I was hoping maybe we'd finish up at Ben and Jerry's."

1-6   The Pack

Written by Joe Reinkemeyer, Directed by Bruce Seth Green

On a field trip at the zoo, Xander and a group of the bullies from school are possessed by hyena spirits. While Xander is cornering Buffy to satisfy his own appetite, the others kill and eat the principal. After returning to normal, Xander protects his bruised dignity by pretending not to remember what happened.

 Music in this Episode

"All You Want" by Dashboard Prophets
"Job's Eyes" by Far
"Reluctant Man" by Sprung Monkey

Heimlich Maneuver

"It was like the Heimlich, with stripes." (Willow describing zebras mating.)

Winged Monkeys, Wizard of Oz (1939 film)

"Oh Great. It's the winged monkeys." (Buffy about the gang of bullies when they enter the Bronze.)

Box of Raisins

Willow is again snacking on a little box of raisins as she sits in the Bronze.

Pizza

XANDER: "Why do I need to learn this."

WILLOW: "Because otherwise you'll flunk math."

XANDER: "Explain the part why that's bad."

WILLOW: "You fail math, you flunk out of school, you end up being the guy at the pizza place who sweeps the floor and says 'Hey kids, where're the cool parties this weekend.'"

Showtime, Cable

"You kids today have no school spirit. Today it's all gangs and drugs and those movies on Showtime with the nudity. I don't have cable—I heard of it." (Principal Flutie complaining about the students.)

Dodgeball

"All right, it's raining. All regular gym classes have been postponed, so you know what that means: Dodgeball. Now for those of you who may have forgotten, the rules are as follows: You dodge." (P.E. teacher to the students.)

Testosterone

"Xander has taken to teasing the less fortunate? And there's a noticeable change in both clothing and demeanor? And otherwise, all his spare time is spent lounging about with imbeciles? It's devastating—he's turned into a 16 year old boy. Of course, you'll have to kill him.... Testosterone is a great equalizer. It turns all men into morons. He will, however, get over it." (Giles to worried Willow and Buffy about Xander's recent behavior.)

X-Files ('90s TV show), Scully

"I can't believe you're trying to Scully me." (Buffy to Giles when he asserts that something is normal and explainable.)

Yanni, Chianti

"It's safe to say that in his animal state, his idea of wooing doesn't involve a Yanni CD and a bottle of Chianti." (Buffy about Xander's over-zealous advances while possessed by an evil hyena spirit.)

1-7   Angel

Written by David Greenwalt, Directed by Scott Brazil

Angel comes to Buffy's house, where she learns that their attraction is mutual and that he is a vampire. In an effort to chase Angel from Buffy's arms and back to the Master's fold, Darla attacks Joyce and makes it look like Angel was the attacker.

 Music in this Episode

"I'll Remember You" by Sophie Zelmani

Gatorade

XANDER: "Guys will do anything to impress a girl. I once drank an entire gallon of Gatorade without taking a breath."

WILLOW: "It was pretty impressive. Although later there was an ick-factor."

Friar Tuck

"Giles, 20th century. I'm not going to be fighting Friar Tuck." (Buffy when Giles says she must train with a quarterstaff.)

Umpire

XANDER: (To Buffy) "You're in love with a vampire? What, are you out of your mind?"

CORDELIA: "What?"

XANDER: "Not a vampire... How could you love an *umpire*. Everyone hates 'em."

Todd Oldham (Fashion designer), Free-trade agreements

"Where did you get that dress? This is a one-of-a-kind Todd Oldham! Do you know how much this dress cost? Is this a knockoff? This is a knockoff, isn't it! A cheesy knockoff! This is exactly what happens when you sign those free-trade agreements." (Cordelia to a girl who walks by at school wearing the same dress that Cordelia is wearing.)

Quiche

DARLA: "You're not one of them, are you?"

ANGEL: "No. And I'm not exactly one of you either."

DARLA: "Is that what you tell yourself these days? You're not exactly living off quiche." (Referring to the bags of blood in Angel's refrigerator.)

Reconstruction, Civil War

BUFFY: "Reconstruction began after the construction which was shoddy so they had to reconstruct."

WILLOW: "After the destruction of the Civil War."

Buffy and Angel's first kiss

For their first-ever kissing scene in this episode, David and Sarah Michelle thought they'd be funny by eating the worst stuff they could think of before shooting the scene to make their breath as awful as possible.

Columbus

"Well, if you've been around since Columbus then you're bound to pile up a few exes." (Buffy, cattily, to Darla.)

1-8   I, Robot... You, Jane

Written by Ashley Gable, Directed by Stephen Posey

While scanning books into the computer to archive them, a demon who had been imprisoned in a book is accidentally let loose on the Internet. It controls students, lures Willow into a relationship, and tries to kill Buffy.

Idiot Box

GILES: "Ms. Calendar, I'm sure your computer science class is fascinating, but I happen to believe that one can survive in modern society without being enslaved to the idiot box."

JENNY: "That's TV. The idiot box is TV. This is the good box."

Spider-Man, Spider Sense, Pop Culture

BUFFY: "My spider sense is tingling."

GILES: "Your spider sense?"

BUFFY: "Pop culture reference. Sorry."

With a Little Help From My Friends (1967 song), Beatles

BUFFY: "Dave. He's dead. Well, it looked like suicide."

XANDER: "With a little help from our friends?"

1-9   The Puppet Show

Written by Dean Batali, Directed by Ellen S. Pressman

The school talent show is rocked by violence and a mysterious murder. The gang allies itself with a possessed ventriloquist's dummy to solve the crime, and nearly become victims themselves.

The Slayer Intro

"Giles, into every generation is born one who must run the annual talentless show. You cannot escape your destiny." (Buffy, teasing Giles because he has been ordered by Principal Snyder to run the annual talent show.)

The Greatest Love of All (song popularized by Whitney Houston, 1986)

This is the song that Cordelia sang, very badly, in the school talent show.

Dummies

WILLOW: "I think dummies are cute, don't you?"

BUFFY: "No they give me the wig, ever since I was little."

WILLOW: "What happened?"

BUFFY: "I saw a dummy, it gave me the wig... there's no story there."

The Shining (1980 film), Redrum

"Redrum! Redrum!" (Xander has a ventriloquist's dummy say that in an effort to jokingly make it be scary and creepy.)

Duraflame

DUMMY: "You know what they say: Once you go wood, nothing's as good!"

BUFFY: "Okay, we get the joke, horny dummy, ha ha. It's very funny, but you might want to consider getting some new shtick, unless you want your prop ending up as a Duraflame log."

※ *Episode Reference*

When Principal Snyder says: "Principal Flutie would have said kids need understanding. Kids are human beings. That's the kind of woolly-headed liberal thinking that leads to being eaten. This place has quite a reputation, suicide, missing persons, spontaneous cheerleader combustion," he is referring to, among other things, episode 1-6, "The Pack," and episode 1-2, "Witch."

Smoking

"There are things I will not tolerate. Students loitering on campus after school, horrible murders with hearts being removed. Also smoking." (Principal Snyder warning the gang to stay out of trouble.)

Keyser Söze, Usual Suspects (1995 film)

"So the dummy says that he's a demon hunter, and we're like, fine, la la la la la. Then he takes off, and now there's a brain. Does anyone else feel like they were Keyser Söze'd?" (Xander when they think they've been duped by Sid.)

❧ *A scene plays over the credits*

This is the only episode in which they show a scene over the credits: Buffy, Willow, and Xander reciting their dramatic scene for the talent show, in the middle of which Willow runs away.

1-10 Nightmares

Written by Joss Whedon, Directed by Bruce Seth Green

Everyone's worst nightmares come true, caused by a boy in a coma who is desperately trying to escape the evil that attacked him. As the nightmares get more severe and endanger the lives of everyone in Sunnydale, Buffy helps the boy destroy the source of the evil and to awaken from his coma.

Nerf Herder

When Willow opens her locker, you see a bumper sticker for Nerf Herders.

Who are the Nerf Herders?

This is the band who wrote and performs the Buffy the Vampire Slayer theme song, and which Joss Whedon says was recommended to him by Allison Hannigan.

Nazis

WILLOW: "Well, I don't like spiders, okay? Their hairy bodies and their sticky webs. And what do they need all those legs for anyway? I'll tell you: for crawling across your face in the middle of the night. Egh! How do they not ruffle you?"

XANDER: "I'm sorry, I'm unruffled by spiders. Now a bunch of Nazis crawling across my face...."

Middle East

WENDELL: "They're not insects, they're arachnids."

XANDER: "They're from the Middle East?"

Astral projection

GILES: "Well, there's astral projection—the theory that while one sleeps one has another body, an astral body which can travel through time and space."

BUFFY: "Billy's in a coma, that's like sleep, right? Could I be seeing Billy's astroid body?"

Chess team

The boys drag Cordelia, with frizzy hair and unfashionable clothes, to a meeting of the chess team—her nightmare of the ultimate in unpopularity.

Evita Peron

"Why is she so Evita-like?" (Willow wondering why Cordelia is so self-important.)

Madame Butterfly (Opera)

Willow's nightmare is of being on stage to perform *Madame Butterfly*.

Clown, Balloon animals

"You were a lousy clown. Your balloon animals were pathetic. Everyone can make a giraffe." (Xander to his nightmare of the clown from his sixth birthday party.)

Snow White (1937 Disney film)

"A dream is a wish your heart makes." (Master quoting the song to Buffy right before he buries her alive.)

Wizard of Oz (1939 film)

"I had the strangest dream, and you were there, and you.... Who are you people?" (Billy after waking from his coma, pointing at Buffy and the gang.)

1-11 Out of Mind, Out of Sight

Written by Joss Whedon, Directed by Reza Badiyi

Ignored to the point of actual invisibility, unpopular girl Marcie takes her vengeance out on Cordelia right before the ceremony to crown the May Queen.

❖ *Scooby shirt*

Willow wears a "Scooby Doo" t-shirt in this episode.

Helen Keller

"My eyes are hazel, Helen Keller." (Cordelia to her boyfriend, Mitch, when he says her eyes are blue.)

Shakespeare, Merchant of Venice, Shylock, Twinkie Defense

TEACHER: "Has Shylock suffered? What's his place in Venice society?"

WILLOW: "Well, everyone looked down on him."

CORDELIA: "That's such a Twinkie defense. Shylock should get over himself. People who think their problems are so huge craze me."

(This discussion of *Merchant of Venice* sets up the theme of the episode: the anger of the outcast.)

※ *Episode Reference*

Talking about the invisible girl's powers, Willow says: "How'd she get it? Is she a witch? 'Cuz we can fight a witch." This is a reference to episode 1-3, "Witch."

Chinese food

WILLOW: "Oh Hey do you want to come over to our place for dinner? Mom's making her famous phone call to the Chinese place."

XANDER: "Do you guys even have a stove?"

Generation gap

"Once again I teeter at the precipice of the generation gap." (Giles, not understanding what the gang is talking about.)

Laura Ashley (Fashion designer)

"God. Is she really wearing Laura Ashley?" (Cordelia's response when shown a photo of the girl who is attacking her.)

Gangs

"You're always around when all this weird stuff is happening, and I know you're very strong, and you've got all those weapons. I was kind of hoping you were in a gang." (Cordelia to Buffy.)

FBI

> FBI AGENT: "FBI! Nobody move! We're here for the girl. We can rehabilitate her. In time, she'll learn to be a useful member of society again. It would be best for you to forget this whole incident."
>
> BUFFY: "Did you know that you guys are very creepy?"

1-12 Prophecy Girl

Written and Directed by Joss Whedon

Although one of Giles' books foretells that it will mean her death, Buffy confronts the Master in his underground lair and ultimately defeats him—but not before he kills her first.

 Music in this Episode

"I Fall To Pieces" by Patsy Cline
"Inconsolable" by Jonatha Brooke

 The Buffy theme plays during the show

This episode includes the only scene in which the Buffy theme is played during the show. The scene shows Buffy, Xander, and Angel marching toward battle with the Master at Sunnydale High.

Box of Raisins

Willow has her box of raisins again.

Press-on Nails

> BUFFY: "Giles, care? I'm putting my life on the line battling the undead. Look I broke a nail, okay? I'm wearing a press-on. The least you could do is exhibit some casual interest. You could go 'Hmm.'"

Country Music

"I'm just gonna go home, lie down, and listen to country music, the music of pain." (Xander when Buffy turns him down.)

I Fall to Pieces, (1961 Patsy Cline song)

This is the song playing in Xander's room when Willow tries to call him.

Borg, Star Trek Next Generation ('80s TV show), Locutus

"I'm sorry. Calm may work for Locutus the Borg here, but I'm freaked out and I intend to stay that way." (Xander when Giles doesn't show alarm about Buffy's whereabouts.)

Feeble Banter

BUFFY: "You know you really should talk to your contractor. Looks like you've got some water damage."

MASTER: "Oh good. The feeble banter portion of the fight."

Fruit Punch

"You have fruit-punch mouth." (Buffy commenting on the redness around the Master's mouth.)

Season Two:
Buffy Loses It All

Aired: 1997-1998
Big-bad: Spike, and later Angel
(Episode Table starts on page 238)

---

*"I'm an old-fashioned gal.
I was raised to believe that men dig up the corpses
and the women have the babies."*

  – Buffy

*"I was at Woodstock. I fed off a flower person, and I
spent the next six hours watching my hand move."*

  – Spike

*"You know, computers are on the way out.
I think paper's going to make a big comeback."*
  – Xander

"Don't warn the tadpoles!"

  – Willow

Season Two:
Buffy Loses It All

Death can really ruin your day. After a long summer in Los Angeles with her father, Buffy is showing the strain of dealing with her death and her battle with the Master. Being the Chosen One may sound like an honor, but she knows it's a curse that will keep her from filling any other role her life might have promised. This is brought home when a new vampire, Spike, comes to town who considers himself a slayer of Slayers.

When Spike learns that a Slayer has the local underworld shaking in its collective boots, he figures he will take care of things and set himself up as the biggest big-bad. But Buffy is a Slayer that Spike cannot seem to conquer, and indeed the rest of his days on Earth revolve around her.

Buffy pushes against her limits and grapples with her future. Her friends are thinking about what they'll be when they grow up, but she knows that all she will be is a Slayer until her early death. While any seventeen-year-old is dealing with big decisions and life changes, Buffy's duties as a Slayer bring death and darkness to her everyday life. While she takes on more responsibility as the Slayer—leading the others in the fight against evil and guarding their very lives—she is treated as an adolescent at home and at school. She saves the world one day, and the next is told she is too irresponsible to get a driver's license.

Her situation takes a turn for the serious when Buffy and Angel give in to their passions and make love. Buffy is understandably traumatized to learn that this moment of bliss has resulted in Angel losing his soul. She has lost her lover, and added a very dangerous vampire to the world. The new Angel surpasses the evil she has previously known, taking a perverse pleasure in killing and torturing those she loves.

In season two, Buffy loses almost everything. She falls for a trick which leaves her friends unprotected and they are seriously hurt. With her identity revealed to her mother, an argument between them sends Buffy out of the house. To stop yet another apocalypse, she makes the right choice when she must choose between having Angel back and saving the world. And accused of murder, she is expelled from school and hunted by the police.

Buffy has nothing left but herself, and she's not so sure that's enough. She is haunted by having killed Angel and sent him to hell, and she is tired of fighting. Unable to deal with all that has happened, Buffy leaves Sunnydale. Alone.

Season Two Episodes and Pop Culture References

2-1   When She Was Bad

Written and Directed by Joss Whedon

Buffy's stress over her experience with the Master has her sporting a sour attitude that worries her parents and her friends.

 Music in this Episode

> "It Doesn't Matter" by Alison Krauss and Union Station
> "Spoon" and "Sugar Water" by Cibo Matto

 DVD Alert: Don't miss the first two scenes

> On the DVD, the first two scenes after the theme are grouped in the same chapter as the theme. If you skip the theme you may miss these scenes!

Terminator, Planet of the Apes, Star Wars (Films), The Force, Luke Skywalker

WILLOW: "In the few hours that we had together, we loved a lifetime's worth."

XANDER: "Terminator!"

XANDER: "Its a Madhouse—a Madhouse."

WILLOW: "Planet of the Apes!"

WILLOW: "Use the Force, Luke."

XANDER: "Do I even have to dignify that with a guess?"

(The movie-guessing game that Xander and Willow play as they walk through the graveyard.)

Rock, Paper, Scissors

XANDER: "We already played rock, paper, scissors. My hand's cramped up."

WILLOW: "Well yes, if you're always scissors of course...."

Amish, Witness (1985 film)

XANDER: "I've got a movie for you." (Puts ice cream on Willow's nose.) "You're Amish. You can't fight back 'cause you're Amish. I mock you with my ice cream cone, Amish guy!"

WILLOW: "Witness!"

Locusts

PRINCIPAL SNYDER: "The first day back. It always gets me. I mean it's incredible. One day the campus is completely bare, empty. The next there are children everywhere, like locusts, crawling around mindlessly bent on feeding and mating, destroying everything in sight with their relentless, pointless desire to exist."

Burning Man, Raves

"I did Burning Man in Black Rock. Such a great festival. You should have been there. They had drum rituals, mobile sculptures, raves, naked mud dances. You would have just—hated it with a fiery passion." (Jenny to Giles on what she did over the summer.)

Cibo Matto, Clog Dancing

XANDER: "Oh hey, did you hear Cibo Matto is gonna be at the Bronze tonight."

WILLOW: "Cibo Matto. They're playing?"

XANDER: "No, Will they're clog dancing."

WILLOW: "Cibo Matto can clog dance? Oh sarcasm, right."

Three Musketeers, Three Stooges ('40s-50s TV show)

CORDELIA: "Oh look, it's the three musketeers!"

WILLOW: "The three musketeers were cool."

XANDER: "I would have gone with stooges."

Sixth sense

PRINCIPAL SNYDER: "There are some things I can just smell. It's like a sixth sense."

GILES: "That would be one of the five."

Joan Collins, Dynasty ('70s TV show)

"You know, we've never really been close, which is nice because I don't really like you that much. But, you have on occasion saved the world and stuff so I'm going to do you a favor. I'm going to give some advice. Get over it. Whatever is causing the Joan Collins 'tude, deal with it. Embrace the pain, spank your inner moppet, whatever." (Cordelia to Buffy about what a bitch she is being.)

Spelling

WILLOW: "Why else would she be acting like such a B-I-T-C-H?"

GILES: "Willow, I think we're a little too old to be spelling things out."

XANDER: "A *bitca*?"

Political correctness

"I don't trust you—you're a vampire. Oh, I'm sorry, was that an offensive term? Should I say Undead American?" (Buffy to Angel.)

Stains

"What an ordeal. And you know what the worst part is? It stays with you forever. No matter what they tell you, none of that rust and blood and grime comes out. I mean, you can dry clean 'til judgement day. You are living with those stains." (Very shallow Cordelia to Jenny after they survive an ordeal.)

Cable

GILES: "What are you going to do—crawl into a cave for the rest of your life?"

BUFFY: "Would it have cable?"

2-2   Some Assembly Required

Written by Dean Batali, Directed by Bruce Seth Green

When emptied graves turn out to be the work of grave robbers, not vampires, the gang discovers that a Sunnydale High student is building a girlfriend.

Gene Siskel and Roger Ebert

"If you wouldn't mind a little Gene and Roger, you might want to leave off the 'idiot' part." (Buffy when she walks in on Giles, having just declared himself an idiot while rehearsing how he will ask Jenny on a date.)

Cyrano de Bergerac

BUFFY: "Speak English. Not whatever it is they speak in, uh…"

GILES: "England?"

BUFFY: "Yeah. You just say: 'I got a thing. You maybe have a thing. Maybe we could have a thing.'"

GILES: "Oh thank you, Cyrano."

Yodeling

"Are you crazy? You don't just sneak up on people in a graveyard! You make noise when you walk. You stomp, or you yodel." (Buffy when Angel startles her in the graveyard while on patrol.)

Zombies

XANDER: "That makes three girls signed up for the army of zombies."

WILLOW: "Is it an army if you just have three?"

BUFFY: "Zombie drill team then."

Scientific American (Magazine)

"Nothing in here but back issues of *Scientific American*. Ooh—I haven't read this one!" (Willow as they are searching lockers looking for evidence.)

Football, Basketball, Baseball, Rugby

JENNY: "I don't know what it is about football that does it for me. I mean, it lacks the grace of basketball, the poetry of baseball. At its best, it's unadorned aggression. It's such a rugged contest."

GILES: "Rugged. American football (chuckles). I just think it's rather odd that a nation that prides itself on its virility should feel compelled to strap on forty pounds of protective gear just in order to play rugby."

Batman, Bat-Signal

"Sorry to interrupt, Willow, but it's the Bat-Signal." (Buffy letting Willow know she is needed.)

My Girl ('60s song)

Eric sings this song as Chris works on stitching the body together.

Musical Chairs

"Well I guess that makes it official—everybody's paired off. Vampires get dates. Hell, even the school librarian sees more action than me. Do you ever think that the world is a giant game of musical chairs, and the music stopped, and we're the only ones who don't have a chair?" (Xander to Willow.)

2-3   School Hard

Written by Joss Whedon, Directed by John T. Kretchmer

Vampires from Angel's past, Spike and Drusilla, arrive in Sunnydale. While Buffy tries to keep her mother away from Principal Snyder at parent-teacher night, Spike invades the school and Buffy saves the day.

 Music in this Episode

"1000 Nights" and "Stupid Thing" by Nickel

Crucifixion, Woodstock, LSD

VAMPIRE: "When I kill her, it will be the greatest event since the Crucifixion. And I should know, 'cause I was there."

SPIKE: "You were there? Oh please. If every vampire who said he was at the Crucifixion was actually there, it would have been like Woodstock. I was actually at Woodstock. That was a weird gig. I fed off a flower person, and I spent the next six hours watching my hand move."

Reform

GILES: "That's a little unorthodox, isn't it?" (Discussing Spike's unusual name.)

BUFFY: "Maybe he's Reform."

✳ *Episode Reference | Where did Spike get his name?*

One possible origin for both the names "William the Bloody" and "Spike" is revealed in Spike's backstory shown in episode 5-7, "Fool for Love." When poetry by the bumbling human, William, is read aloud at a party in 1880 London, someone says, "They call him William the Bloody because of his bloody awful poetry," to which someone replies, "It suits him. I'd rather have a railroad spike through my head than listen to that awful stuff!"

Balloon animals

"Let me guess: he didn't make balloon animals." (Buffy when Giles says that the following Saturday will be the night of St. Vigeous.)

Anne Rice

ANGEL: "I gave the puppy-dog 'I'm all tortured' act. Keeps her off my back when I feed."

SPIKE: "People still fall for that Anne Rice routine! What a world!"

Uncle Tom's Cabin (1852 book), Yoda, Star Wars (1977 Film)

SPIKE: "You were my sire, man. You were my... Yoda!"

ANGEL: "Things change."

SPIKE: "Not us. Not demons! Man, I can't believe this! You Uncle Tom!"

Jack and the Beanstalk

"Fee, fie, fo, fum. I smell the blood of a nice, ripe girl." (Spike while stalking the halls at school.)

2-4 Inca Mummy Girl

Written by Joe Reinkemeyer, Directed by Ellen S. Pressman

The foreign exchange student staying with Buffy turns out to be a dangerous mummy who of course Xander is attracted to. Like Buffy, the Inca Princess was a chosen one—one girl in a generation—chosen to sacrifice and die to protect her people from the nether world.

 ### *Music in this Episode*

"Shadows" and "Fate" by Four Star Mary (as Dingoes Ate My Baby)

 ### *What's up with all the cheese?*

There must be an inside joke about cheese. In this episode, bored Willow builds a structure out of cheese, and in episode 16 of this season, Buffy is returned from being a rat and says she recalls a "sudden need for cheese." In season 4, Willow tells Riley that Buffy loves cheese, and in Season 6, a man with cheese slices haunts the Scoobies' dreams.

Bell curve

"That's Rodney Munsen. He's God's gift to the bell curve. What he lacks in smarts, he makes up in lack of smarts." (Xander to Buffy about the mischievous student in the museum.)

Scone

"Oh I know this one: Slaying entails certain sacrifices. Blah blah bitty-blah. I'm so stuffy. Give me a scone." (Buffy when Giles says she can't go to a dance because she's the Slayer and has responsibilities.)

Doritos, Chihuahua

"Do we have to speak Spanish when we see him? Because I don't know anything much besides *Doritos* and *Chihuahua*." (Xander as they look for the South American foreign exchange student at the bus station.)

A Summer Place (1959 film), Oz likely refers to the 1960 Percy Faith arrangement

DEVON: "What does a girl have to do to impress you?"

OZ: "Well, it involves a feather boa and the theme to *A Summer Place*. I can't discuss it here." (When Oz says that Cordelia is not his type.)

Twinkies

"This is called a snack food. It's a delicious, spongy, golden cake, stuffed with a delightful, creamy white substance of goodness." (Xander introducing Ampata to Twinkies.)

Chess club

"We're not in the archeology club. We're in… we're in the… crime club. Which is kind of like a chess club, but with crime. And no chess." (Xander explaining to Ampata why they are investigating the seal.)

Praying Mantis

AMPATA: "Can I tell you a secret? I like you too."

XANDER: "Really? That's great! You're not a praying mantis, are you?"

※ *Episode Reference*

The above comment from Xander is a reference to episode 1-4, "Teacher's Pet," in which he was seduced by a demon who resembled a giant praying mantis.

Sergio Leone, Clint Eastwood

"I'm from the country of Leone. It's in Italy, pretending to be Montana." (Xander explaining his Eastwood-esque costume.)

Grand Canyon

CORDELIA'S POSSE: "Where's Sven?"

CORDELIA: "Oh, I keep trying to ditch him. He's like one of those dogs that you leave at the Grand Canyon on vacation. It follows you back across four states."

Mommy Dearest (1981 film)

"I'll get Xander before he gets smoochy with mummy dearest." (Buffy to Xander about rescuing Xander from Ampata the mummy.)

※ *The true identity of Dingoes*

When Oz's band, Dingoes Ate My Baby, performs, you are actually hearing performances of the band Four Star Mary.

2-5   Reptile Boy

Written and Directed by David Greenwalt

Tired of everyone telling her what she can and cannot do, Buffy lies to Angel and Giles and goes to a frat party with Cordelia. The frat boys drug the girls and offer them up to a demon in exchange for a promise of prosperity.

 Music in this Episode

> "Wolves" by Clement & Murray
> "She" by Louie Says
> "Bring Me On" by Act of Faith

Kind of Hush ('60s hit song)

"I for one am giddy and up. There's a kind of hush all over Sunnydale. No demons or vampires to slay. I'm here with my friends." (Buffy talking about how nice and quiet it's been in Sunnydale lately.)

Corndog

WILLOW: "You lied to Giles!"

BUFFY: "Look I wasn't lying. I was just protecting him from information he wouldn't be able to digest properly."

XANDER: "Like a corndog."

Bizarro (DC Comics supervillain who is the mirror-image of Superman)

"You could belong to a fraternity of rich and powerful men... in the Bizarro World." (Cordelia to Xander.)

The Hulk

"The Hulk is gone, so you don't have to dance with me." (Buffy's date, having 'rescued' her from an obnoxious party guest, saying the other guy is gone now.)

2-6   Halloween

Written by Carl Ellsworth, Directed by Bruce Seth Green

Ethan Rayne from Giles' past comes to Sunnydale and casts a spell which causes Buffy and the gang to be transformed into expressions of their Halloween costumes.

 Music in this Episode

> "Shy" by Epperley
> "How She Died" by Treble Charger

Barbie Dream Car

"So I told Devon: You call that leather interior? My Barbie Dream Car had nicer seats." (Cordelia making small talk with Angel at the Bronze as he waits for Buffy for their coffee date.)

Carpal Tunnel Syndrome

PRINCIPAL SNYDER: "Halloween must be a big night for you. Tossing eggs, keying cars, bobbing for apples: one pathetic cry for help after another. Well, not this year, Missy."

BUFFY: "Gosh, I'd love to sign up. But I recently contracted carpal tunnel syndrome and I tragically can no longer hold a flashlight."

Care Bears ('80s TV show)

WILLOW: "Angel's a vampire. I thought you knew."

CORDELIA: "Oh, Angel's a vampire. But the cuddly kind, like a Care Bear with fangs."

Xena: Warrior Princess ('90s TV show)

"She couldn't have dressed up like Xena?" (Willow wryly commenting that Buffy's costume led to her being helpless.)

Amnesia

XANDER: "She must be right. We must have some kind of amnesia."

BUFFY: "I don't know what that is, but I'm certain I don't have it. I bathe quite often."

Peanut Butter

GILES: "Primarily the division of self: male and female. Light and dark."

ETHAN: "Chunky and Creamy—oh, sorry that's peanut butter."

2-7   Lie to Me

Written and Directed by Joss Whedon

Buffy's old friend from Los Angeles moves to Sunnydale. She's thrilled until she learns that he has made a deal with Spike to trade her in exchange for immortality as a vampire.

Music in this Episode

"Lois, On The Brink" by Willoughby
"Never Land" by Sisters Of Mercy
"Reptile" by Creaming Jesus

Chanterelle will be back as Lily

The character Chanterelle appears again as Lily in episode 3-1, "Anne."

Marie Antoinette

CORDELIA: "I just don't see why everyone's always picking on Marie Antoinette. I can so relate to her. She worked really hard to look that good. And people just don't appreciate that kind of effort. And I know the peasants were all depressed."

XANDER: "I think you mean oppressed."

CORDELIA: "Whatever. They were cranky. So they were like, 'Let's lose some heads!' That's fair! And Marie Antoinette cared about them! She was gonna let them have cake."

Oreos

"I'd suggest a box of Oreos dunked in apple juice, but maybe she's over that phase." (Ford on what Buffy used to like to eat.)

I Touch Myself (1991 song), Divinyls

"I moped over you for months. Sitting in my room listening to that Divinyls song *I Touch Myself*. Of course I had no idea what it was about." (Buffy telling Ford that she used to have a crush on him.)

Sore thumbs

WILLOW: "Okay, but do they really stick out? I mean have you ever seen a thumb and gone 'Wow! That baby is sore!'"

XANDER: "You have too many thoughts."

Monster Trucks

GILES: "Honestly. I've always been interested in Monster trucks."

BUFFY: "You took him to Monster Trucks?"

JENNY: "I thought it would be a change. We could have just left."

GILES: "What, and miss the nitro-burning funny cars? We couldn't have that."

Black Hat (Western film genre bad-guy stereotype), Happily ever after

GILES: "Yes, it's terribly simple. The good guys are always stalwart and true. The bad guys are easily distinguished by the pointy horns or black hats. And we always defeat them and save the day. No one ever dies, and everyone lives happily ever after."

BUFFY: "Liar."

2-8 The Dark Age

Written by Rob Des Hotel, Directed by Bruce Seth Green

A demon from Giles' wildest young days comes to Sunnydale to kill him and Ethan. The demon possesses Jenny, and Ethan tricks it into targeting Buffy instead.

Gavin Rossdale, John Cusack, Amy Yip

The celebrities that Buffy, Willow, and Xander include in their fantasies when they play a game of "Anywhere But Here."

Meals on Wheels

GILES: "A Medical transport is delivering the monthly blood supply to the hospital."

BUFFY: "Vampire meals on wheels."

Seven Deadly Sins

ANGEL: "Maybe he's late."

BUFFY: "Giles? Who counts tardiness as the eighth deadly sin?"

Halloween

BUFFY: "I know you. You were in that costume shop."

ETHAN: "I'm pleased you remembered."

BUFFY: "You sold me that dress for Halloween and nearly got us all killed!"

ETHAN: "But you looked great."

※ *Episode Reference*

Buffy is referring to what happened in episode 2-6, "Halloween," in which Buffy, Willow, Xander, and other Sunnydale kids were transformed into whatever was portrayed by their Halloween costumes.

Abacus

XANDER: "You know, computers are on the way out. I think paper's going to make a big comeback."

WILLOW: "And the abacus."

Lost Weekend (1945 film)

"I don't like you *Lost-Weekend*ing…." (Buffy commenting on Giles' drinking.)

The Sound of Music (1965 film)

"I'm fine. I'm not running around with the wind in my hair, the-hills-are-alive-with-the-sound-of-music fine, but I'm coping." (Jenny in answer to Giles when he asks how she is feeling.)

The Sound of Music (1965 film)

"The hills are not alive." (Giles when Buffy asks if Jenny is okay.)

Bay City Rollers ('80s band)

"Bay City Rollers—now that's music!" (Giles to Buffy.)

2-9   What's My Line (Part 1)

Written by Marti Noxon, Directed by David Solomon

Assassins sent by Spike hunt Buffy as the gang ponders their future careers. Kendra, a new Slayer in town, targets Angel, and Oz meets Willow at last.

The gang is first called the Scoobies | Why "Scoobies"?

This episode is the first in which the gang is referred to as the Scoobies.

Why that name? The Scooby Doo cartoon from the 1970s and 1980s featured a group of teens and their dog Scooby Doo. They solved mysteries which skirted on the edge of the supernatural and often were hoaxes.

Department of Motor Vehicles (DMV)

"You know, with that kind of attitude, you could have had a bright future as an employee at the DMV." (Xander to Buffy about her pessimistic attitude.)

What's My Line ('50s game show)

"You know its a whole week of *What's My Line*, but I don't get to play." (Buffy to Angel that it's career week at school.)

Cliff Notes

"*Cliff Notes* version? I want a normal life." (Buffy to Angel.)

Dorothy Hamill

"Oh my god! My Dorothy Hamill phase. My room in L.A. was pretty much a shrine. Dorothy dolls, Dorothy posters. I even got a Dorothy haircut, thereby securing a place for myself in the geek hall of fame." (Buffy on how she was a Dorothy Hamill fan as a child.)

Polyester

XANDER: "They assigned you to the booth for law enforcement professionals."

BUFFY: "As in police?"

XANDER: "As in polyester, donuts, and brutality."

Tony Robbins

"First I have to deal with Giles. He's on this Tony Robbins hyper-efficiency kick. Expects me to check in every day after homeroom." (Buffy to Willow and Xander.)

No. 2 Pencil

"But I handed in my test! I used a number-two pencil!" (Willow to Xander, anxious because her test results were not posted along with everyone else's.)

Ho Hos (Snack cakes)

"But Ho Hos are a vital part of my cognitive process." (Xander at the prospect of not getting to have snacks while they work.)

Super Bowl

ANGEL: "Do you know what that ring means?" (About a ring left behind by a vamp that Buffy dusted.)

BUFFY: "I just killed a Super Bowl champ?"

King Solomon, Elks, Bowling

GILES: "It's a society of deadly assassins dating back to King Solomon."

XANDER: "And didn't they beat the Elks this year in the Sunnydale adult bowling league championships?"

GILES: "Their credo is to sow discord and kill the unwary."

XANDER: "Bowling is a vicious game."

GILES: "That's enough Xander!"

The Whole Nine Yards

"They had tools, flashlights, whole nine yards. What does that mean, anyway? Whole nine yards. Nine yards of what?" (Buffy telling Giles about the thieving vampires.)

Tadpoles, Frog fear

WILLOW: "Don't warn the tadpoles!"

GILES: "You all right?"

WILLOW: "Giles what are doing here?"

GILES: "It's the library. You fell asleep. Don't warn the tadpoles?"

WILLOW: "I have frog fear."

※ *Episode Reference*

Willow's frog-fear will come up again when she feigns it to distract a security guard in episode 2-18, "Killed By Death."

Scooby Doo ('70s TV show)

"If you want to be a member of the Scooby gang, you have to be willing to be inconvenienced now and then." (Xander to Cordelia.)

2-10 What's My Line (Part 2)

Written by Marti Noxon, Directed by David Semel

Spike captures Angel in a plot to cure Drusilla, so Buffy and Kendra must work together to save him. Xander and Cordelia secretly develop a new aspect of their relationship.

Power Rangers ('90s TV show)

"Back off Pink Ranger!" (Buffy to Kendra when she confronts Willow.)

Mary Kay (Cosmetics)

XANDER: "Okay Mary Kay, time to… time to run!" (To the assassin posing as a cosmetics salesperson.)

Crispy Critters (1980s breakfast cereal)

"My buddy Angel? You think I'd let him fry? I saved him in the nick. He was about five minutes away from being a Crispy Critter." (Willy the barman to Buffy when she comes to him looking for Angel.)

Baguette

"I was dreaming. We were in Paris. You had a branding iron. And there were worms in my baguette." (Drusilla when Spike awakens her.)

T-Shirt, Slayer Handbook

KENDRA: "I study because it is required. The Slayer Handbook insists on it."

WILLOW: "There's a Slayer Handbook?"

BUFFY: "Handbook? What handbook? How come I don't have a handbook?"

WILLOW: "Is there a t-shirt too? Because that would be cool."

Pocket protector

"Hello and welcome to planet pocket-protector." (Buffy commenting on Giles and Kendra talking about books.)

Disneyland

BUFFY: "I wonder if it would be so bad being replaced."

WILLOW: "You mean like letting Kendra take over?"

BUFFY: "Maybe. I mean, maybe after this thing with Spike and the assassins is over I can say Kendra! You slay, I'm going to Disneyland."

E-flat diminished ninth

WILLOW: "Don't you have any ambition?"

OZ: "Oh yeah: E-flat diminished ninth."

WILLOW: "Huh?"

OZ: "E-flat, that's doable. But that diminished ninth. You know—it's a man's chord. You could lose a finger."

Soccer

"Who sponsored Career Day today, the British soccer fan association?" (Xander, because of the violence and gun-play that took place at career day.)

Molly Ringwald, Pizza

"... teen videofest. Possibly something from the Ringwald oeuvre. When this is over I'm thinking pineapple pizza and teen video moviefest." (Buffy to Kendra on what to do after the fight.)

Beatles, I am the Walrus (1967 song)

"I am the bug-man, coo-coo-ca-choo." (Xander when he spots a reference to a bug demon in a book.)

※ *Episode Reference*

Xander says: "No but this dude was completely different than praying mantis lady. He was a man of bugs, not a man who was a bug." This is a reference to episode 1-4, "Teacher's Pet."

Rebecca of Sunnybrook Farm (1932, 1938 film)

"And if Dru dies, your little Rebecca of Sunnyhell Farm and her mates are spared her coming-out party." (Spike talking to Angel referring to Buffy.)

Animal Crackers, Hippo

"Oh look. Monkey. And he has a little hat, and little pants. The monkey's the only cookie animal that gets to wear clothes, you know that? So I'm wondering, do the other cookie animals feel kind of ripped. Like is the hippo going, 'Hey man—where are my pants? I have my hippo dignity'." (Oz, charming Willow.)

Chevy Chase

"Relax. You earned it. Sit in your seat, you eat your peanuts, you watch the movie… unless it's about a dog or Chevy Chase." (Buffy instructing Kendra on how to relax while she is on her flight home.)

2-11 Ted

Written by Joss Whedon, Directed by Bruce Seth Green

Buffy's is suspicious of Joyce's new boyfriend, and her suspicions are confirmed when he hits her when Joyce isn't looking. When she fights back, the results are severe. Later she learns that he is a robot—which she never suspected.

Captain & Tennille

XANDER: "You don't know what you're talking about."

WILLOW: "Xander, he was obviously in charge."

XANDER: "He was a puppet. She was using him."

WILLOW: "He didn't seem like the type of guy that would let himself be used."

XANDER: "That was her genius! He didn't even know he was playing second fiddle. Buffy—who was the real power: the Captain, or Tennille?"

Miniature golf

TED: "Buffy, do you like miniature golf?"

XANDER: "Who doesn't!"

Sigmund Freud

XANDER: "Buf, you're lacking evidence. I think maybe we're in Sigmund Freud territory... You're having parental issues!"

BUFFY: "Freud would have said the exact same thing. Except he might not have added in that little dance."

Stepford Wives (1975 film)

BUFFY: "Mom's been totally different since he's been around."

WILLOW: "Like happy?"

BUFFY: "Like Stepford."

Creature Feature ('60s film genre)

"What was he? A demon? A giant bug? Some kind of dark god with secrets of nouveau cuisine? I mean, we're talking creature feature here—right?" (Xander wondering what kind of dangerous creature Ted might be.)

※ *Episode Reference*

When Xander includes "giant bug" in his list, this is a reference to episode 1-4, "Teacher's Pet," in which he is seduced by a demon who resembles a giant praying mantis.

Parcheesi (Game)

"Buffy? How about a nice game of Parcheesi?" (Robot Ted as he malfunctions.)

Thelma and Louise (1991 film)

JOYCE: "Do you want to rent a movie tonight? Just nothing with horror in it. Or romance. Or men."

BUFFY: "I guess we're *Thelma and Louise*-ing it again?"

2-12 Bad Eggs

Written by Marti Noxon, Directed by David Greenwalt

When the health class teacher gives the students eggs to teach them about the responsibilities of parenting, they soon learn that the eggs are actually evil body-snatchers in disguise.

 Gorch the Slayer hunter

Lyle Gorch, the vampire that Buffy annoys at the beginning of this episode is one of those who hunt her in episode 3-5, "Homecoming."

Muumuus

"Everyday Woman? Why didn't you just go to Muumuus R Us?" (Buffy poking fun at her mother's fashion sense.)

Dreidel Song, Jewish, Christian

XANDER: "It's the whole sex-leads-to-responsibility thing, which I personally don't get. You've got to take care of the egg. It's a baby. You've got to keep it safe and teach it Christian values."

WILLOW: "My egg is Jewish."

XANDER: "Then teach it that Dreidel song."

Gigapet

"I can't do this. I can't take care of things! I killed my Gigapet. Literally. I sat on it and it broke." (Buffy about how she can't take care of her egg because she's so negligent she even killed an inanimate object.)

Red Cross

"That's okay. I figured there were all sorts of things vampires can't do. You know, like work for the telephone company or volunteer for the Red Cross, or have little vampires." (Buffy when Angel points out that he can't be a father.)

2-13 Surprise (Part 1)

Written by Marti Noxon, Directed by Michael Lange

Buffy's birthday is interrupted when they learn that Drusilla is planning to destroy the world by reassembling the Judge. Angel gives Buffy a claddagh ring, and they consummate their relationship, resulting in something that neither of them suspected.

 Music in this Episode

"Transylvanian Concubine" by Rasputina
"Anything" by Cari Howe

 Emmy award for Best Makeup

This episode plus the next one ("Innocence") won an Emmy Award in 1998 for Best Makeup in a Series.

Discretion is the better part of valor, Drama queen

GILES: "Now remember: discretion is the better part of valor."

XANDER: "You coulda' just said 'Shh!' Are all you Brits such drama queens?"

Jack and the Beanstalk

GILES: "Dreams aren't prophecies, Buffy. You dreamed that the Master was rising but you stopped it from happening."

XANDER: "You ground his bones to make your bread."

BUFFY: "That's true. Except for the bread part."

Snakes in a Can

XANDER: "What, uh, vamp's version of snakes-in-a-can, or do you care to share?" (Asking Angel about the disembodied arm in the box.)

Denny's (Restaurant)

"It's sad, granted. But let's look at the upside for a moment. I mean, what kind of a future could she have really had with him. She's got two jobs: Denny's waitress by day, Slayer by night. And Angel's always in front of the TV with a big blood-belly. And he's dreaming of the glory days when Buffy still thought this whole 'creature of the night' routine was a big turn-on." (Xander on the future for Buffy and Angel.)

※ Episode Reference

Willow says to Buffy: "Carpe Diem—you told me that once." This is a reference to episode 1-1, "Welcome to the Hellmouth," although Buffy's exact words in that episode was "Seize the moment").

2-14 Innocence (Part 2)

Written and Directed by Joss Whedon

When his single moment of complete bliss reverses the gypsy curse, Angel turns back into a demon and is bent on torturing Buffy. This dark episode presents a major turning point in the lives and relationships of almost every character.

 Multiple Roles: The Judge

The actor who plays The Judge also played the vampire Luke in season 1.

911

LADY: "Hey, are you okay? Want me to call 911?"

ANGEL: "No. The pain is gone. I feel just fine."

I Can Read (Children's book series)

XANDER: "After class I'll come help you research."

CORDELIA: "You might find something useful if it's in an 'I Can Read' book."

Episode Reference

Xander says: "Remember Halloween I got turned into a Soldier? Well I still remember all of it. I know procedure, ordinance, access codes, everything. I know the whole layout of this base, and I'm pretty sure I could put together an M16 in 57 seconds." This is a reference to episode 2-6, "Halloween."

Linoleum

CORDELIA: "Does looking at guns make you wanna have sex?"

XANDER: "I'm 17. Looking at Linoleum makes me wanna have sex."

Cable Television

OZ: "So do you guys steal weapons from the army a lot?"

WILLOW: "We don't have cable, so we have to make our own fun."

Smurfs ('80s TV show)

"Everybody keep back: damage control only. Get any of the vamps you can, and I'll handle the Smurf." (Buffy about the Judge, who is blue.)

Stowaway (1936 film)

The film Joyce and Buffy watch together at the end of the evening.

2-15 Phases

Written by Dean Batali, Directed by Bruce Seth Green

Buffy stops a poacher from killing a werewolf. When Oz awakens, naked, in the forest, he suspects that the bite he got from his baby cousin Geordi may have turned him into the werewolf the gang has been looking for.

 Music in this Episode

"Blind For Now" by Lotion

Cheerleading

WILLOW "What are you looking at?"

Oz: (Looking at the school trophy case) "This cheerleading trophy. It's like its eyes are following you wherever you go. I like it."

※ *Episode Reference*

The cheerleading trophy Oz mentions in the above quote first appears at the end of episode 1-3, "Witch."

Popcorn

"Today's movies are kind of like popcorn—you know, you forget about them as soon as they're done? I do remember I liked the popcorn though." (Oz when Willow asked about the movie he saw.)

Thighmaster

"Oh thank you, Thighmaster!" (Larry, crudely, when he knocks the books out of a girl's hands just to get her to bend over.)

Almanac

GILES: "Meaning the accepted legend that werewolves only prowl during the full moon might be erroneous."

CORDELIA: "Or it cold be a crock."

XANDER: "Unless the werewolf was using last year's almanac."

Obsession (Cologne)

"I think you splashed on just a little too much Obsession for Dorks." (Cordelia to Xander when he hushes Oz for touching Willow.)

Moon Pie

GILES: "While there is absolutely no scientific explanation for the lunar effect on the human psyche, the phases of the moon do seem to exert a great deal of psychological influence. And the full moon seems to bring out our darkest qualities."

XANDER: "And yet ironically led to the invention of the Moon Pie."

Hitler (Mein Führer)

"I hope we find him before Mein Furrier." (Buffy to Giles about finding a werewolf before the hunter does.)

Robby the Robot, Forbidden Planet (1956 film)

"If it wasn't for you, people would be lined up five-deep to get buried. Willow would be Robby the Robot's love slave, I wouldn't even have a head...."

※ *Episode Reference*

This reference to Robby the Robot is a reference to Moloch in episode 1-8, "I, Robot... You, Jane"

Roadrunner and Coyote

BUFFY: "Have you dropped any hints?"

WILLOW: "I've dropped anvils."

BUFFY: "He'll come around. What guy could resist your wily Willow charms."

(Willow wishes Oz would take their relationship to the next level.)

※ *Episode Reference*

Xander says: "I know what it's like to crave the taste of freshly killed meat. To be taken over by those uncontrollable urges." This is a reference to Xander's possession by a hyena-demon in episode 1-6, "The Pack."

2-16 Bewitched, Bothered, and Bewildered
Written by Marti Noxon, Directed by James A. Contner

Xander gets Amy to cast a love spell on Cordelia, but it has the opposite effect, causing every woman in Sunnydale *except* Cordelia to pursue him at any cost.

 Music in this Episode

"Drift Away" by Naked
"Got the Love" by The Average White Band
"Pain" by Four Star Mary (as Dingoes Ate My Baby)

No Muss, No Fuss (Advertising slogan)

"I wish dating was like slaying—you know, simple, direct, stake to the heart, no muss, no fuss." (Xander on how complicated Valentine's Day is.)

Say It with Flowers (Advertising slogan)

GILES: "Where did this come from?" (Discussing a note from Angel.)

BUFFY: "He said it with flowers."

Walmart

"All you gave me was that Smallmart-looking thing." (Cordelia to Xander about the necklace he gave her.)

Midol

"Okay Harmony, if you need to borrow my Midol, just ask." (Cordelia subtly telling Harmony that she is being a bitch.)

Roofie, Date drug

"She loved you before you invoked the great roofie-spirit." (Buffy to Xander about Willow.)

2-17 Passion

Written by Ty King, Directed by Michael Gershman

Jenny finally completes her translation program for the spell to give Angel back his soul, but before she can tell anybody, Angel comes to the school and kills her. He then arranges her in Giles' bed in order to torment him.

 Music in this Episode

"Never An Easy Way" by Morcheeba

"O soave fanciulla" from La Boheme, Puccini, Performed by Jonathon Welch

Tooth Fairy

"A visit from the pointed-tooth fairy." (Xander on how Angel visited Buffy's room during the night.)

Naa nana, na naaa

GILES: "He's trying to taunt you. To goad you into a mishap."

XANDER: "The 'Nana na nana, naaa' approach to battle."

GILES: "Once more you've managed to boil a complex thought down to its simplest possible form."

※ *Episode Reference*

Joyce says: "Angel... the college boy who was tutoring you in history." This is a reference to the lie Buffy told Joyce in episode 1-7, "Angel."

Snoopy, A Charlie Brown Christmas (1965 TV special), Crucifix

WILLOW: "I'm gonna have a hard time explaining this to my dad."

BUFFY: "You really think it'll bother him?"

WILLOW: "Ira Rosenberg's only daughter nailing crucifixes to the bedroom wall? I have to go to Xander's house to watch *A Charlie Brown Christmas* every year. Although it is worthwhile to see him do the Snoopy dance!"

Faster, Pussycat! Kill! Kill! (1965 film)

Xander says this to Giles, saying he thinks Giles should kill Angel.

2-18 Killed by Death

Written by Dean Batali, Directed by Deran Sarafian

When the flu and a high fever put Buffy in the hospital, she battles an invisible monster that kills sick children.

Gwyneth Paltrow, Mr. Potato Head

"I don't know. Lysette got her nose done here, and she came in looking for the Gwyneth Paltrow and it looked more like Mr. Potato Head." (Cordelia on how the Sunnydale Hospital might not be the best place.)

The Seventh Seal (1957 Swedish film), Chess

"If he wants you to play chess, don't even do it, the guy's like a wiz." (Xander when Buffy says she thinks she saw Death in the hospital.)

Firemen, Security Guards

SECURITY GUARD: "You know, most people think that security guards are just guys who failed the police exam, but that's not me. This is my career."

CORDELIA: "Stereotypes are so unfair."

SECURITY GUARD: "I did take the firemen's exam though. I didn't do so good."

CORDELIA: "You know, I think that security guards are way sexier than firemen. They're all sooty."

SECURITY GUARD: "Well this is where all the action is, anyhow. I'm all the time restraining people."

Rogaine

XANDER: "Could you make a little more with the touchy-gropey?"

CORDELIA: "Jealous?"

XANDER: "Of Rogaine Boy? I think not."

Post-Its

"I'll check Backer's office and see if I can find any Post-Its marked 'Why a monster might want me dead'." (Willow to Buffy as they investigate children's deaths at the hospital.)

Playing Doctor

WILLOW: "I'm good at medical stuff. Xander and I used to
time."

XANDER: "She's being literal. She had the medical volume
with stuff. I didn't have the heart to tell her she w

WILLOW: "Wrong? Why?" (Turning to Buffy....) "How did you play doctor?"

BUFFY: "I never have."

Invisible Man (1933 film)

XANDER: "Maybe I'll get lucky with the Death guy."

CORDELIA: "He's invisible."

XANDER: "Yeah, but if I see a pipe and a smoking jacket then he's dropped."

Sherlock Holmes

WILLOW: "Hey wait, I think I have something."

BUFFY: "Okay, Sherlock."

Frogs

"Frogs. Frogs! Get them off of me!" (Willow, using her frog-fear as a way to
distract the hospital security guards.)

❋ *Episode Reference*

*The above quote is the second reference to Willow's "frog-fear." We first learned
of this when she woke up from a nightmare about tadpoles in episode 2-9,
"What's My Line, Part 1."*

2-19 I Only Have Eyes for You

Written by Marti Noxon, Directed by James Whitmore, Jr.

The spirits of a lovelorn high school boy and the teacher who was the object of
his desire endlessly reenact the murder-suicide that ended their lives in 1955 at
Sunnydale High.

 ### *Music in this Episode*

"Charge" by Splendid
"I Only Have Eyes For You" by The Flamingos

Vegan

SECRETARY: "Mr. Snyder, Billy Crandon chained himself to the snack machine
again."

SNYDER: "Pathetic little no-life vegan!"

...mpson

"You just went OJ on your girlfriend." (Buffy to a kid who was threatening to kill his girlfriend.)

JFK (1991 film)

"People can be coerced, Summers. I'm no stranger to conspiracy. I saw *JFK*." (Principal Snyder when Buffy says that the janitor can confirm her story.)

Loch Ness Monster

XANDER: "I was just accosted by some kind of... locker monster." (A phantom demon hand attacked Xander at his school locker.)

GILES: "Loch Ness monster?"

Wall Street (1987 film)

"I'm dead as hell and I'm not going to take it any more." (Xander describing the anger from a ghost.)

Dr. Laura Schlessinger

"Fabulous! Now we're Dr. Laura for the deceased." (Buffy when Giles said the only way to stop the haunting of the school is to help the ghosts resolve the issue that holds them there.)

Final Solution, The Exorcist (1973 film)

WILLOW: "The only solution is the final solution."

XANDER: "Nuke the school? I like that."

WILLOW: "Not quite. Exorcism."

CORDELIA: "Are you crazy? I saw that movie. Even the priest died!"

I Only Have Eyes for You ('50s song)

Title of episode, and the song the ghosts dance to.

Raid (insecticide)

"So what now? Not even a mega-vat of Raid's going to do the trick here." (Xander as the gang stands before Sunnydale High, which is guarded by an impenetrable wall of wasps.)

2-20 Go Fish

Written by Elin Hampton, Directed by David Semel

The gang investigates when members of the swim team begin to disappear. To get a look on the inside, Xander joins the team. The gang solves the mystery, and Xander saves Buffy's life for the second time.

 Music in this Episode

"Mann's Chinese" by Naked
"If You'd Listen" by Nero's Rome

Yankees, Abott and Costello, The A-Team ('80s TV show)

"... The Yankees, Abott and Costello, The A—now that was a team." (Xander complaining about the swim team.)

Solitaire

"Your pie chart is looking a lot like solitaire. With naked ladies on the cards." (Willow to a student who is goofing off in computer class.)

Abraham Lincoln, Thomas Jefferson, All men are created equal

CORDELIA: "Xander I know you take pride in being the voice of the common wuss, but the truth is, certain people are entitled to special privileges. They're called winners. That's the way the world works."

XANDER: "And what about that nutty 'All men are created equal' thing?"

CORDELIA: "Propaganda spouted out by the ugly and less deserving."

XANDER: "I think that was Lincoln."

CORDELIA: "Disgusting mole and stupid hat."

WILLOW: "Actually it was Jefferson."

CORDELIA: "Kept slaves, remember?"

Gertrude Ederle

"When I'm in the vastness of the ocean, it's like I'm never alone. You ever hear of a woman named Gertrude Ederle? First woman to swim the English Channel." (Self-absorbed swim-team jock Ken babbling to Buffy.)

Velcro

BUFFY: "Where's Gage?"

XANDER: "He was right behind me, putting his sneakers on. But it's not the Velcro kind, so give him a couple of extra minutes."

Steroids, Discus Throwers, Crucifixion

WILLOW: "If steroids are that dangerous, why would they do that to themselves?"

BUFFY: "They needed to win. And winning equals trophies which equals prestige for the school. And you see how they're treated. It's been like that forever."

XANDER: "Sure, the discus throwers got the best seats at all the crucifixions."

Steroids, Aromatherapy, You're Soaking In It (Advertising slogan)

XANDER: "The steroids. Where are they?"

CAM: "You're soaking in it, bud. Aromatherapy. It's in the steam."

Oreos

BUFFY: "So something ripped him open and ate out his insides?"

WILLOW: "Like an Oreo cookie, but without, you know, the chocolatey Oreo goodness."

Chicken Little

"We couldn't find any sea demon that matched the description that Xander gave us. Not like Chicken Little is much of a witness." (Cordelia saying that her research hadn't found anything, and taking the opportunity to insult Xander.)

Three Times a Lady (1978 song), Tartar sauce

BUFFY: "I wouldn't break out the tartar sauce just yet. It's not like you were exposed more than once."

WILLOW: "Twice?"

XANDER: "Three times a fish guy."

(The gang is talking about the steam that has been turning the swim team into sea demons.)

The Blue Lagoon (1980 film), Creature From the Black Lagoon (1954 film), Brooke Shields

CORDELIA: "It's one thing to be dating the lame unpopular guy, but it's another to be dating the creature from the Blue Lagoon."

XANDER: "Black Lagoon. The creature from the Blue Lagoon was Brooke Shields."

Skinnydipping

"We found Sean. He was in the pool skinless dipping." (Cordelia to the gang explaining where the missing member of the swim team is.)

2-21 Becoming (Part 1)

Written and Directed by Joss Whedon

When an evil demon long since turned into stone is unearthed by a local archaeologist, Angel and Drusilla plot to revive it to destroy the world. Meanwhile Willow finds a disk with Jenny's program to give Angel his soul. In this episode we see Drusilla's backstory, Angel's journey from a young Glasgow drunkard to a vampire cursed by gypsies, and Angel's first glimpse of the pre-Sunnydale Buffy.

 Emmy award for Music Composition

This episode won an Emmy for Outstanding Music Composition for a Series.

 "Angel" Episode Cross Reference

You can see more of Angel's backstory in "Angel" episode 1-15, "The Prodigal."

Buy American, Fish Sticks

XANDER: (Playing with fish sticks—one of which has a toothpick) "Tell Angel I'm gonna kill him. No wait… I'm gonna kill you! Die! Die. Die. Argh. Mother?"

BUFFY: "Exactly how it happened."

OZ: "I thought it was riveting. I was a little unclear about some of the themes."

BUFFY: "The theme is Angel is too much of a coward to take me on face to face."

XANDER: "Yeah the other thing was Buy American but it got kind of buried."

Alfalfa, Our Gang ('30s TV show)

BUFFY: "And you're sure this is the tomb of Alfalfa?"

GILES: "Alcatha."

Bullock's

"You're not from Bullock's are you? Because I meant to pay for that lipstick."
(Fifteen-year-old Buffy upon meeting her first Watcher.)

Al Franken

"Shouldn't you be pulling a sword out of Al Franken or whatever his name is?"
(Buffy not getting Alcatha's name yet again while small-talking with Angel before fighting.)

2-22 Becoming (Part 2)

Written and Directed by Joss Whedon

Buffy must stop Angel's evil plan to destroy the world, although Buffy hopes that Willow can return Angel's soul before she is forced to kill him. Things get worse when the police think she killed Kendra, her mother learns she is the Slayer, and Principal Snyder expels her from school.

Music in this Episode

"Full Of Grace" by Sarah McLachlan

Mutant Enemy Monster needs a hug

After the credits at the end of the episode, instead of his usual "Grr, Argh," the Mutant Enemy Monster says, "Oh, I need a hug."

Manchester United, McDonald's, Happy Meals

"We like to talk big, vampires do: 'I'm going to destroy the world.' It's just tough-guy talk. Strutting around with your friends over a pint of blood. The truth is, I like this world. You've got dog racing, and Manchester United, and you've got people. Billions of people walking around like Happy Meals on legs." (Spike explaining to Buffy why he doesn't want the world to end.)

Piccadilly, Leicester Square, It's a Long Way to Tipperary (1912 song)

"Angel could pull it off. Goodbye Piccadilly, farewell Leicester bloody Square. You know what I'm saying?" (Spike on why he wants to help Buffy stop Angel.)

Episode Reference

Joyce asks Spike if they've met, and he says: "You hit me on the head with an axe one time. Remember: 'Get the hell away from my daughter'?" This is a reference to episode 2-3, "School Hard."

Postal Worker, Going postal

JOYCE: "I am sure that they will understand."

BUFFY: "Get them involved and you get them killed."

JOYCE: "Well you're not going to hurt them are you?"

BUFFY: "I'm a Slayer, not a postal worker. Cops can't fight demons. I have to do it."

Sit 'N Spin

"Keep out of it, Sit 'N Spin!" (Angel, disparaging Spike and his wheelchair.)

Season Three:
Buffy Graduates

Aired: 1998-1999

Big-bad: The Mayor

(Episode Table starts on page 240)

---

*"Chemistry's easy.
It's a lot like witchcraft, only less newt."*

— Willow

*"What about home schooling? You know, it's not
just for scary religious people any more."*

— Buffy

*"... What would Tollhouse Cookies be without the
chocolate chips? A pretty darn big disappointment,
I can tell you."*

— Mayor Richard Wilkins III

"I like the quiet."

— Xander

Season Three:
Buffy Graduates

Buffy began to dream about a future. With Faith on board as a new Slayer, perhaps Buffy could actually lead a normal life. But soon she stops hoping.

Battling evil and dealing out death every night is bound to lead to accidental casualties. While Buffy and Faith are battling vamps, Faith stakes a man who turns out to have been human. At first the girls keep the accident a secret. The guilt and remorse haunt Buffy, while the experience causes Faith to spin wildly to her darkest side. Buffy finally turns to Giles for help, revealing the depth of Buffy's longing for a father figure, as well as the extent to which Giles has filled that role.

Willow and Xander are having their own adventures and see their horizons expand. Willow's deepening relationship with Oz has helped her grow and find greater confidence, even to stand up to her mother. Her academic success means she has been accepted "to every college with a stamp," yet she decides her life path is to stay at Buffy's side to fight evil. Xander comes into his own when he finds that he can stand up to anyone—even an undead homicidal bully. This is a rare case of a character finding strength and power, not from what he does or what others see in him, but entirely based on what he knows that he has within himself. There are those around him who think he is a loser, but he knows otherwise—or at least, he usually does.

Buffy's positive impact on the world is brought into focus when we are shown what Sunnydale is like in an alternate reality in which she never came to town. But Buffy never sees that world. In her own reality, Buffy is scorned by the school principal, shunned by the popular kids, and she struggles to do well on her SATs. When she battles hellhounds to save the day yet again, the Sunnydale High student body acknowledges her at last, naming her the Class Protector.

The school year ends with another potential apocalypse averted and with a graduation for Buffy and the Scoobies not only from high school, but into adulthood.

Season Three Episodes and Pop Culture References

3-1   Anne

Written and Directed by Joss Whedon

Struggling to come to terms with having killed Angel after he had regained his soul, Buffy has run away from Sunnydale and is living in Los Angeles under an assumed name. After battling an evil that preys on the homeless, she decides it's time to return to Sunnydale.

 Music in this Episode

"Back To Freedom" by Bellylove

 Lily was Chanterelle

The character Lily was Chanterelle in episode 2-7, "Lie To Me," and appears in the series Angel, still using the name Buffy gives her.

Jaws: The Revenge (1987 film)

"'This time it's personal.' There's a reason that's a classic." (Oz on a good quip to use while slaying.)

Duck and Cover

"I'm psyched! There's going to be some heat, if you know what I mean. So you guys had better duck and cover." (Xander to the gang on how much he's looking forward to seeing Cordelia after a long summer without her.)

Summer School

Oz: "You remember when I didn't graduate?"

WILLOW: "Well, I know you had a lot of incompletes, but that's what summer school was for."

Oz: "Yeah. Remember when I didn't go?"

Episode Reference

Lily says: "I was calling myself Chanterelle then. I used to, well, I was in this cult that worshipped vampires." She is referring to episode 2-7, "Lie to Me."

Gandhi

"Wanna see my impression of Gandhi?" (Buffy kills a demon.) "Well, you know, he was really pissed off."

Episode Reference

Cordelia says to Xander: "Oh yeah, Mr. Faithful. Probably met up with some hot little Inca Mummy girl. Yeah. I heard about her!" She is referring to Xander's unfortunate romance in episode 2-4, "Inca Mummy Girl."

3-2   Dead Man's Party

Written by Marti Noxon, Directed by James A. Whitmore, Jr.

Being home is much more difficult than Buffy expected. She is on the verge of leaving again when zombies flock to her house in response to a tribal mask Joyce has on the wall.

 Music in this Episode

"Never Mind," "Pain," and "Sway" by Four Star Mary (as Dingoes Ate My Baby)

Rambo ('80s film series), Hilfiger (Fashion designer)

"The outfits suck. This *Rambo* thing is so over. I'm thinking, more sporty, like Hilfiger maybe." (Cordelia on dressing for slaying.)

Hot Dog on a Stick

"I noticed when I came to work this morning that Hot Dog on a Stick was hiring. You'll look so cute in that hat." (Principal Snyder to Buffy after telling her she will not be allowed to come back to school.)

Home Schooling

"What about home schooling? You know, it's not just for scary religious people any more." (Buffy when her mom suggests a strict local private school as an alternative to Sunnydale High.)

Deep End of the Ocean (1996 book)

Joyce reads this in book club.

Deep End of the Ocean

This is possibly the least appropriate book that Joyce could have read while worrying about Buffy's whereabouts and safety, as it is about a family dealing with the aftermath when their son is kidnapped.

Foot binding

"A girl's school. So now it's jackets, kilts, and no boys? Care to throw in a little foot binding?" (Buffy when Joyce suggests she go to a private girl's school.)

Little Bus

JOYCE: "It's not your fault you have a special circumstance. They should make allowances for you."

BUFFY: "Mom, I'm a Slayer. It's not like I have to ride the little bus to school."

USA Today (Newspaper), Golf

"Nice pet, Giles. Don't you like anything regular? Golf? *USA Today*? Anything? (Cordelia when she sees he has a zombie cat in a cage in the library.)

Mr. Belvedere ('80s TV show)

"Sorry, you've got the wrong house, Mr. Belvedere." (One of the party goers at Buffy's welcome-back party when Giles tries to reach her on the phone.)

Weebles (Toy)

"This sucker wobbles but he won't fall down!" (Xander as he repeatedly hits a zombie that doesn't stop coming at him.)

Schnapps

"I don't care what people think of me or of you. You've put me through the ringer, and I've had Schnapps." (Joyce to Buffy.)

Bad Seed (1956 film)

Willow jokingly calls Buffy this at the end of the episode.

3-3   Faith, Hope, and Trick

Written by David Greenwalt, Directed by James A. Contner

Kendra's replacement, Faith, comes to town, on the run from an ancient vampire who is hunting her. On the same night, vampire Mr. Trick comes to town. Buffy, trying to get back to normal, is interested in a boy at school named Scott Hope.

 Music in this Episode

"Cure" and "Blue Sun" by Darling Violetta
"Going To Hell" by The Brian Jonestown Massacre
"Background" by Third Eye Blind

※ *Episode Reference*

All the references in this episode to Alcatha are in reference to episodes 2-21 and 2-22, "Becoming," parts 1 and 2.

Martha Stewart, Prosciutto, Picnic

CORDELIA: "When did you become Martha Stewart?"(As Buffy prepares an elaborate picnic for the gang.)

BUFFY: "First of all, Martha Stewart doesn't know jack about hand-cut prosciutto."

XANDER: "I don't believe she slays, either."

OZ: "Oh, I hear she can, but she doesn't like to."

Mayberry R.F.D. ('60s TV show)

"I ran a statistical analysis and, Hello darkness! Makes D.C. look like Mayberry! And ain't nobody saying boo about it." (Mr. Trick on entering Sunnydale.)

Naa nana, na na naaa

"I think what my daughter is trying to say is: Naa nana, na na naaa!" (Joyce to Principal Snyder when he tells them that he has to allow Buffy back in school.)

KC & the Sunshine Band

CORDELIA: "What's the last thing that guy danced to—KC & the Sunshine Band?" (Cordelia remarking on a disco-dancing vampire.)

BUFFY: "I don't think that guy thrives on sunshine."

Five by five

"Five by five!" (Faith's catchphrase.)

 ### *What does 5 by 5 mean?*

Radio operators report on the signal strength and clarity of signals on a scale of one to five, with five being the best quality. "Five by five" means the signal has excellent strength and clarity, and in slang it means everything is great.

DEFCON 1

"The vamps though—they'd better get their asses to DEFCON 1, 'cuz you and I are gonna have fun!" (Faith to Buffy about how much fun they're going to have slaying together.)

Single White Female (1992 film)

"I'm the one getting *Single White Female*d." (Buffy to Joyce talking about Faith.)

Gay Pride

"I've tried to march in the Slayer-pride parade." (Joyce to Buffy that she's tried to be supportive of her.)

※ *Episode Reference*

WILLOW: "And over here we have the cafeteria where we were mauled by snakes."

XANDER: "And this is the spot where Angel tried to kill Willow."

WILLOW: "And over there in the lounge is where Spike and his gang nearly massacred us all on Parent Teacher night. Oh and up those stairs I was sucked into a muddy grave."

In the above quote, Willow's references to snakes as well as getting sucked into a muddy grave are from episode 2-19, "I Only Have Eyes For You." Willow's reference to Spike is from episode 2-3, "School Hard." Xander's reference to Angel trying to kill Willow is from episode 2-17 "Passion."

Playing With a Full Deck

"The girl isn't playing with a full deck. She has no deck. She has a three." (Buffy to Giles about how Faith is too much into violence.)

Taquitos

"'Kissing toast'. He lived for 'kissing toast.' Or maybe it was taquitos." (Buffy not remembering the word *Conquistos*.)

Leprechauns

BUFFY: "Giles there are two things I don't believe in: Coincidence, and leprechauns."

GILES: "Buffy, Its entirely possibly that they both arrived here by chance simultaneously."

BUFFY: "Okay, but I was right about the leprechauns, right?"

GILES: "As far as I know."

Buster Keaton

SCOTT: "Think of this as my last-ditch effort. I realize that one more is going to qualify as stalking. I've given a lot of thought, some might say too much thought, to how I might be a part of your life. It begins with conversation, we all know this. Maybe over a cup of coffee. Or maybe over the Buster Keaton festival playing on State Street all this weekend."

BUFFY: "Come to think of it, I don't think I've given a fair chance to Buster Keaton. I like what I've seen of him so far."

※ *Why is Angel back?*

The reason Angel is returned to this world is revealed in episode 3-10, "Amends."

3-4   Beauty and the Beasts

Written by Marti Noxon, Directed by James A. Whitmore, Jr.

When a student is brutally murdered in the woods during a full moon, the gang suspects that werewolf Oz may have escaped from his cage. Buffy goes to investigate and encounters Angel—somehow back from hell and in a wild state.

 Scooby lunch box

When Willow, Cordy, and Xander go into the morgue to examine the body, Willow carries her forensic tools in a Scooby-Doo lunch box.

Call of the Wild (1903 book), Cliff Notes

"Ah, *Call of the Wild*—aren't we reading the *Cliff Notes* to this for English?" (Xander to Willow when he hears her reading to werewolf-Oz.)

The Full Monty (1997 film)

XANDER: "I can handle Oz's full monty."

WILLOW: "I'm still getting used to half a monty."

Manimal (1983 TV show), The English Patient (1996 film)

"Every guy from Manimal down to Mr. I-love-*The-English-Patient* has beast in him. I don't care how sensitive they act, they're all still just in it for the chase." (Faith telling Buffy her pessimistic view of men.)

Get Out of Jail Free, Monopoly

BUFFY: "I came to give you the rest of the night off."

FAITH: "'Get out of jail free,' huh?"

Sensurround, Sound of Music (1965 film)

"This was vivid. Really vivid. Three-dimensional, Sensurround, the hills are alive." (Buffy, lying, telling Giles about a dream.)

Barbie, Ken

"What's that? Like a Barbie thing? 'Dear Dream Journal: how come Ken hasn't come around since he got that earring?'" (Pete joking about the school counselor and dream journals.)

Zippo

"Your mom has the wattage of a Zippo lighter." (Pete when Scott says his mom thinks therapy can be helpful.)

Jekyll and Hyde, The Mr. Science Show

"Mr. Science was doing a Jekyll-Hyde deal. He was afraid Debbie was going to leave him so he makes this potion to became *super mas macho*." (Willow on what happened with Pete.)

3-5   Homecoming

Written and Directed by David by Greenwalt

Buffy and Cordelia's competition over the Homecoming Queen crown puts the gang on edge. Tired of the squabbling, they send the girls off to settle their differences, not realizing they were putting them in the path of competitive Slayer-hunters.

 Music in this Episode

"Jodi Foster" by The Pinehurst Kids
"How" by Lisa Loeb
"Fire Escape" by Fastball
"She Knows" by Four Star Mary (as Dingoes Ate My Baby)
"Fell Into The Loneliness" by Lori Carson

※ ***Episode Reference***

Buffy says: "I can't believe it. My favorite teacher and she didn't even remember who I was. I'm like a non-person. Am I invisible? Can you see me?" This is a reference to the unnoticed girl who became invisible in episode 1-11, "Out of Mind, Out of Sight."

As Maine goes, so goes my nation (1800s political slogan)

"As Willow goes, so goes my nation." (Oz telling Buffy why he's siding with Cordelia.)

Zombies

BUFFY: "This is just like any other popularity contest. I've done this before... the only difference being I'm not actually popular. Although I'm not exactly unpopular: A lot of people came to my welcome-home party."

WILLOW: "They were killed by Zombies."

BUFFY: "Good point."

※ ***Episode Reference***

The above quote is a reference to episode 3-2, "Dead Man's Party."

Star Trek ('60s TV show), Vulcan Death Grip

"Are you kidding? I've been doing the Vulcan death grip since I was four!" (Cordelia trying to appeal to nerds.)

Chia Pet

BUFFY: "You really love Xander?"

CORDELIA: "Well, he grows on you, like a Chia Pet." (Cordelia telling Buffy why she loves Xander.)

※ *Episode Reference*

The vampire Lyle Gorch's girlfriend says: "I want to do Buffy. My wedding present for what she did to your poor brother!" She is referring to episode 2-12, "Bad Eggs."

3-6 Band Candy

Written by Jane Espenson, Directed by Michael Lange

When enchanted candy makes the adults of Sunnydale revert to their younger selves, the gang must stop the Mayor from offering the town's newborns to a demon—and keep Giles, Joyce, and Principal Snyder out of trouble.

 ### *Music in this Episode*

"Violent" by Four Star Mary (as Dingoes Ate My Baby)
"Slip Jimmy" by Every Bit of Nothing
"Blasé" by Mad Cow
"Tales of Brave Ulysses" by Cream

No. 2 Pencil

"I broke my No. 2 pencil. We'll have to do this again sometime." (Buffy to Giles after staking a vamp with her pencil, trying to get out of studying for the SATs.)

SAT, Connect-the-dots

GILES: "This is the SATs, Buffy, not connect-the-dots. Please pay attention."

Real World (TV show)

"It's like being in the *Real World* house, only real." (Buffy about being overscheduled by Giles and her mom.)

A Christmas Carol (1984 film)

XANDER: "Were you visited by the ghost of Christmas Past, by any chance?"

SNYDER: "It's band candy."

BUFFY: "Let's hear it for the band, huh? Very generous."

Death of a Salesman, Willy Loman

"We love the idea of going all Willy Loman." (Buffy to Principal Snyder about selling candy for the band.)

※ *Episode Reference*

Buffy says to her mother: "I can't believe you, I'm not taking off again. Besides, if I wanted to I could just get on the bus." Buffy's comment about "taking off" is a reference to her running away at the end of episode 2-22, "Becoming."

Seals and Croft

JOYCE: "You've got good albums."

GILES: "Yeah, they're okay."

JOYCE: "Do you like Seals and Croft?"

GILES: (glares)

JOYCE: "Heh. Me neither."

Rocky Horror Picture Show (1975 film), Time Warp

"Let's do the time warp again." (Buffy commenting on how the Bronze is full of middle-aged people.)

※ *Anthony Head as Frank-N-Furter*

What makes a reference to Rocky Horror a double-reference is that Anthony Head starred as Frank-N-Furter in the 1990-91 stage production in London.

Billy Joel

"Maybe there's a reunion in town, or a Billy Joel tour or something." (Willow to Buffy, speculating on why the Bronze is full of partying adults.)

Barbarino, Welcome Back Kotter ('70s TV show)

"Call me Snyder—just the last name. Like Barbarino." (Principal Snyder to Buffy when they see him at the Bronze.)

YMCA, Taekwondo

"I took taekwondo at the Y." (Drugged Principal Snyder to Ethan.)

Juice Newton

"That's cool! Very Juice Newton." (Drugged Joyce admiring a jacket in a store window.)

Burt Reynolds

"You're so cool. You're like Burt Reynolds." (Joyce to Giles.)

Kiss

"Kiss rocks? Why would anybody– Oh." (Willow wondering about what the graffiti means.)

3-7 Revelations

Written by Douglas Petrie, Directed by James A. Contner

Gwendolyn Post, Faith's new Watcher, arrives in Sunnydale. She is remarkably critical of Giles and Buffy, diverting their attention from her real intentions. Meanwhile, Xander sees Buffy with Angel and their secret is out.

 Music in this Episode

"Run" by Four Star Mary (as Dingoes Ate My Baby)
"West of Here" by Lotion

Mary Poppins (1964 film)

"Excuse me Mary Poppins, I don't think you're listening." (Faith to Gwendolyn Post.)

Nicotine Patch

"Cold turkey. It's the key to quitting. Do you think they make a patch for this?" (Buffy to Angel about how they need to stop being attracted to each other.)

Intervention, Alcoholics Anonymous

WILLOW: "Nobody's here to blame you, but this is serious. You need help."

BUFFY: "What is this, Demons Anonymous? I don't need an intervention."

Marathon Man (1976 film)

BUFFY: "How long do you think he can stay angry with me anyway?" (Giles is angry about her keeping Angel's return a secret.)

WILLOW: "The emotional marathon man?"

Going Postal

"Just seein' the two of you kissing after everything that happened, I leaned toward the postal." (Xander to Buffy, explaining his behavior toward Angel.)

Spartans

GWENDOLYN POST: "Do you know who the Spartans were?"

FAITH: "Wild stab: A bunch of guys from Spart?"

GWENDOLYN POST: "They were the fiercest warriors known to ancient Greece, and they lived in quarters very much like these. Do you know why? Because a true fighter needs nothing else."

(Later when Buffy tells Faith that her place looks nice, Faith replies "Yeah, it's real spottin'," not realizing that she was mispronouncing the word.)

3-8   Lovers Walk

Written by Dan Vebber, Directed by David Semel

As Xander and Willow try to quell the feelings they have for each other, Spike returns to Sunnydale, having been left by Drusilla. Heartbroken, he kidnaps Willow and Xander. Oz and Cordelia rescue them—just in time to find them in a compromising position. Meanwhile, Buffy finally sets boundaries on her relationship with Angel.

 Music in this Episode

> "My Way" performed by Gary Oldman (from the film Sid and Nancy)

Cletus the Slack-jawed Yokel (The Simpsons, TV show), SATs, Village idiot

WILLOW: "This is a nightmare. My world is spinning."

XANDER: "It's not that bad, Willow. Really."

WILLOW: "740? Verbal? I'm Pathetic! Illiterate! I'm Cletus the slack-jawed yokel!"

XANDER: "That's right. And the fact that your 740 verbal closely resembles my combined score in no way compromises your position as the village idiot."

My Way (1967 song)

Spike begins and ends his parts in this episode with this song.

Pez

WILLOW: "It's a little Pez-witch!" (Oz gives Willow a witch-themed Pez dispenser.)

Video Rentals, Be kind, rewind

"Okay. Be kind, rewind." (Buffy asking Giles to repeat what he said.)

La Nausea (1938 novel by Jean Paul Sartre)

This is the book Angel is reading when Spike spies on him.

✳ *Episode reference*

> Xander says, "Are you nuts? Or have you forgotten that I tend to have bad luck with these sorts of spells?" This is a reference to events in episode 2-16, "Bewitched, Bothered, and Bewildered."

Weird Science (1985 film)

"What is all this stuff? I'm thinking *Weird Science*." (Buffy when she and Cordelia find the aftermath of where Willow and Xander were taken from the science lab.)

3-9   The Wish

Written by Marti Noxon, Directed by David Greenwalt

When Cordelia wishes that Buffy had never come to Sunnydale, Anya, a vengeance demon in disguise, makes her wish come true. The world is plunged into an alternate reality in which Buffy never came to town to stop the Master from rising, leaving vampires in deadly control over Sunnydale.

 Music in this Episode

"Tired of Being Alone" by The Spies
"Never Noticed" by Gingersol

Nerf

"What kills a demon… oh nerf! Not nerf—knife!" (Willow struggling to understand what Buffy is asking for as a demon holds her by the throat.)

No fuss, no muss (Advertising slogan)

WILLOW: "Isn't he going to go poof?"

BUFFY: "I guess these guys don't. We'll have to bury him or something. Makes you appreciate vamps though. No fuss, no muss."

Prada, Payless

ANYA: "Nice bag. Prada?"

CORDELIA: "Good call! Most people around here can't tell Prada from Payless."

W (Magazine), Gucci

CORDELIA: "Ever since we met this morning, it was like, Thank God there's another person in this town who actually reads *W*."

ANYA: "But Harmony?"

CORDELIA: "Oh, she follows me around. If that girl had an original thought her head would explode. Is that Gucci?"

ANYA: "No, it's an actual old thing. Sort of a good-luck charm my dad gave me."

Crazy Little Thing Called Love (1980 song)

"Starting this minute, I'm gonna grab a hold of that crazy little thing called life and let it do its magical little heal-ey thing. What's done is done. Let's be in the moment. Behold the beauty that is now." (Xander to Willow about needing to move on after they were caught kissing.)

Bizarro (DC Comics supervillain who is the mirror image of Superman)

"No way! I wish us into Bizarro Land and you guys are still together? I cannot win!" (Cordelia to evil Willow and evil Xander.)

White Hats (Western film genre good-guy stereotype)

"Oh swell, it's the White Hats." (Evil Xander when Giles and the others rescue Cordelia.)

※ *Episode reference*

Giles mentions demonic activity in Cleveland, and indeed this is where Buffy lives and slays in this alternate reality. The presence of another Hellmouth in Cleveland is mentioned in the final episode of the series, episode 7-22, "Chosen."

3-10 Amends

Written and Directed by Joss Whedon

Still adjusting to being back in the world, Angel turns to Giles for help with hauntings from his former victims who urge him to kill Buffy in order to find peace. We learn more of Angel's backstory.

Music in this Episode

"Can't Get Enough of Your Love, Babe" by Barry White

※ *Introducing the Bringers*

This episode introduces the Bringers and the big-bad they serve, The First. These characters are prominently featured in season 7.

※ *Mutant Enemy Monster has Christmas Spirit*

After the credits, the Mutant Enemy monster is wearing a Santa hat.

Jewish, Santa, Christmas, How the Grinch Stole Christmas (1966 TV show)

XANDER: "So, you doing anything special?"

BUFFY: "Tree, nog, roast beast. Just me and Mom and hopefully an excess of gifts. What are you doing for Christmas?"

WILLOW: "I'm Jewish, remember people? Not everyone worships Santa!"

※ *Episode reference*

BUFFY: "What about Giles, he doesn't have—"

JOYCE: "No, I'm sure he's fine."

Joyce's emphatic rejection of Buffy's idea to invite Giles over for Christmas Eve is in response to events in episode 3-6, "Band Candy."

Syphilis

ANGEL: "I was young. I never had a chance to—"

APPARITION: "To die of syphilis?"

Deck the Halls

BUFFY: "I don't know what to do."

XANDER: "I think right now the best plan is to deck the halls with boughs of holly. Then we'll catch the bad guys, sooner or later."

Barry White, Can't Get Enough of Your Love (1974 song)

"You look great, and you've got the Barry working for you, and it's all good. But when it happens, I want it to be because we both need it for the same reason." Oz when Willow plays Barry White in an effort to seduce him.)

※ *Episode Reference*

BUFFY: "I don't want to bug Giles. He's still kind of twitchy when it comes to the subject of Angel."

XANDER: "Well, it must be the whole Angel-killed-his-girlfriend-and-tortured-him thing. Giles is pretty petty when it comes to stuff like that."

This is a reference to episode 2-22, "Becoming," in which Angel wreaked havoc and Buffy sent him to hell.

3-11 Gingerbread

Written by Thania St. John, Directed by James A. Whitmore, Jr.

Shaken when she sees children who apparently were ritually murdered, Joyce and the other Sunnydale parents form a mob to stamp out anything occult in town, not realizing that they are being controlled by a demon.

⬧ *Episode Reference*

In this episode, Amy turns herself into a rat to escape being burned at the stake. She remains a rat in Willow's care until episode 6-9, "Smashed," not counting a mere moment of humanity in episode 4-9, "Something Blue."

Doodle

BUFFY: "What is this?" (Holding Willow's notebook with a symbol on it.)

WILLOW: "A doodle. I do doodle. You too! You do doodle too."

Playboy (Magazine), Nazi

XANDER: "Oh man, it's Nazi Germany and I've got *Playboys* in my locker!"

My Friend Flicka (1941 book)

GILES: "Ordinarily I'd say let's widen our research."

BUFFY: "Using what, a dictionary and *My Friend Flicka*?"

Apocalypse Now (1979 film), Chess Club

PRINCIPAL SNYDER: "I love the smell of desperate librarian in the morning."

GILES: "Get out. And take your marauders with you."

PRINCIPAL SNYDER: "Oh my, so fierce. I suppose I should hear you out. Just how is 'Blood Rites and Sacrifices' appropriate material for a public school library. Is the chess club branching out?"

Mister Rogers' Neighborhood (Children's TV show), King Friday

WILLOW: "The last time we had a conversation over three minutes it was about the patriarchal bias of the *Mister Rogers* show."

MRS. ROSENBERG: "Well with King Friday lording it over all the lesser puppets...."

Boy with his finger in the dike

BUFFY: "The bad keeps coming and getting stronger, like the boy that stuck his finger in the duck."

ANGEL: "Dike. It's another word for dam."

BUFFY: "Okay. That story makes more sense now."

Hansel and Gretel

"Hansel and Gretel? Bread crumbs, ovens, gingerbread house?" (Xander when they identify the murdered children as Hansel and Gretel.)

Jack and the Beanstalk

OZ: "So what do we do?" (When he is told that some fairly tales are real.)

XANDER: "I don't know about you, but I'm going to go trade my cow in for some beans."

3-12 Helpless

Written by David Fury, Directed by James A. Contner

Buffy is dismayed to find herself losing her Slayer powers, and even more upset when she learns that Giles has been secretly drugging her on the orders of the Watcher's Council to test her on her birthday. Giles' affection for Buffy and his efforts to help her result in his being fired from the Watchers' Council.

 Multiple Roles: Vampire Zach

The actor who plays the criminally-insane vampire Zachary Kralik also plays the warlock Rack in season 6.

Wash Me

"How do you know if your aura is dirty? Does someone come by with their finger and write *wash me* on it?" (Buffy when Giles says a certain crystal is good for cleaning auras.)

Cuernavaca

"I'm way off my game. My game has left the country. It's in Cuernavaca! Giles, what's going on here?" (Buffy, upset and very confused by her new weakness.)

Peanuts, Woodstock, Snoopy On Ice

"I went to *Snoopy On Ice* when I was little. My dad took me backstage, and I got so scared I threw up on Woodstock." (Willow to Xander and Buffy when Buffy says she is going to the ice show with her father.)

※ *Episode Reference*

Buffy, suggesting to Xander that they should perhaps not have a birthday party for her, says: "I don't know. I think it might be time to put a moratorium on parties in my honor. They tend to go badly. Monsters crash, people die." This is a reference to the zombie attack at her welcome-home party in episode 3-2, "Dead Man's Party."

Brian Boitano, Carmen (Opera)

"It's not just cartoon characters. They do pieces from operas and ballets. Brian Boitano doing Carmen is a life changer. He doesn't actually play Carmen, but a lot of sophisticated people go. It's usually something that families do together. If someone were free they would take their daughter, or their student, or their Slayer." (Buffy blatantly hinting to Giles that he should take her to the ice show.)

※ *Episode Reference*

When Buffy tells him she likes his gift, Angel says, "Then why did you seem more excited last year when you got a severed arm in a box?" This is a reference to episode 2-13, "Surprise," in which the gang attempted to prevent Drusilla from reassembling an ancient demon.

❈ *Buffy's birthday book*

The book that Angel gave to Buffy is the very romantic "Sonnets from the Portuguese" by Elizabeth Barrett Browning, published in 1850.

Superman, Kryptonite

XANDER: "You know, maybe we're on the wrong track with the whole spell curse and whammy thing... maybe what we should be looking for is Slayer-kryptonite."

OZ: "Faulty metaphor. Kryptonite kills."

XANDER: "You assume I was referring to the green kryptonite. I was referring of course to the red kryptonite which drains Superman of his powers."

OZ: "Wrong. The gold kryptonite's the power-sucker. The red kryptonite mutates Superman into some kind of weird—"

BUFFY: "Guys? Reality?"

※ *Episode reference*

Angel tells Buffy: "I saw you before you were the Slayer…." This is a reference to a brief scene in episode 2-21, "Becoming," in which Angel sees Buffy and feels drawn to protect her.

Wrong Number

"Suddenly there's a chance that my calling is a wrong number, and it's just freaking me out a little." (Buffy on how bad she feels about being weak.)

Red Riding Hood

"Why did she come through the dark in the woods, to bring all these sweets to grandmother's house." (The vampire to Buffy, who wore a red hooded jacket earlier in the episode.)

Gold Star

"Do I get a gold star?" (Buffy to Quentin when he says she passed the Slayer test.)

3-13 The Zeppo

Written by Dan Vebber, Directed by James A. Whitmore, Jr.

The butt of Cordelia's put-downs and intimidated by local toughs, Xander tries on a new cool identity through the use of his uncle's car—and finds himself battling danger on his own and surprising himself with strength he never knew he had.

Music in this Episode

"G-Song" by Supergrass
"Easy" by Tricky Woo

Marshmallows

BUFFY: "What should we do with the trio here. Should we burn them?"

WILLOW: "I brought marshmallows! Occasionally I'm callous and strange."

Jimmy Olsen, Superman, Clark Kent, Lois Lane, Perry White

"'But gee Mr. White. If Clark and Lois get all the good stories I'll never be a good reporter.' Jimmy Olsen jokes are pretty lost on you, huh?" (Xander to Giles.)

Wanna Be Startin' Somethin' (1982 song), Michael Jackson

"What—starting something? Like that Michael Jackson song, right? That was a lot of fun. 'Too high to get over. Yeah, yeah.' Remember that fun song?" (Xander to O'Toole, who threatened him.)

Jimmy Olsen, Superman

"It must be really hard when all your friends have like super powers: Slayer, werewolf, witches, vampires and you're like this little nothing. You must feel like... Jimmy Olsen!" (Cordelia, insulting Xander.)

Zeppo Marx

"Xander, you're the useless part of the group. You're the Zeppo." (Cordelia comparing his usefulness in the Scooby gang to Zeppo in the Marx brothers.)

※ *Episode Reference*

BUFFY: "Remember the demon that almost got out the night I died?"

WILLOW: "Every nightmare I have that doesn't revolve around academic failure or public nudity is about that thing. In fact, once I dreamed that it attacked me while I was late for test and naked."

This is a reference to the tentacled creature that emerged from the Hellmouth in episode 1-12, "Prophecy Girl."

Gatorade

GILES "The Sisterhood of Jhe: Race of female demons, fierce warriors, they celebrate victory in battle by eating their foes."

BUFFY: "Can't they just pour Gatorade on each other?"

Walker, Texas Ranger ('90s TV show)

BOB: "How long've I been down?"

O'TOOLE: "Eight months—I had to wait til the stars aligned."

BOB: "Eight months! I've got some catching up to do. *Walker Texas Ranger*—you been recording them?"

Taco Bell

"We'll hang out at Taco Bell, get some girls...." (Teen zombie to other teen zombie.)

Up With People ('70s music group)

FAITH: "You up for it?"

XANDER: "Oh I'm up. I'm suddenly very up. It's just, I've never been up with people before."

3-14 Bad Girls

Written by Douglas Petrie, Directed by Michael Lange

New Watcher, Wesley Wyndam-Pryce, arrives to replace Giles just as Faith gets Buffy to let her hair down and try being a bad girl. While fighting vampires, Faith accidentally kills a human, and suddenly things become very serious.

 Music in this Episode

"Chinese Burn" by Curve

Tupperware, Sesame Street

BUFFY: "Okay, count of three. One—" (Faith jumps into action.)

FAITH: "This isn't a Tupperware party. It's a little hard to plan."

BUFFY: "The count of three isn't a plan. It's *Sesame Street*."

Family Circus, Marmaduke, Cathy (Comics)

MAYOR: "I just love the Family Circus. That PJ! He's getting to be quite a handful. ... Do you like Family Circus?"

MR. TRICK: "I like Marmaduke."

MAYOR: "Oh, Ech. He's always on the furniture—unsanitary!"

MR. TRICK: "Nobody can tell Marmaduke what to do. That's my kind of dog."

ALAN: "I like to read Cathy."

※ *Episode Reference*

Cordelia says, "Well Xander, I could dress more like you but, oh, my father has a job." Xander replies, "I'm not gonna waste the perfect comeback on you now, but don't think I don't have it. Oh, yes. It's time will come." Watch for Xander's comeback in episode 3-20, "The Prom." When Cordelia's father no longer has a job and she can't afford a new dress, Xander buys it for her.

Chemistry

"Chemistry's easy. It's a lot like witchcraft, only less newt." (Willow when she offers to help Buffy study for her chemistry test.)

※ *Episode Reference*

When she sees Wesley, Buffy asks Giles: "Is he evil? The last one was evil." This is a reference to Mrs. Gwendolyn Post in episode 3-7, "Revelations."

Lather, Rinse, and Repeat

GILES: "Are you all right?"

BUFFY: "I had to lather, rinse, and repeat about five million times to get the sewer out of my hair, but otherwise I am of the good. Thanks for asking."

Stairmaster

"Okay, we've got 10, maybe 12 bad guys and one big demon in desperate need of a Stairmaster." (Buffy to Faith as they peek in a window at Balthazar and his minions.)

※ *Episode Reference*

When the Eliminati vampire tries to drown Buffy, she comes back up and says: "I hate it when they drown me." This is a reference to her death by drowning in episode 1-12, "Prophecy Girl."

Uzi

"Why do they always gotta be using swords? It's called an Uzi, chump. Would have saved your ass right about now." (Mr. Trick to the Eliminati vampire as he takes his sword.)

Captains Courageous (1937 film)

"Look, you, tell you what. Let Captain Courageous here go and I'll tell you what you need to know." (Giles to Balthazar as Wesley trembles with fear.)

3-15 Consequences

Written by Marti Noxon, Directed by Michael Gershman

Buffy is miserable about the accidental killing and resolves to tell Giles—only to learn that Faith has already told him a different version of the story. Deciding that she is irretrievably lost to the world of doing right, Faith asks the Mayor for a job.

 ### *Music in this Episode*

"Wish We Never Met" by Kathleen Wilhoite

Star Trek Next Generation ('80s TV show)

"Check out Giles the Next Generation." (Cordelia on seeing Wesley.)

Black Hat (Western film genre bad-guy stereotype)

"So the mayor of Sunnydale is a Black Hat. It's a shocker, huh?" (Faith to Buffy when they see the Mayor with Mr. Trick.)

Zip-a-Dee-Doo-Dah (1946 song)

"Look at you Faith. Less than 24 hours ago you killed a man. And now you're all Zip-a-dee-doo-dah." (Buffy concerned and confused about Faith's lack of remorse.)

Chains, Safety word

FAITH: "Finally decided to tie me up, huh? I always knew you weren't a one-Slayer guy."

ANGEL: "Sorry about the chains. It's not that I don't trust you... actually it is that I don't trust you."

FAITH: "The thing with Xander: I know what it looked like, but we were just playin'."

ANGEL: "And he forgot the safety word, is that it?"

FAITH: "Safety words are for wusses."

Mastercard

ANGEL: "Going down this path will ruin you. You can't imagine the price for true evil."

FAITH: "Yeah. I hope evil takes Mastercard."

Mother Country

WESLEY: "What can I do? I want to help."

BUFFY: "Still got your ticket to the Mother Country?"

(Buffy is understandably miffed after Wesley notifies the Watchers' Council and attempts to kidnap Faith to take her to England to face justice.)

3-16 Dopplegangland

Written and Directed by Joss Whedon

When Anya asks Willow for help with a spell, they accidentally bring Evil Willow to this world from the alternate reality glimpsed in episode 3-9, "The Wish," in which Buffy never stopped the Master from rising.

Music in this Episode

"Priced 2 Move" by Spectator Pump
"Virgin State of Mind" by k's Choice

Rorschach, Psychology Tests, TAT (Thematic Apperception Test)

"The Watcher's Council shrink is heavy into tests. He's got tests for everything. TATs, Rorschach, associative logic. He even has that test that sees if you're crazy that asks if you hear voices or ever wanted to be a florist." (Buffy to Willow about the testing the Council is running on her and Faith.)

Vanity Fair (Magazine)

"I know Faith's not going to be on the cover of Sanity Fair, but she had it rough. In different circumstances, that could be me." (Buffy agreeing with Willow that Faith is unstable. One could argue that Buffy, in the alternate reality of episode 3-9, "The Wish," turned out very much like Faith.)

Princess Margaret

"Well that was a blast. Princess Margaret here had a little trouble keeping up." (Faith on the physical evaluation and Wesley's lack of stamina.)

Playstation

"Let's take a look at the rest of the apartment. If I'm not mistaken, some lucky girl has herself a Playstation." (The Mayor to Faith, showing off her new apartment.)

Old Reliable, Old Faithful, Old Yeller (1957 Film)

WILLOW: "Old Reliable? Yeah, great. There's a sexy nickname."

XANDER: "She just means, you know, the geyser. You're a geyser of fun that goes off at regular intervals."

WILLOW: "That's Old Faithful."

XANDER: "Isn't that the dog that the guy had to shoot?"

WILLOW: "That's *Old Yeller*."

BUFFY: "Xander, I beg you not to help me."

(Later Willow says to Anya: "That's me. Reliable dog geyser person.")

※ *Episode Reference*

When Anya asks Willow for help to perform a spell, she is trying to recover the necklace which was the source of her power as a vengeance demon in episode 3-9, "The Wish." The troubling scenes shown as the spell was cast are from the alternate reality in which the necklace was lost.

🁢 *Sandy will be back*

The girl Sandy, who Evil Willow bites in the Bronze, is seen again as a vampire in season 5: episodes 5-6, "Family," and 5-8, "Shadow."

Mistress of Pain, Dominatrix

WILLOW: "This is creepy. I don't like the thought that there's a vampire out there that looks like me."

XANDER: "Not looks like—is."

BUFFY: "It was exactly you, Will, every detail, Except for you not being a dominatrix... as far as we know."

WILLOW: "Oh right! Me and Oz play Mistress of Pain every night."

XANDER: "Did anyone else just go to a scary visual place?"

Creature From the Black Lagoon (1954 film)

"If she's a vampire then I'm the creature from the Black Lagoon." (Anya about Willow masquerading as Evil Willow.)

John Wayne

"So we charge in—much in the style of John Wayne?" (Xander suggesting that they should go back to the Bronze.)

3-17 Enemies

Written by Douglas Petrie, Directed by David Greenwalt

Seeing the potential for a helpful ally, the Mayor has a demon work magic to evict Angel's soul. When Giles and the gang learn of the plan, they move quickly to put their own plan in place to use the Mayor's scheme to get information about the ascension.

Cold Shower

"So... feel like getting some hot chocolate? Or some cold shower?" (Buffy to Angel after the movie they saw was more erotically charged than they expected.)

Superfriends

"It's just a matter of time before this demon guy is gonna spill—and then Buffy and the Superfriends are gonna...." (Faith to the Mayor on how she should hurry and kill the demon before he tells Buffy about the ascension.)

12-Step, Alcoholics Anonymous

"I don't want to get all twelve-steppy...." (Faith asking Angel for help dealing with her feelings about killing.)

Waiting for Godot (1953 play by Samuel Beckett)

"That could be hours. The girl makes Godot look punctual." (Buffy to Giles when he says she should wait for Faith.)

Reader's Digest

ANGEL: "Had a soul. Now I'm free."

MAYOR: "That's terrific! Poetic, too. Not that I read much poetry, except for those little ones in the Readers Digest. You know, some are quite catchy."

Chains

"You know what I can't believe? All of our time together and we never tried chains." (Angel to Buffy, in chains, as he and Faith prepare to torture her.)

Scoobies

"You get the Watcher. You get the mom. You get the little Scooby gang. What do I get? Jack squat! This was supposed to be my town!" (Faith to Buffy.)

Miniature Golf

"I've got two words that are going to make all the pain go away: Miniature. Golf." (The Mayor trying to cheer Faith up.)

3-18 Earshot

Written by Jane Espenson, Directed by Regis Kimble

An encounter with a demon leaves Buffy with the ability to read minds, which she quickly realizes is more a curse than a gift. But before the chaos engulfs her completely, she hears someone at the school with murderous thoughts.

Lubriderm

"Just another problem for the people at Lubriderm." (Buffy to Giles about a rash on her hand after a demon touched her.)

Pierce Brosnan

XANDER: "He's got his filthy adult Pierce Brosnan-ey eyes all over my Cordy."

OZ: "You're a very complex man aren't you?"

Walk Like an Egyptian (1984 song), The Bangles

"Principal Snyder has 'Walk Like an Egyptian' stuck in his head. And the boys at this school are seriously disturbed." (Buffy about what she hears at the school while she can read minds.)

❋ Episode Reference

BUFFY: "Mom please—just come sit with me."

JOYCE: "Um… I've, uh… I've got laundry."

BUFFY: "Why are you– You had sex with Giles?"

JOYCE: "It was the candy! We were teenagers!"

BUFFY: "On the hood of a police car? Twice?"

When Buffy's telepathy reveals too much information about her mother, this is a reference to episode 3-6, "Band Candy."

3-19 Choices

Written by David Fury, Directed by James A. Contner

As the gang ponders what they will do after graduation, assuming they survive, Buffy plans a heist to take the box from the Mayor's office in order to prevent the ascension. When they make it back to the library with the box, they find that Willow was captured and they must arrange a trade.

Tollhouse Cookies

"A package is arriving tomorrow night from Central America—something, and I can't stress this enough, something that is crucially important to my ascension. Without it, well– what would Tollhouse Cookies be without the chocolate chips? A pretty darn big disappointment, I can tell you." (The Mayor telling Faith why he needs her to go to the airport for him.)

The Force, Star Wars, Dark Side

WILLOW: "Sounds like your mom's in a state of denial."

BUFFY: "More like a continent. She just has to realize that I can't go away."

WILLOW: "Well, maybe not now, but soon, maybe. Or maybe I too hail from denial-land."

BUFFY: "Faith's turn to the dark side of the force pretty much put the proverbial kibosh on any away plans for me."

Jack Kerouac, On the Road (1957 book)

XANDER: "Kerouac, he's my teacher. The open road, my school. Everything in life is foreign territory…."

BUFFY: "Making the open dumpster your cafeteria?"

XANDER: "Go ahead, mock me."

Clearasil, MIT

"MIT is a Clearasil ad with housing." (Cordelia to Willow when Xander brags about the list of colleges that Willow was accepted into.)

Mayor McCheese (Advertising character for McDonald's)

"I'm tired of waiting for Mayor McSleaze to make his move while we sit on our hands counting down to ascension day. Let's take the fight to him." (Buffy telling Giles and Wesley that she wants to force the Mayor's hand so she can solve the ascension problem and make plans to go away for college.)

Duck and Cover

BUFFY: "Look, we call the mayor and arrange a meeting."

WESLEY: "This box must be destroyed!"

XANDER: "I need a volunteer to hit Wesley."

WESLEY: "Giles, you know I'm right."

BUFFY: "Wes, you want to duck and cover at this point?"

Nancy Drew

"You just can't stop Nancy Drewing." (Faith when she catches Willow snooping around the Mayor's office.)

3-20 The Prom

Written by Marti Noxon, Directed by David Solomon

The gang discovers that evil is planned for the prom by Tucker and his hellhounds. Angel and Buffy break up, and Angel announces he plans to leave Sunnydale after they defeat the Mayor. Buffy goes to the prom after saving the day again, and the school kids acknowledge her years of protection at last.

 Music in this Episode

"Praise You" by Fatboy Slim
"Celebration" by Kool & the Gang
"The Good Life" by Cracker
"El Rey" by The Lassie Foundation
"Wild Horses" by The Sundays

 SMG loves The Prom

In a Q&A on Reddit, Sarah Michelle Gellar said that her favorite episode is "The Prom," followed by "Hush" and "The Body."

James Bond, 007

WESLEY: "It's safe to say, we shouldn't waste any time on such trifling matters as a school dance."

CORDELIA: "Well that's too bad, because I bet you would look way 007 in a tux."

WESLEY: "Except of course on the actual night, when I will be aiding Mr. Giles in his chaperoning duties."

Miles to Go…, Stopping By the Woods on a Snowy Evening, Robert Frost

"Giles, we get it: 'Miles to go before we sleep.'" (Buffy when Giles complains that the gang is not taking the ascension seriously enough.)

 Miles to go?

"Stopping By Woods On A Snowy Evening" is a poem by Robert Frost which is referred to several times in Buffy the Vampire Slayer. The poem ends with the lines: The woods are lovely, dark and deep / But I have promises to keep, / And miles to go before I sleep, / And miles to go before I sleep.

Fish Story

"Couldn't we say it was the vamp that got away? We could say it was *that* big!" (Buffy complaining about going into the sewers again.)

Women's Wear Daily (Magazine)

CORDELIA: "You know the part that totally weirded me out? That thing had good taste. I mean, he chucked Xander and went right for the formal wear."

XANDER: "That's right, he left behind his copy of Monster's Wear Daily."

Hellraiser (1987 film)

CORDELIA: "Wait! Right there! Zoom in on that!"

XANDER: "It's a video tape."

CORDELIA: "So? They do it on television all the time."

XANDER: "Not with a regular VCR they don't."

...

OZ: "What's that? Pause it."

XANDER: "Guys! It's just a normal VCR. It doesn't... oh wait. It can do Pause. Hello Hell-HoundRaiser."

Carrie (1976 film)

"Gotta stop a crazy from pulling a *Carrie* at the prom." (Buffy to Angel about stopping violence at the prom.)

Snausages

BUFFY: "And could you check the magic shop? It's right next to the dress store on Main."

XANDER: "I can swing that one. What's the mission?"

BUFFY: "See if anyone's been in, buying supplies to raise a hell hound."

XANDER: "Gotcha. Or check and see who's been stocking up on hell hound Snausages. I hear those pups do anything for a tasty treat."

Prom Night, Pump Up the Volume, Pretty in Pink, The Club, Carrie (films from the '70s, '80s, and '90s that feature high school proms)

"So that's how you did it? That's how you brainwashed the hounds to go psycho on the prom?" (Buffy when see sees the stack of videos on the TV in Tucker's basement.)

Class Clown

"Please! Anybody can be a prop class clown. You know, none of the people who vote these things are funny." (Xander complaining indignantly to Anya about the winner of the year's class clown.)

✳ *Episode Reference*

During Jonathan's speech before giving the award to Buffy at the prom, someone calls out, "Hyena people!" This is a reference to episode 1-6, "The Pack."

3-21 Graduation Day (Part 1)

Written and Directed by Joss Whedon

As the gang struggles to find a way to stop the Mayor's ascension on graduation day, Faith poisons Angel to take him out of the fight and distract Buffy. When the Council refuses to help, Buffy announces she is done working for them. To get the Slayer blood needed to counteract the poison that is killing Angel, Buffy sets out to kill Faith.

 Music in this Episode

"Sunday Mail" by Spectator Pump

The Sixties

"The whole senior class has turned into the sixties—or what I imagine the sixties would have been without the war and hairy armpits." (Buffy to Willow on how oddly friendly everyone is being on the last day of school.)

Siegfried and Roy

XANDER: "You guys didn't hear? Guess who our commencement speaker is?"

WILLOW: "Siegfried?"

XANDER: "No."

WILLOW: "Roy?"

XANDER: "No."

WILLOW: "One of the tigers?"

XANDER: "Come out of the fantasy, Will."

Mutiny

BUFFY: "Until the next Slayer comes along, they close up shop. I'm not working for them any more."

WESLEY: "This is mutiny."

BUFFY: "I like to think of it as graduation."

Icee

"Change back into your street clothes. I'll buy you an Icee." (The Mayor to Faith after a touching, father-ey speech.)

Sports, Action Movies

XANDER: "Yes. Men like sports. Men watch the action movie. They eat of the beef and enjoy to look of the bosoms."

ANYA: "Men like sports, I'm sure of it."

XANDER: "Yes. A thousand years of avenging our wrongs and that's all that you learned?"

Habitrail

"But you've got the swingin' Habitrail goin'. I think Amy's in a good place emotionally." (Oz reassuring Willow when she questions her magical ability because she still can't change Amy back into a human.)

Jaws (1975 film)

"We're going to need a bigger boat." (Xander to Giles when he sees the massive size of the demon the Mayor will become.)

3-22 Graduation Day (Part 2)

Written and Directed by Joss Whedon

Preparing for the biggest battle yet, Buffy organizes the Sunnydale senior class to fight the Mayor as soon as he has ascended into demon form. With the battle won, Angel leaves Sunnydale, and the gang revels not only in a battle won, but in having survived high school.

 Mutant Enemy Monster graduates

> *After the credits, the Mutant Enemy monster is wearing a graduation hat.*

Cricket

"Still battin' zero—but I mean, uh—in cricket." (Xander to Giles on how no information on the demon has yet been found.)

Spinach, Popeye

"It looks like someone's been eating his spinach." (Mayor Wilkins when Angel pushes him away from Buffy at the hospital.)

✳ *Episode Reference*

> BUFFY: "Do you remember any of your military training from when you became soldier guy?"
>
> XANDER: "Oh—rocket launcher!"
>
> *Buffy is referring to Xander's transformation in episode 2-6, "Halloween," and Xander is referring to the gang's success using heavy artillery in episode 2-14, "Innocence."*

Miles to go…, Stopping By Woods On A Snowy Evening, Little Miss Muffet

"Oh yeah. Miles to go. Little Miss Muffet counting down from 7-3-0." (Faith to Buffy as they commune, with both girls unconscious in the hospital.)

 7-3-0?

> *What does Faith mean by 7-3-0? This is the number of days until Buffy dies at the end of season five. While probably unrelated, 730 is also slang for "crazy," referring to the legal motion that someone would have to file in order to be found mentally fit to go to trial.*

Season Four:
Buffy and the Gang Come Together

Aired: 1999-2000

Big-bad: Adam

(Episode Table starts on page 242)

"Sometimes I think about two women doing a spell, and then I do a spell by myself."

— *Xander*

"Frankly it's ludicrous to have these interlocking bodies and not... interlock."

— *Anya*

"Thanks for the Dadaist pep talk. I feel much more abstract now."

— *Buffy*

"Nowadays every girl with a henna tattoo and a spice rack thinks she's a sister of the dark ones."

— *Willow*

"I'm a comfortidor."

— *Xander*

Season Four:
Buffy and the Gang Come Together

No longer in the microcosm of high school, the Scoobies start off in their own directions, only to come together in the end.

Buffy, Willow, and Oz enroll at UC Sunnydale. After a summer on the road to see America, Xander is living in his parents' basement, working menial jobs, and trying to stay connected with his college-bound friends. Willow is eager for all that she will learn, not just in class but in her continuing study of magic. When Oz leaves Sunnydale, she starts a relationship with Tara—making good on the hint dropped in season three's *Dopplegangland* about her sexual orientation.

Buffy struggles to adjust to college life. Sunnydale High, with its occasional hauntings and position above the Hellmouth, was at least familiar. Giles encourages her to stand on her own, but Buffy questions whether she has what it takes, not only as a Slayer, but as a college student and even as an adult. Eventually she gets back in control, finding her center in what she does best: fighting evil. Even Faith grows when she finally learns that, while leading to darkness and death, the responsibilities of a Slayer cannot be denied.

Season four is about self discovery and the power not only of the individual but of the group. Each of our heroes, even Giles, struggles to be an adult, to forge a productive life, and to define his or her individuality.

This focus on the importance of individuality is contrasted by the season's big-bads: a government/military organization called the Initiative and its manufactured super-demon, Adam. It is the Initiative which puts an aggression-control chip in Spike's head, essentially de-fanging him and making him defenseless. Buffy's boyfriend Riley bases his self-worth in his work with the Initiative and the power he feels as one of its leaders; so he begins to slowly unravel when he questions their values and decides to leave.

Each of the Scoobies follows a self-discovery path—but it's from their relationships and shared goals that they draw their ultimate strengths. It is when the unity of the gang is splintered that they see the power they have as a group, especially when they each contribute the best of who they are as individuals: Giles as the guiding father, Willow as a powerful witch, Buffy the warrior, and Xander as the loyal heart of the group.

Season Four Episodes and Pop Culture References

4-1 The Freshmen

Written and Directed by Joss Whedon

Buffy feels out of her depth in college. New vampires intimidate her, and she wonders if she is Slayer enough. When she asks Giles for help, he encourages her to be more self-sufficient.

 Music in this Episode

"Universe" by Stretch Princess
"I Wish I Could Be You" by The Muffs
"Memory Of A Free Festival" by David Bowie
"You and Me" by Splendid

 The UC Sunnydale campus

Many of the exterior UC Sunnydale scenes were filmed at the UC Los Angeles campus. The UC Sunnydale campus buildings were named after buildings at the real UC Santa Cruz.

 "Angel" Episode Cross Reference

The phone rings at Buffy's house and nobody is there. This correlates to the season opener of Angel (episode 1-1, "City Of"), when Angel calls Buffy just to hear her voice.

Planet of the Apes (1968 film)

"It's pretty much a madhouse, a madhouse." (Oz, using Charlton Heston's famous line from *Planet of the Apes* to describe how busy it is on campus.)

Nuremberg Rallies

"This is great, if you need a place for the Nuremberg Rallies." (Buffy commenting on the large size of the UC Sunnydale library.)

Celine Dion

Buffy's perky roommate, Kathy, shows her dorkitude by putting up a Celine Dion poster.

Of Human Bondage (1915 book), Porn

EDDIE: "Of Human Bondage—have you ever read it?"

BUFFY: "I'm not really into porn—I'm trying to cut way back." (Buffy when Eddie mentions the book *Of Human Bondage*.)

Klimt, Monet

Vamps say freshmen are predictable when they have Monet and Klimt posters.

Hugh Hefner

"Remember before you became Hugh Hefner when you used to be a Watcher?" (Buffy to Giles, when, in his bathrobe, he suggests she should deal with her problem without his help.)

Thai Stick

"I'm thinkin' Slayer's blood must be, whoa, like Thai stick." (Sunday's stoner-vamp minion hungering after Buffy's blood.)

Purple Mountain Majesty, Star Spangled Banner, Grand Canyon (1991 film)

BUFFY: "How was your trip? Is America nice? I hear it's nice."

XANDER: "There are some purple mountains majesty, I have to say."

BUFFY: "What'd you do? What'd you see?"

XANDER: "Well, Grand Canyon."

BUFFY: "You saw the Grand Canyon?"

XANDER: "I saw the movie *Grand Canyon* on cable. Really lame."

Avengers (Marvel comic series)

"Where's the gang? Avengers assemble—Let's get it going!" (Xander when Buffy says there's a vamp on campus who's giving her trouble.)

Star Wars (1977 film), Dark Side

"Hate leads to the dark side... no wait." (Xander trying and failing to give Buffy a pep talk.)

Dada

"Thanks for the Dadaist pep talk. I feel much more abstract now." (Buffy responding to Xander's pep talk.)

Stripping

XANDER: "Nothing says 'thank you' like dollars in the waistband."

Renaissance

XANDER: "Up for a little reconnaissance?"

BUFFY: "You mean where we all paint and sculpt and stuff?"

XANDER: "That's the Renaissance."

4-2   Living Conditions

Written by Marti Noxon, Directed by David Grossman

Buffy hates her roommate so much that the gang begins to wonder about her sanity. Xander and Anya become an item.

 Music in this Episode

"Believe" by Cher

Cher, Believe (1998 song)

Buffy's roommate, Kathy, repeatedly listens to Cher's *Believe*.

VH1 (Music video cable channel)

"Listening to the best of VH1 all day put me on edge." (Buffy commenting on her roommate's taste in music.)

Mod (1960s British subculture)

GILES: "Congratulations, you found me out. I'm a Mod jogger."

BUFFY: "Okay, you're not having one of those mid-life things, are you? Because I'm still going ish from the last time you tried to recapture your youth."

※ *Episode Reference*

In the above quote, Buffy is referring to Giles' transformation to his reckless teenaged self in episode 3-6, "Band Candy."

Terminator (1984 film)

XANDER: "He got hit by the Buffinator, and now he's powerless." (Referring to a guy Buffy was flirting with.)

BUFFY: "You think?"

OZ: "No question—he'll be back."

Scooby

BUFFY: "I did get jumped by a demon of non-specific origin last night."

XANDER: "Yeah? Something apocalyps-ey? Do we need to assemble the Scooby gang?"

Madonna, Whitney Houston

"Lots of popular artists who don't get their due. Madonna, Whitney…." (Parker chatting with Kathy as he waits for Buffy to get back.)

Red Wings (Hockey team)

"We sort of got caught up talking Red Wings. It turns out Kathy's a closet hockey fan. I think it's the violence." (Parker when Buffy asks how long he had been there.)

Mime

BUFFY: "And I'm like, Oh yeah? Share this!" (Mimes punching.)

Oz: "So either you hit her or you did your wacky mime routine for her."

BUFFY: "Well, I didn't do either, actually, but she deserved it, don't you think?"

Oz: "Nobody deserves mime, Buffy."

BUFFY: "Kathy does. She deserves to be locked in an invisible box and blown away by an invisible wind, and—"

Oz: "Forced to wear a binding unitard?"

Titanic (1997 film)

"She's even affecting my work now! She's *Titanic*! She's a crawling black cancer. She's other really bad things!" (Buffy to Oz about how much she hates her roommate.)

Linda Blair, The Exorcist (1973 film)

"Wait, are you saying Buffy has been doing a Linda Blair on us because Kathy's been sucking her soul?" (Xander on the reason Giles gives for why Buffy has been acting so crazy.)

4-3 The Harsh Light of Day

Written by Jane Espenson, Directed by James A. Contner

While Spike is searching for a jewel that makes vampires indestructible, Buffy, Anya, and Harmony find unhappiness in their relationships.

Music in this Episode

"Moment Of Weakness," "Anything," and "Lucky" by Bif Naked
"It's Over, It's Under" by Dollshead
"Dilate" by Four Star Mary (as Dingoes Ate My Baby)

※ Episode Reference

WILLOW: "Harmony. I haven't seen you since—"

HARMONY: "Graduation. Big snake, huh?"

This is a reference to the Mayor in episode 3-22, "Graduation Day."

Walmart

"If I'm naked in the checkout line at the Walmart then I've had the same one." (Xander to Anya about having nightmares of public nudity.)

✳ *Episode Reference*

ANYA: "I like you. You're funny and nicely shaped. Frankly it's ludicrous to have these interlocking bodies and not... interlock. Please remove your clothing now."

XANDER: "And the amazing thing: Still more romantic than Faith."

Xander is referring to his very odd sexual encounter with Faith in episode 3-13, "The Zeppo."

Holy Grail

"The Gem of Amara—are you sure? It's not real. It's the vampire equivalent of the Holy Grail." (Giles telling Buffy what the Gem of Amara is.)

Antonio Banderas, Melanie Griffith

HARMONY: "Can I make Antonio Banderas a vampire?"

SPIKE: "No. On second thought, yeah. Do Melanie and the kids as well."

Velvet Underground

"Either I'm borrowing all your albums or I'm moving in." (Oz, looking through Giles' record collection, finds Velvet Underground's *Loaded*.)

Public Television

XANDER: "Whoa. Giles has a TV! He's shallow like us!"

WILLOW: "Well, maybe it doesn't work!"

OZ: "I've got to admit. I'm a little disappointed."

GILES: "Public television!"

Syphilis

HARMONY: "You love that tunnel more than me!"

SPIKE: "I love syphilis more than you."

✳ *"Angel" Episode Cross Reference*

Following the events of this episode, Oz drives to Los Angeles to bring the Gem of Amara to Angel. He says, "Your old buddy Spike dug up Sunnydale looking for it. Got a fistful of Buffy and left it behind," in "Angel" episode 1-3, "In the Dark."

4-4   Fear, Itself

Written by David Fury & Marti Noxon, Directed by Tucker Gates

The gang goes to a Halloween party in a frat house decorated to be a haunted house. However the frat boys did too good of a job in decorating, accidentally summoning a demon that makes your deepest fears real.

 Music in this Episode

"Ow Ow Ow" by Third Grade Teacher

"Pretty Please" by Verbena

Fantasia (1940 film), Phantasm (1979 film), Hippo

XANDER: "Got a treat for tomorrow night's second annual Halloween screening. People, prepare to have your spines tingled and your gooses bumped by the terrifying *Fantasia*. *Fantasia*? It was supposed to be *Phantasm*!"

Oz: "Maybe it's because of all the horrific things we've seen, but hippos wearing tutus just don't unnerve me the way they used to."

Brutus, Caesar

"Okay Brutus. Brutus. Uh, Caesar? Betrayal, trusted friend... back-stabby?" (Willow when Oz expresses concern over her use of magic.)

Arbor Day, Halloween

FRAT BOY 1: "If we cannot scare the young women, they will not fall into our arms. We'll have womanless arms. Halloween's not about thrills , chills, and funny costumes. It's about getting laid."

FRAT BOY 2: "Is there any holiday that's not about getting laid?"

FRAT BOY 1: "Arbor Day."

Schnapps

ANYA: "Does he always smell like peppermint?" (About Xander's Uncle Rory.)

XANDER: "The man likes his Schnapps."

Casio

"*Mi Casio es su Casio*." (Oz to his friends when they thank him for lending them his sound system for their Halloween party.)

Star Wars (1977 film), The Force

"Sensing a disturbance in the Force, Master?" (Xander, when he sees an odd look on Oz's face.)

Red Riding Hood

JOYCE: "I'm thinking about that little girl who wore that five, six years ago." (Joyce is altering Buffy's old Halloween costume.)

BUFFY: "When Little Red Riding Hood was the cutting edge in costumes."

✵ *Episode Reference*

Joyce says, "I didn't believe I could trust anyone again. It's taken time and a lot of effort, but I've got a nice circle of friends now. I mean, don't get me wrong, I'm still a little gun shy. It certainly didn't help that my last boyfriend turned out to be a homicidal robot." She is referring to episode 2-11, "Ted."

James Bond

BUFFY: "I like the tux, Xander."

XANDER: "Bond. James Bond. Insurance. You know, in case we get turned into our costumes again. I'm goin' for cool secret-agent guy."

BUFFY: "I hate to break it to you, but you'll probably end up cool head-waiter guy."

✵ *Episode Reference*

In the above quote, Xander is referring to events in episode 2-6, "Halloween."

NATO

BUFFY: "Nice costumes. Very stealthy." (They see Initiative commandos.)

WILLOW: "Who are they supposed to be?"

OZ: "NATO?"

Joan of Arc

"I'm Joan of Arc. I figured we had a lot in common. Seeing as how I was almost burned at the stake." (Willow explaining her Halloween costume.)

✵ *Episode Reference*

In the above quote, being burned to the stake is a reference to episode 3-11, "Gingerbread."

Abbot and Costello

"Terrifying. If I was Abbot and Costello this would be fairly traumatic." (Buffy commenting on a Halloween haunted house.)

4-5 Beer Bad

Written by Tracey Forbes, Directed by David Solomon

Xander is a bartender, Buffy drinks enchanted beer that makes her cave-girly, and Oz is strangely attracted to Veruca.

 Music in this Episode

"Overfire" by Thc (as Veruca's band, "Shy")
"Nothing But You" by Kim Ferron
"Ladyfingers" by Luscious Jackson

Cocktail (1988 film)

"I saw *Cocktail*—I can do the hippy-hippy shake." (Xander explaining that he can be a bartender.)

Oscars, Academy Awards

WILLOW: "I'm pregnant by my stepbrother, who'd rather be with my best friend, who's left me with no place to live, no food, except for this bottle of wild turkey, which I've drank all up. That was me being all tanked and friendless for ya."

XANDER: "Gets my Oscar nod."

 The true identity of Shy

When Veruca's band, Shy, performs, you are actually hearing performances of the band Thc.

Groupie

"'This is Willow.' 'Oh how fun—a groupie!'" (Willow in a mocking voice on what Oz and Veruca just said.)

The Sixties, Electric Kool-Aid Acid Test (1968 book)

GILES: "I can't believe you served Buffy that beer."

XANDER: "I didn't know it was evil."

GILES: "You knew it was beer."

XANDER: "Well excuse me, Mr. 'I Spent the Sixties in an Electric Kool-Aid Funky-Satan Groove.'"

GILES: "It was the seventies, and you should know better."

4-6   Wild at Heart

Written by Marti Noxon, Directed by David Grossman

Spike is captured by the Initiative, and meanwhile Giles isn't sure what to do with himself. Oz starts to question how much control he has over his wolf side. After struggling with a powerful, intuitive attraction to a dangerous female werewolf, he leaves Willow and Sunnydale.

 Music in this Episode

"Dip" and "Need to Destroy" by Thc (as Veruca's band, "Shy")

 Oz' Cibo Matto poster

Oz has a Cibo Matto poster on his dorm room wall. This was the band that Willow was excited to see in Episode 2-1, "When She Was Bad."

8-tracks, Rolling Stones

GILES: "Well it's ages since I've been to a gig. Don't look that way. I'm down with the new music, and I have the albums to prove it."

BUFFY: "Yes, but it's your cutting-edge 8-tracks that keep you ahead of the scene."

OZ: "Don't scoff, gang. I've seen Giles' collection. He was an animal in his day."

BUFFY: "Hey, why not? If the Stones can still keep rolling, why can't Giles?"

Jerry Garcia

"I don't know about tonight, unless the extreme Jerry Garcia look turns you on." (Oz telling Willow they can't be intimate tonight because of the full moon.)

Elvis Presley, Hound Dog (1956 recording), Dingoes Ate My Baby

OZ: "Number one? No, I gotta go with Hound Dog."

WILLOW: "Me too. That's a great song. I mean, Elvis, what a guy."

VERUCA: "You a big Elvis fan?"

WILLOW: "The biggest. Well, I mean, after Dingoes, of course."

OZ: "We're actually talking amps."

Sarah McLachlan

"Wild monkey sex? Or tender Sarah McLachlan love?" (Xander asking Willow to clarify what she means exactly by "making love.")

Habitrail

"So this is why you called me here? To see your Habitrail?" (Veruca when Oz has her meet him at sunset at his cage.)

 Episode Reference

When Willow tells Oz, referring to his night with Veruca, "What happened with Xander, it doesn't compare," she is referring to her romantic interlude with Xander in episode 3-8, "Lovers Walk."

4-7   The Initiative

Written by Douglas Petrie, Directed by James A. Contner

Spike escapes from the Initiative with a chip in his head that prevents him from hurting humans. Meanwhile Riley realizes that he's interested in Buffy, and Willow is overcome with grief over losing Oz.

🎵 **Music in this Episode**

"Never Say Never" by That Dog
"Fate" by Four Star Mary (as Dingoes Ate My Baby)

Canadian

RILEY: "There's just something off about her."

GRAHAM: "Maybe she's Canadian."

Supermodel

"No studying! Damn! Next thing you're going to tell me is I'll have to eat jelly doughnuts or sleep with a supermodel to get things done around here." (Xander on Giles saying no research is needed this time.)

Ouija

XANDER: "Well how about this: We whip out the Ouija board, light a few candles, summon some ancient, unstoppable evil, mayhem, mayhem, mayhem. We show up and kick its ass."

GILES: "Wee bit unethical."

Nazis

"And they are? The government? Nazis? A major cosmetics company?" (Spike when he awakens in a lab and another vampire warns him not to drink the blood they provide him.)

 What happened to Sunday's minion?

The vampire who warns Spike not to drink the drugged blood is Sunday's minion who ran from Buffy at the end of episode 4-1, "The Freshmen," only to be captured by the Initiative.

Marines, Semper Fi

XANDER: "Here we go... gear for tonight. If some commando squads are out there, fully loaded, these babies might give us the edge we need."

GILES: "That's a very impressive array. Where'd it all come from?"

XANDER: "Requisitioned it. Back when I was military guy."

GILES: "That was two years ago. You still 100%?"

XANDER: "Are you kidding? I put the semper in *Semper Fi.*"

※ *Episode Reference*

When Xander says he was military guy in the above quote, this is a reference to Episode 2-6, "Halloween."

Swiss Army Knife, Cabernet

"Right now I don't have the technical skills to join the Swiss Army, and all those guys ask you to do is uncork a couple of sassy cabernets." (Xander admitting he no longer has military skills.)

Fruit Punch

XANDER'S MOM: "Xander! I made a nice fruit punch for you and your friend. Would you boys like some?"

GILES: "Is it raspberry fruit punch?"

Denver Broncos (Football team)

"'How 'bout them Broncos' won't really cut it." (Riley to Willow about wanting to learn more about Buffy so he'll have something to talk to her about.)

※ *Episode Reference*

Harmony says to Spike: "Bastard! You dumped me and staked me and hurt me and left me...." This is a reference to episode 4-3, "The Harsh Light of Day."

Sex Pistols

"Like I'd listen to the Sex Pistols. Eww. This crap belongs to Spike." (Harmony to Xander about the pile of things she's about to burn.)

Cheese, Ice Capades

"I'm not saying it's the key to her heart, but Buffy... she likes cheese. She has a stuffed piggy named Mr. Gordo, and loves the Ice Capades without the irony." (Willow telling Riley about Buffy.)

John Wayne

"It's a free campus. Who died and made you John Wayne?" (Buffy to Riley when he tries to get her to go home so he can hunt for Hostile 17.)

Spike's pet names for Harmony

Spike had delightful pet names for Harmony in this episode, including: My little Foam latte, Mon petite Crème brûlée, and My little Mentholated pack of smokes

4-8 Pangs

Written by Jane Espenson, Directed by Michael Lange

Buffy puts on a Thanksgiving feast, and Xander gets a disease from a vengeful spirit. The gang feeds Spike in exchange for information about the Initiative, and Angel lurks to keep watch over Buffy.

 "Angel" Episode Cross Reference

When Angel tells Giles that a friend had a vision that Buffy was in danger, this happens at the end of the "Angel" episode 1-7, "The Bachelor Party."

Village People, Hot Dog on a Stick

BUFFY: "Very manly. Not at all Village People." (Describing Xander, who is dressed for his job as a construction worker.)

ANYA: "So much sexier than the outfit from his last job."

WILLOW: "Oh, I miss the free hotdogs on sticks."

Yams

WILLOW: "Earlier you agreed with me about Thanksgiving. It's a sham. It's all about death."

BUFFY: "It is a sham. But it's a sham with yams. It's a yam-sham."

WILLOW: "You're not going to jokey-rhyme your way out of this."

Squanto, Thanksgiving

WILLOW: "Thanksgiving isn't about blending of two cultures! It's about one culture wiping out another. And then they make animated specials about the part where, with the maize and the big, big belt buckles. They don't show you the next scene where all the bison die and Squanto takes a musket ball in the stomach."

Thanksgiving

ANYA: "I love a ritual sacrifice."

BUFFY: "It's not really a one of those."

ANYA: "To commemorate a past event you kill and eat an animal. A ritual sacrifice with pie." (Anya describing Thanksgiving.)

Van Gogh

"We're just assuming someone else cut off the ear. What if it was self-inflicted, like Van Gogh?" (Willow speculating on a scene of violence they are investigating.)

Ralph's

"It was more like a riot than a Ralph's." (Buffy telling Giles how crowded the grocery store was.)

Grant Wood

RILEY: "You're thinking it's like I grew up in a Grant Wood painting."

BUFFY: "Exactly, if I knew who that was."

RILEY: "Just a guy who painted stuff that looked like what I grew up in."

Home is that place…, Robert Frost

"What's the line? 'Home is the place that, when you have to go there, they have to take you in.'" (Buffy and Riley after Riley describes his idyllic home in Iowa.)

Indians, Native Americans, Political correctness

GILES: "It's very common for Indian spirits to change to animal form."

BUFFY: "And, 'Native American'. We don't say 'Indian'."

GILES: "Oh, right. Yes. I'm always behind on the terms. Still trying not to refer to you lot as bloody Colonials."

Casinos

"Uh, you can have casinos now!" (Buffy trying to placate the angry Chumash spirit.)

Gentle Ben ('60s TV show), Syphilis

"Hey Gentle Ben—over here! That's for giving me syphilis!" (Xander trying to distract the spirit, in bear form, so Buffy can kill it.)

General Custer

"Did you see me? Two seconds of conflict with an indigenous person and I turn into General Custer." (Willow feeling bad about her part in the battle.)

Black Hat (Western film genre bad-guy stereotype)

"I like my evil like I like my men: Evil. You know, straight up, 'black hat, tied to the train tracks, soon my electro-ray will destroy metropolis' bad." (Buffy, on how she feels conflicted about killing the Native American spirit.)

※ *"Angel" Episode Cross Reference*

The "Angel" episode 1-8, "I Will Remember You" takes place immediately following the events of this episode. Buffy goes to Los Angeles to confront Angel about coming to Sunnydale without seeing her, and they have a romantic day.

Near the end of this episode is a scene in which Buffy is in Angel's arms, sobbing at the prospect of losing him again. Sarah Michelle Gellar says this was a very emotional scene for both of them and her tears were real. If you listen closely you can hear David Boreanz say, "Please, Sara please."

4-9   Something Blue

Written by Marti Noxon & Tracey Forbes, Directed by Nick Marck

Willow's spell backfires as she struggles with the loss of Oz. As a result, Giles loses his sight, Spike and Buffy get engaged, and Xander becomes a demon magnet.

 ### Music in this Episode

"All the Small Things" by Blink 182
"Night Time Company" by Sue Willett

Zagat's Guide

BUFFY: "I don't think you want us to let you go. Maybe we made it too comfy in here for you."

SPIKE: "Comfy? I'm chained in a bathtub drinking pig's blood from a novelty mug. Doesn't rate huge in the Zagat's guide."

※ "Angel" Episode Cross Reference

When Buffy mentions seeing Angel in LA "even for 5 minutes" refers to the "Angel" episode 1-8, "I Will Remember You."

The English Patient (1996 film)

GILES: "Truth spell. Why didn't I think of that?"

WILLOW: "Because you had your hands full with the undead English Patient."

Brave Little Toaster (1987 film)

"I believe that's the dance of a brave little toaster." (Xander commenting on Willow's seemingly carefree dancing at the Bronze.)

One Million Years BC (1966 film)

BUFFY: "Anybody remember when Buffy had the fun beer-fest and went *One Million Years BC*?"

XANDER: "Sadly without the fuzzy bikini."

※ Episode Reference

Buffy's comment in the above quote is a reference to episode 4-5, "Beer Bad."

Passions

SPIKE: "Come on now, it's telly time! *Passions* is on! Timmy's down a bloody well! And if you make me miss it I'll—"

GILES: "You'll what? Lick me to death?"

Steel Magnolias (1989 film)

"I figured since I'm kind of griefy we could have a girls' night. You know, eat sundaes, watch *Steel Magnolias*, and you could tell me how, at least I don't have diabetes." (Willow asking Buffy to stay in and hang out with her instead of going out to find Spike.)

❋ *Episode Reference*

Willow says: "... and I didn't have the guts to do the spell on Veruca." She is referring to events in episode 4-6, "Wild at Heart."

❋ *Episode Reference*

WILLOW: "I think we're all doomed to badness."

XANDER: "We're not doomed."

WILLOW: "Let's look at your bio. Insect lady. Mummy girl. Anya. You're a demon magnet!"

When Willow mentions Insect Lady, she is referring to episode 1-4, "Teacher's Pet," and Mummy girl is a reference to episode 2-4, "Inca Mummy Girl."

Fruit Roll-ups

"Consider my lips your Fruit Roll-ups of love. Okay, that was gross." (Xander to Anya.)

Wind Beneath My Wings (1982 song)

"Yeah, well I'm not the one who wanted *Wind Beneath My Wings* for the first dance." (Spike to Buffy when she calls him a pig.)

4-10 Hush

Written and Directed by Joss Whedon

The town is struck silent. As Buffy and Riley both seek a solution, they discover each other's secrets. Willow connects with a new friend.

 ### *Music in this Episode*
"Fairy Tale Rhyme" by Joss Whedon

❖ *Oscar nominations for Cinematography and Writing*

This episode was nominated for Outstanding Cinematography for a Single Camera Series and also for Outstanding Writing for a Drama Series.

Fortune favors the brave

This is what Buffy says in her dream when Riley's kiss makes the sun go down.

Weetabix

"Sometimes I like to crumble up the Weetabix into the blood. Give a little texture." (Spike when Giles asks why he needs Weetabix if he lives on blood.)

Henna

BUFFY: "No actual witches in your witch group?"

WILLOW: "No. A bunch of wannablessedbes. Nowadays every girl with a henna tattoo and a spice rack thinks she's a sister of the dark ones."

Clark Kent

"This is the burden we bear. We have a gig that would inevitably cause any girl living to think we are cool upon cool. Yet we must Clark Kent our way through the dating scene." (Forrest reminding Riley that they have to keep their identities as members of the Initiative a secret.)

Baseball Movie

OLIVIA: "Sorry I'm so late. The flight was a horror."

GILES: "Oh no. Bad weather?"

OLIVIA: "Baseball movie."

Centers for Disease Control (CDC)

"The Centers for Disease Control have ordered the entire town quarantined." (Newscaster talking about the mysterious case of every resident of Sunnydale suddenly being rendered silent.)

Pink Floyd

OLIVIA: "All those times you used to talk to me about witchcraft and darkness and the like, I just thought you were being pretentious."

GILES: "Oh I was. I was also right."

OLIVIA: "So everything you told me was true?"

GILES: "Well, I wasn't actually one of the original members of Pink Floyd, but the monster stuff, yes."

OLIVIA: "Scary."

GILES: "Too scary?"

OLIVIA: "I don't know."

4-11 Doomed

Written by David Fury, Jane Espenson & Thania St. John,
Directed by James A. Contner

Buffy and Riley struggle to come to terms with discovering each other's secrets. The gang must stop another apocalypse, and Riley helps—drawing Buffy and Riley back together. Spike learns that he can hurt non-humans.

 Music in this Episode

"Hey" by Hellacopters

Capricorn, Aquarius, Astrology

RILEY: "What are you?"

BUFFY: "Capricorn on the cusp of Aquarius. You?"

Pizza

"Delivering melted cheese on bread: doing your part to keep America constipated." (Spike about Xander's job.)

Slayer, Black Sabbath

"Slayer. Thrash band. Anvil-heavy guitar rock with delusions of Black Sabbath." (Gates' response when Riley asks if he's heard of the Slayer.)

Easter Bunny

"Am I bursting somebody's bubble here? Maybe this is a bad time to tell you about the Easter Bunny." (Forest telling Riley that the Slayer is a myth.)

Smallville, Superman

"They're just animals. Granted, a little rarer than the ones you grew up with on that little farm in Smallville." (Forrest on how he explains the demons they encounter in Sunnydale.)

Limbo

"Hey are you guys serious about naked limbo? I'm in!" (The last thing a drinking college guy says before a demon kills him.)

CBS (Television network), Morley Safer (Host of 60 Minutes)

"Looks like the CBS logo. Could this be the work of one Morley Safer?" (Xander about the symbol carved onto a victim's chest.)

Cereal Boxes

"I wonder where I've seen this before? Where else? The place I spend most of my waking hours memorizing stuff off the sides of mausoleums. Big, freaky cereal boxes of death." (Buffy about recognizing a symbol in the cemetery.)

US Navy (Advertising slogan: It's not a job, it's an adventure.)

RILEY: "It's not just a job!"

BUFFY: "It's an adventure. Great."

Groupie

"Buffy fights the forces of evil. You're her groupies." (Spike when Willow and Xander say they fight evil.)

Donkey Kong (Video game)

"Is this really the time for Donkey Kong?" (Buffy to Riley about a handheld gadget he was using.)

※ *Episode Reference*

In the old Sunnydale High to stop a demon ritual, Xander says: "Sunnydale High. If these walls were still walls, what stories they could tell. Eww. Mayor meat. Extra crispy." This is a reference to episode 3-22, "Graduation Day."

Lunch Money

"You're picking on the wrong guy, dude. I've got a lot of practice with my lunch money." (Xander to the demon beating him near the Hellmouth.)

GI Joe

"You were just passing through in your GI Joe outfit?" (Willow commenting on Riley's uniform.)

4-12 A New Man

Written by Jane Espenson, Directed by Michael Gershman

Giles feels supplanted by Maggie and is upset to learn that Buffy didn't tell him about Riley. Ethan returns and casts a spell that turns Giles into a demon, giving him a unique chance to vent at Maggie. But he must break the spell to prevent it from becoming permanent. This episode begins with Buffy's birthday.

※ *Episode Reference*

When Riley learns that Buffy is the Slayer, he says: "But you killed the... You did the thing with that... You drowned. And the snake? Not to mention daily slayage of... wow." The mention of drowning is a reference to episode 1-12, "Prophecy Girl," and the mention of the snake is a reference to episode 3-22, "Graduation Day."

Treacle

GILES: "One time I was up to a bit of a prank with the dartboard."

ANYA: "I'm bored. Let's eat."

XANDER: "Anya, we talked about this."

ANYA: "I'm sorry. That was rude. Please continue your story. Hopefully it involves treacle and a headmaster."

GILES: "Go and eat."

I Spy (Game)

"What do I spy with my little eye?" (Spike to Giles-demon.)

Spider-Man

RILEY: "You're really strong—like, Spider-Man-strong."

BUFFY: "Yeah, but I don't stick to stuff."

4-13 The I in Team

Written by David Fury, Directed by James A. Contner

Willow and Tara get closer, but Willow is hesitant to tell anyone. Buffy joins the Initiative. Maggie, spying on Riley, knows that Buffy is learning too much. She tries to get Buffy killed, but her plan backfires and results in Riley leaving the Initiative.

 Music in this Episode

"Keep Myself Awake" by Black Lab
"Trashed" by Lavish

Poker

WILLOW: "I implore you Neisa, blessed goddess of chance and fortune, heed my call. Send to me the heart I desire."

XANDER: "You know, magic at the poker table qualifies as cheating!"

WILLOW: "That wasn't magic. I was praying!"

Spanking

WILLOW: "I guess she's out with Riley. You know how it is with the spanking new boyfriend."

ANYA: "Yes, we've enjoyed spanking."

Sabrina the Teenage Witch (Comic, '90s TV show)

"And I don't want you crawling back here knocking on my door pleading for help the second Teen Witch's magic goes all wonky or little Xander cuts a new tooth." (Spike when Giles comes to pay him and thank him for his help.)

Discovery Channel

MAGGIE WALSH: "We've made significant advances in reconditioning the subterrestrials. We're bringing them to the point where they no longer pose a threat."

BUFFY: "So I've seen… on the Discovery Channel. With gorillas and sharks. They made them all nice. You haven't seen it?" (Buffy covering up that she already knows some of what the Initiative is doing.)

Life of Riley ('50s TV show)

"Let's face it, Will, she's almost an hour late. She's probably off living the *Life of Riley*. I don't think she's coming." (Xander saying Buffy is hanging out with Riley.)

Scooby

WILLOW: "I just thought this was supposed to be, you know, us. Just the Scooby corps, you know? I mean, I could have invited somebody else if I knew it was an open free-for-all."

BUFFY: "I'm sorry. I had no idea. My total bad."

Walmart

WILLOW: "What's the ultimate agenda? I mean, okay, yeah, they neuter vampires and demons. But then what? Are they going to reintegrate them into society? Get them jobs as bag boys at Walmart?"

BUFFY: "Does Walmart have bag boys?"

Private Benjamin (1980 film)

MAGGIE WALSH: "You might want to be suited up for this."

BUFFY: "Oh, you mean the camo and stuff? I thought about it, but on me it's gonna look all *Private Benjamin*. Don't worry. I've patrolled in this halter many times."

Rock the Casbah (1982 song), Jews Harp

"I don't care if it's playing *Rock the Casbah* on a bloody Jews harp—I just want it out!" (Spike, on the object the Initiative put in his back.)

※ *Episode Reference*

Xander, talking about electronic gadget the Initiative shot into Spike's back, says: "That blinking thing? My pseudo-soldier memory bank tells me that's a tracer." This is a reference to episode 2-6, "Halloween."

4-14 Goodbye Iowa

Written by Marti Noxon, Directed by David Solomon

Having walked away from the Initiative, Riley begins to behave strangely and realizes that he is addicted to drugs that the Initiative had been giving him. Maggie is killed by Adam, who is now on the loose, and the gang must hide from the Initiative.

Scooby

"I'm guessing the mad scientist isn't too keen on the fact that the entire Scooby gang knows that the Initiative is up to no good." (Xander as the gang is discussing the ramifications of Professor Walsh's attempt on Buffy's life.)

Roadrunner and Coyote cartoon

BUFFY: "That would never happen."

WILLOW: "Well no, Buf, that's why they call them cartoons and not documentaries."

Richard Wagner

GILES: "I can't imagine why I didn't sleep well in my beach ball."

ANYA: "Every time you moved it made squeaky noises. It was irritating."

GILES: "Really? I'm surprised you could hear it over your Wagnerian snoring."

Pajamas

"That probably would have sounded more commanding if I wasn't wearing my yummy sushi pajamas." (Buffy after delivering an inspirational speech.)

Viet Nam, GI Joe, Xerox

ANYA: "Not Xander. Not in a boyfriend way or a lead-him-to-certain-death way."

BUFFY: "He's the only one with military experience."

ANYA: "It's not like he was in the Nam. He was GI Joe for one night."

XANDER: "It's okay, Anya. I've backed up Buffy before."

ANYA: "Can't you do something else... like Xerox handouts or something?"

※ *Episode Reference*

In the above quote, when Anya says that Xander was GI Joe for one night, she is referring to episode 2-6, "Halloween."

Dumb Blonde

"Spell it out for me. I feel a case of dumb blonde coming on." (Buffy demanding an explanation from Dr. Angleman of the Initiative on why Professor Walsh wanted to kill her.)

4-15 This Year's Girl (Part 1)
Written by Douglas Petrie & Marti Noxon, Directed by Michael Gershman

Riley returns from the hospital. Faith wakes from her coma to a package left her by the Mayor with a gizmo which she uses to swap bodies with Buffy. She gets Buffy (in Faith's body) arrested, and plans a new life in her new body—starting with Riley.

Terminator (1984 film), Slayer Handbook

BUFFY: "Just get the blaster working, that's all the strength I need."

WILLOW: "Why, because ray guns aren't in the Slayer Handbook?"

BUFFY: "You haven't seen this Adam guy. He's the Terminator without the bashful charm. I mean, he's deadly, and the last time we met, he kicked my ass."

Napalm

"Been there, done that. Not unlike smothering a forest fire with napalm." (Xander on how badly it worked out to turn Faith over to the Council.)

※ Episode Reference

BUFFY: "Giles used to be part of this council. And for years, all they ever did was give me orders."

RILEY: "Ever obey them?"

BUFFY: "Sure. The ones I was going to do anyway. The point is, I quit the council. And I was scared, but it's okay now."

Buffy is referring to when she stopped cooperating with the council in episode 3-21, "Graduation Day."

The Patty Duke Show ('60s TV show)

WILLOW: "What did you tell him?"

BUFFY: "The truth. That she's my wacky identical cousin from England, and whenever she visits, hijinks ensue." (Buffy joking about who Faith is.)

Gunsmoke ('50s TV show)

WILLOW: "I'll bet every cop in Sunnydale is out there looking for her right now."

BUFFY: "Pressure's definitely high. I'll tell you, if I was her, I'd get out of Dodge post-hasty."

FAITH: "You're not me."

Freudian Symbols

FAITH: "So that's my dream. That and some stuff about cigars and a tunnel...."

5 by 5

WILLOW: "We're sure to spot Faith first. She's like this cleavag-ey slutbomb walking around going 'Oh, I'm wicked cool, I'm five by five!'"

TARA: "Five by five? Five what by five what?"

WILLOW: "See, that's the thing. No one knows!"

(For an explanation of "5 by 5," see the note on page 86.)

Scooby Doo

"Can't any one of your damned little Scooby club at least try to remember that I hate you all? Just because I can't do the damage myself doesn't stop me from aiming a loose canon your way." (Spike to Giles and Xander when they encounter him in an alley and ask for his help to find Faith.)

Gumball Machine

"You don't get these in any gumball machines." (Mayor Wilkins, on tape, telling Faith about the soul-exchanging gadget.)

4-16 Who Are You (Part 2)

Written and Directed by Joss Whedon

As Buffy battles against the Watchers who think she is Faith, Faith—in Buffy's body—begins to realize that while being the Slayer comes with responsibility, it also is very meaningful. Meanwhile Adam grows ever stronger and begins reaching out to local vampires to help them overcome their fears.

Bondage

GILES: "If you are Buffy, then you'll let me tie you up without killing me until we find out wether you're telling the truth."

BUFFY/FAITH: "Giles, Faith has taken my body, and for all I know she's taken it to Mexico by now. I don't have time for bondage fun."

※ *Episode Reference*

Willow asks Anya: "You didn't sense a hyena energy at all did you? Because hyena possession is just unpleasant." She is referring to Xander's possession by a Hyena demon in episode 1-6, "The Pack."

Stevedore

BUFFY: "Giles, you turned into a demon and I knew it was you. Can't you look in my eyes and be all intuitive?"

GILES: (Testing her) "How did I turn into a demon?"

BUFFY: "Oh, 'cuz Ethan Rayne. And you have a girlfriend named Olivia, and you haven't had a job since we blew up the school—which is valid, life-style wise. I mean, its not like you're a slacker-type. Oh, when I had psychic powers I heard my mom think you were like a stevedore during sex. Do you want me to continue?"

※ *Episode Reference*

In the above quote, Giles turning into a demon is a reference to episode 4-12, "A New Man," blowing up the school is a reference to episode 3-22, "Graduation Day." Her psychic powers is a reference to episode 3-18, "Earshot," and her mom's sexual encounter with Giles was in episode 3-6, "Band Candy."

※ *"Angel" Episode Cross Reference*

After this episode, Faith runs to Los Angeles where she tortures Wesley and is hired by an evil law firm, Wolfram & Hart, to kill Angel. At first she agrees, but she finally turns to Angel for help. This is shown in the "Angel" episodes 1-18, "Five by Five" and 1-19 "Sanctuary."

4-17 Superstar

Written by Jane Espenson, Directed by David Grossman

Jonathan is a superstar, and the gang all but worship the ground he walks on. Buffy is the only one who senses that something is wrong, and it is soon revealed that Jonathan used magic to create an alternate reality in which everyone would like him.

🎵 *Music in this Episode*

"Serenade in Blue" by Royal Crown Revue (performed by Brad Kane)

※ *It's the Jonathan Show!*

Be sure to watch the delightfully Jonathan-esque revised opening to this episode.

Scooby

TARA: "Come on. You have fun, admit it. Living the Scooby life."

WILLOW: "I was going for a kind of stoic bravery, but yeah."

Joseph and the Amazing Technicolor Dreamcoat

RILEY: "A lot stronger. I mean, no Jonathan, but I'm doing okay."

BUFFY: "Are you… I mean, you're not eating the Initiative's technicolor food of strongness?" (Buffy checking that Riley is being careful not to eat the potentially drugged food from the Initiative.)

 Episode Reference

BUFFY: "He seemed a little scared."

WILLOW: "Buffy, this is Jonathan. You know he doesn't get scared. You talked about it when you gave him the class protector award at the prom."

This is a twist of a reference to episode 3-20, "The Prom."

Internet

"Hey! I was just at the part where he invents the Internet." (Anya when Buffy takes her book about Jonathan.)

Being John Malkovich

The scene that pans by the Sunnydale theater marquee shows that the film showing is *"Being Jonathan Levinson."*

President McKinley

BUFFY: "Anya, when you were a demon, you granted wishes, right?"

ANYA: "Vengeance wishes, on ex-boyfriends. I'd wish he was a dog, or ugly, or in love with President McKinley or something."

The Matrix (1999 film)

"He starred in *The Matrix* but he never left town. I'm just saying, it doesn't make sense." (Buffy wondering how Jonathan could have done all that they believe he did.)

U.S. Women's Soccer Team, World Cup

"He crushed the bones of the Master, he blew up a big snake made up of the Mayor, and he coached the U.S. Women's Soccer Team to a stunning World Cup victory." (Xander on the amazing things Jonathan had done.)

※ *Episode Reference*

In the above quote, crushing the bones of the master is a reference to episode 2-1, "When She Was Bad," and blowing up the big snake is a reference to episode 3-22, "Graduation Day."

Superman, Kryptonite

"He's like your kryptonite!" (Xander to Jonathan about the monster.)

※ *Episode Reference*

Jonathan says, "After the thing with the bell tower and the gun, I went to counseling with, you know, other kids with problems, and one of them had this spell." This is a reference to episode 3-18, "Earshot."

4-18 Where the Wild Things Are

Written by Tracey Forbes, Directed by David Solomon

Riley's frat house is haunted by kids who were oppressed by a religious zealot years before, inciting lust in Buffy and Riley and putting everyone in danger. Anya is adjusting to what it means to be in a relationship.

Music in this Episode

"The Devil You Know" by Face to Face
"Behind Blue Eyes" by The Who (performed by Anthony Head)

Stripes, Polka dots

BUFFY: Vamps hate demons. It's like stripes and polka dots. Major clashing.

Martin Luther King

TARA: "So Adam is bridging the gap between the races."

WILLOW: "Huh. Like Martin Luther King."

Stop and Smell the Roses

"You take the killing for granted. Now that it's gone, I wish I'd appreciated it more—you know: stop and smell the corpses." (Spike to Anya about missing killing people.)

Felicity ('90s TV show), Keri Russell

"Look around. There's ghosts, and shaking, and people are going all *Felicity* with their hair. We're fresh out of superpeople, and somebody's got to go back in there." (Xander commenting on, among other things, the girl who hid in a closet and began to cut her hair.)

Munchkins, Wizard of Oz (1939 film)

"We need to work fast. Never know how long before the munchkins get homesick." (Xander as he and Anya go into the haunted frat house to rescue Buffy and Riley while the rest of the gang distract the spirits of the children who control the house.)

Jezebel

"The girls felt the vanity more than the boys. I'd see them preening like Jezebel, doting over their pretty hair." (Old Genevieve Holt on how she disciplined the kids to "save them" from being lost to lust.)

4-19 New Moon Rising

Written by Marti Noxon, Directed by James A. Contner

With new control over his wolfishness, Oz comes back for Willow. But when he suspects he has lost her to Tara, he loses control and the Initiative takes him captive. Riley rescues him, then leaves the Initiative. Willow comes out to Buffy, and chooses Tara over Oz.

Radiohead

"A woman in Tibet traded it to me for a Radiohead record. Got a lot of mileage out of the barter system." (Oz about the scarf he gave to Willow.)

Scoobies

OZ: "I saw you at Giles' yesterday."

TARA: "Yeah, sometimes Willow takes me with her to the Scoobies."

Boy Scouts

SPIKE: "This all goes down, the chip comes out, yeah? No tricks?"

ADAM: "Scouts honor."

SPIKE: "You were a Boy Scout?"

ADAM: "Parts of me."

High Five

ANYA: "Slap my hand now!" (After she succeeds in shutting the power off.)

GILES: "Beg your pardon?"

ANYA: "In celebration."

William Burroughs

BUFFY: "Stay back, or I'll pull a William Burroughs on your leader here."

XANDER: "You'll bore him to death with free prose?"

BUFFY: "Was I the only one awake in English that day? I'll kill him."

4-20 The Yoko Factor (Part 1)

Written by Douglas Petrie & Marti Noxon, Directed by David Grossman

Promising to remove the chip from his head, Adam orders Spike to separate the Slayer from her friends, which Spike does by turning the Scoobies against each other.

 Music in this Episode

"Freebird" by Lynyrd Skynyrd (Performed by Anthony Head)

Tony Robbins, Frankenstein

"I get why the demons fall in line with you. You're like Tony Robbins, if he was a big, scary, Frankenstein-looking— You're exactly like Tony Robbins." (Spike telling Adam he is good at motivating and inspiring others.)

L.A. Woman (1971 song/album)

RILEY: "You know if she's back yet?" (Buffy went to Los Angeles to see Angel.)

XANDER: "L.A. Woman? I haven't heard from her."

※ *"Angel" Episode Cross Reference*

Buffy went to Angel's place in Los Angeles because she heard that Faith had tried to Kill Angel. This is shown in the "Angel" episode 1-19 "Sanctuary."

GI Joe, Clown

XANDER: "Hey—who's your buddy?" (Tosses clothes to Riley). "So you don't have to be GI Joe while your civvies are getting washed. Try those on. You'll feel like a new man."

RILEY: "Does this man have a bright red nose and big, floppy feet?"

Wheaties

"Quite a day, huh? You woke up to a big bowl of Wheaties. Now you're a fugitive." (Buffy to Riley after he leaves the Initiative.)

Wizard of Oz (1939 film)

"I am a wiz—if ever a wiz there was." (Willow to Spike when he says she's not a wiz with the computer any more.)

Be All You Can Be, Army (Advertising slogan)

"Your girlie-mates were talking. Something about, uh, be all you can be. Or all *you* can be." (Spike in an effort to make Xander believe that the rest of the gang wanted him to go join the Army.)

Starbucks, Phone sex

"Xander got fired from Starbucks. Xander got fired from that phone sex line." (Xander complaining about Willow and Buffy disrespecting him.)

Godfather (1972 film), Corleones

FORREST: "The family's tearing apart."

BUFFY: "Family? What kind of family are you? The Corleones?"

Yoko Ono, Beatles, Helter Skelter (1968 song)

SPIKE: "It's called the Yoko factor. Don't tell me you've never heard of the Beatles."

ADAM: "I have. I like *Helter Skelter.*"

SPIKE: "What a surprise. The point is, they were once a real powerful group. It's not a stretch to say they ruled the world. When they broke up, everyone blamed Yoko but the fact is, the group split itself apart. She just happened to be there."

Batman, Alfred

XANDER: "I'll just putter around the bat cave with crusty old Alfred."

GILES: "I'm no Alfred, sir. Alfred had a job."

Fort Dix

"Maybe that all changes when I'm doing sit-ups at Fort Dix." (Xander, upset, thinking the gang is conspiring and saying he should join the army.)

4-21 Primeval (Part 2)

Written by David Fury, Directed by James A. Contner

With Riley under Adam's control because of an implanted chip, Buffy and the gang tap into the deepest magic to band together to defeat Adam and destroy the Initiative.

Nancy Drew

"Look at little Nancy Drew!" (Spike to Buffy that she's investigating Adam.)

Party Pack

"So it's chips all around, is it? Someone must have bought the party pack." (Spike when Adam tells him that Riley has a chip too.)

※ *Episode Reference*

Discussing how to defeat Adam, Xander says, "Does anybody miss the Mayor: 'I just want to be a big snake'?" He is referring to episode 3-22, "Graduation Day."

Trojan Horse

"Adam's in the Initiative. Those overcrowded containment cells of yours— courtesy of Adam. He's pulling a Trojan Horse on you." (Buffy explaining the situation to the Colonel.)

Duck and Cover

"Great plan. That's right up there with 'duck and cover.'" (Xander when the Colonel says his plan is to use Tasers against Adam.)

Open house

WILLOW: "All the locks in the Initiative have been disengaged, except the exits."

XANDER: "Demon Open House!"

(They are locked in the Initiative with all the demons that have just been released from their containment cells.)

Must See TV ('90s advertising slogan for NBC), The Eagle has landed

"It's must-see TV: Bait's been taken. Trap's all set. Slayer has landed." (Spike to Adam as they watch the CCTV monitors and see Buffy and the gang being arrested by the Initiative.)

4-22 Restless

Written and Directed by Joss Whedon

As the Scoobies wind down after their victory at the Initiative, the spirit of the First Slayer visits their dreams and reveals their deepest fears—and cheese.

Bay of Pigs, Honorable Discharge

RILEY: "I might actually get out of this with an honorable discharge."

GILES: "In return for your silence, no doubt."

RILEY: "Oh yeah. Having the inside scoop on the administration's own Bay of Mutated Pigs is definitely an advantage."

WILLOW: "It's like you're blackmailing the government… in a patriotic way."

Microwave Popcorn

XANDER: "Dinner is served. And my very own recipe."

WILLOW: "Ooh! You pushed the button on the microwave that says *Popcorn*?"

XANDER: "Actually I pushed *Defrost*, but Joyce was there in the clinch."

Apocalypse Now (1979 film), Heart of Darkness (1903 book), Chick Flicks

XANDER: "I'm putting in a preemptive bid for *Apocalypse Now*."

WILLOW: "Did you get anything less *Heart of Darkness*-ey?"

XANDER: "*Apocalypse Now* is a gay romp. It's the feel-good movie of whatever year it was."

BUFFY: "What else?"

XANDER: "Don't worry, I have plenty of chick and British-guy flicks too."

Madame Butterfly (Opera)

"This isn't *Madame Butterfly* is it? Because I have a whole problem with opera." (Willow in a panic on the set of a play.)

※ *Episode Reference*

Willow's mention of "a problem with opera" in the above quote is a reference to her nightmare about being on stage and unprepared to sing in an opera in episode 1-10, "Nightmares."

Death of a Salesman

"Now if we can stay in focus, keep our heads, and if Willow will stop stepping on everyone's cues, I know this will be the best production of *Death of a Salesman* we've ever done!" (Giles as director of the play in Willow's dream.)

The Lion, The Witch, and The Wardrobe (1950 book), Chronicles of Narnia

"My book report this summer was *The Lion, The Witch, and The Wardrobe*." (Willow as a nervous nerd in her dream.)

Conquistador

XANDER: "A man's always after—"

JOYCE: "A conquest?"

XANDER: "I'm a conquistador."

JOYCE: "You sure it isn't comfort?"

XANDER: "I'm a comfortidor also."

※ *Episode Reference*

When Xander tells Principal Snyder, "You know, I never got a chance to tell you how glad I was that you were eaten by a snake," he is referring to episode 3-22, "Graduation Day."

※ *Giles' important pianist*

When Giles takes to the stage to sing, the pianist accompanying him is Christophe Becke, the show's composer.

※ *Episode Reference*

In Buffy's dream Buffy says to Tara, "Faith and I just made that bed." At the end of their conversation Tara says, "Be back before Dawn." This is a reference to the dream Faith had while unconscious in episode 4-15, "This Year's Girl," in which she and Buffy made the bed, and is one of the scenes that foreshadows Dawn's addition to Buffy's life.

Season Four: The Cheeseman Cometh

In each of the dream sequences in *Restless*, just when you may think you understand what is going on, the Cheeseman—a meek-looking, bespectacled man bearing cheese slices—will make you think again.

Joss and the other grown-ups behind the show say there is no hidden meaning in these scenes, that they are there just to inject some whimsy and surrealist humor.

In Willow's Dream:

"I've made a little space for the cheese slices." (Cheeseman indicates a small wooden table with eleven neatly-arranged slices of cheese.)

In Xander's Dream:

"These will not protect you." (Cheeseman holds a blue stoneware serving plate with eight neatly-arranged slices of cheese.)

In Giles' Dream:

"I wear the cheese. It does not wear me." (Cheeseman is wearing two slices of cheese on his head and one on his shoulder.)

In Buffy's Dream:

As the First Slayer is telling Buffy that she must not have friends, Cheeseman says nothing as he wiggles two slices of cheese at Buffy.

Season Five:
Buffy Saves the World...a Lot

Aired: 2000-2001

Big-bad: Glorificus

(Episode Table starts on page 244)

---

*"There comes a point where you either have to move on,
or just buy yourself a Klingon costume and go with it."*

   – Xander

*"Ancient shamans were called upon
to do the hokey pokey and turn themselves around."*

   – Buffy

*"We should drop a piano on her. That works
for that creepy cartoon rabbit when he's running
from that nice man with the speech impediment."*

   – Anya

*"No threesomes unless it's boy, boy, girl—
or Charlize Theron."*

   – Harmony

Season Five:
Buffy Saves the World... a Lot

The malleability of reality is highlighted when a little sister is grafted onto Buffy's family tree. Buffy bristles at having to watch out for her little sister. She wishes she had been an only child, and envies the relationship Dawn has with their mother. Buffy soon learns the truth about Dawn: that she is the human manifestation of a mystical energy called the Key who must be protected to prevent all the dimensions of hell to be loosed on earth. Another day, another apocalypse.

Buffy must now face not just a mere demon, but an evil god that has been banished from Hell. As the god searches for the Key that will let it return to its dominion, Buffy must keep Dawn a secret and prepare for the biggest battle of her life.

Against this backdrop, Giles gathers his loose ends and buys the local magic shop, Riley unravels and leaves Sunnydale, and Xander finally finds his personal path and proposes to Anya. Spike proclaims his love for Buffy, which she coldly and cruelly rejects. But when he demonstrates that he would withstand torture and even die for her, she knows she at least has an ally.

Buffy's tenuous grasp on adulthood is tested when her mother becomes ill. She rises well to the challenge, but when her mother dies leaving Buffy in charge of caring for Dawn, it is more responsibility than she wants to bear. She leans heavily on Giles, who is more than willing to help, but is concerned that she is too reliant on him.

Season five is about power. Xander's success takes off when he is given the opportunity to see the power he has within himself. The power of Willow's magic reaches a level that enables her to battle, at least temporarily, against a god. When Buffy seeks to learn more about her power, she is told that death is her gift. Buffy finds that not only does she have power, but she has been giving it away, which she resolves not to do any more—although she'd be happy to give some to Giles.

When Glorificus finally discovers that Dawn is the Key, Buffy lacks confidence and tries running from the inevitable fight. But with the help of her friends, she embraces her power and devises a plan to save Dawn and defeat the god. Death was her gift and the source of her power; in giving her own life, Buffy wins the battle and saves the world. A lot.

Season Five Episodes and Pop Culture References

5-1   Buffy vs. Dracula
Written by Marti Noxon, Directed by David Solomon

Buffy battles Dracula and Riley is jealous. Giles confides to Willow that he is returning to England, but when Buffy tells him she needs a Watcher again he happily decides to stay. We meet Buffy's sister Dawn, who everyone believes was there all along.

 Music in this Episode
"Finding Me" by Vertical Horizon

Kung-Fu
"Willow check you out! Witch-Fu." (Buffy complimenting Willow's ease with magic.)

Horse Whisperer (1998 film)
WILLOW: "There you go, all set." (After fixing he computer)

GILES: "Thank you Willow. Obstinate bloody machine simply refused to work for me."

WILLOW: "Just call me the computer whisperer."

Clowns
DRACULA: "Why else would I come here, for the sun? I came to meet the renowned killer."

BUFFY: "Yeah, I prefer the term Slayer. Killer just sounds so—"

DRACULA: "Naked?"

BUFFY: "Like I paint clowns or something."

Interview with a Vampire (1976 book), Lestat
"Are you sure this isn't a fanboy thing? Because I've fought more than a few pimply, overweight vamps who called themselves Lestat." (Buffy to Dracula.)

Sesame Street
"And where'd you get that accent? *Sesame Street*? One, Two, Three. Three victims. Bwa ha ha ha." (Xander channeling *Sesame Street's* "Count" character, before realizing that the vampire he's talking to is the actual Dracula.)

Frankenstein
"I wonder if he knows Frankenstein?" (Xander, as the gang discusses Buffy's encounter with Dracula.)

Vlad the Impaler, Internet
"There's a great deal of myth about Dracula. I imagine the trick to defeating him lies in separating the fact from the fiction.... All right. Willow, you and Tara find out everything you can about the actual legend of Vlad the Impaler on the Internet, and I'll check the library." (Giles when the gang encounters the actual Dracula.)

Music Video

"You think you can just waft in here with your music-video wind and your hypno-eyes...." (Buffy, a bit mesmerized by Dracula who has come into her bedroom.)

Creature Feature

"You're saying Dracula has some sort of freaky mind control over her? You're watching too many Creature Features, man." (Xander when Riley says he's concerned that Buffy is under the thrall of Dracula.)

Syphilis

XANDER: "I'm sick of this crap. I'm sick of being the guy who eats insects and gets the funny syphilis."

※ *Episode Reference*

In the above quote, Xander's comment about the 'funny syphilis' is a reference to episode 4-8, "Pangs."

5-2   Real Me

Written by David Fury, Directed by David Grossman

A crazy man on the street sees that Dawn is something out of the ordinary. Meanwhile, Harmony has minions and wants to kill Buffy, and Giles buys the magic shop.

※ *Multiple Roles: Andrew (Tucker's brother)*

The actor who plays Harmony's minion Cyrus later returns to the series playing Tucker's brother, Andrew.

Hogwarts, Harry Potter (1997-2007 books)

BUFFY: "We're going to the magic shop. No school supplies there."

DAWN: "Yeah Mom, I'm not going to Hogwarts."

George Clooney, Books on tape

"There are a lot of books on this list. Any of them come on tape? You know, read by George Clooney or someone cute like that?" (Buffy looking over the list Giles has compiled of books for their new training program.)

Little Miss Muffet, Curds and Whey

"I know you. Curds and whey. I know what you are. You don't belong here." (Disheveled man to Dawn outside the magic shop.)

※ *Episode Reference*

This line above ties back to the foreshadowing about Dawn when Faith mentioned Little Miss Muffet near the end of episode 3-22, "Graduation Day."

Scoobies

"They're going to be a little while longer doing the detective thing. Best non-Scoobies like you and me stay out of their way." (Tara to Dawn as they wait outside the Magic Shop for the others.)

Cheese, Pizza

"Check it out. They put cheese on round bread. It's gonna be big." (Xander to Dawn when he comes over with a pizza.)

※ *Episode Reference*

Dawn, always seeing Xander through love-tinted eyes, says, "He builds things, and he's brave too. Just last week he went undercover to stop that Dracula guy." She is referring to episode 5-1, "Buffy vs. Dracula."

Monopoly, Clue, Life (Games)

"Hello there, little girl. We are going to have fun, fun, fun. Look, I've got Monopoly, Clue, and, ooh, the game of Life! That sounds good!" (Anya, her arms full of games, as she and Xander come over to sit with Dawn.)

Scooby

"You're completely one of the gang now. Everyone accepts that. You're one of the good guys. Maybe I can talk to the rest of the group and we can do something. Some kind of Scooby initiation." (Willow when Tara says she's not sure she's welcome in the gang.)

※ *Episode Reference*

Xander says to Harmony, "I'm afraid I don't feel like getting into another hair-pulling contest with you." This is a reference to their epic sissy-fight in episode 4-7, "The Initiative."

This is Spinal Tap (1984 film)

"Most magic shop owners in Sunnydale have the life expectancy of a Spinal Tap drummer." (Buffy to Giles on the magic shop.)

Ruffles Potato Chips

BUFFY: "Harmony has minions."

XANDER: "... and Ruffles have ridges."

Fortress of Solitude, Superman

"Buffy, I left word with Willow. She'll come do a return engagement of her uninvitation spell. She probably still has the stuff from last week. And bang-boom, you're back in the fortress of solitude. All better." (Xander trying to calm Buffy after Dawn invited Harmony in the house.)

Passions (TV daytime drama)

BUFFY: "Just how bored were you last year?"

GILES: "I watched *Passions* with Spike. Let us never speak of it"

5-3   The Replacement

Written by Jane Espenson, Directed by James A. Contner

Xander is sure that a demon is impersonating him and taking over his life. Spike becomes obsessed with Buffy, and Joyce begins to have headaches.

✧ *Xander's double*

The replacement Xander is played by Kelly Donovan, Nick Brendan's identical twin brother.

SpaghettiOs

"I do have SpaghettiOs. Set 'em on top of the dryer and you're a fluff-dry cycle away from lukewarm goodness." (Xander to the gang as they sit in his basement room watching TV.)

Kung Fu, Chinese

"Incompetently dubbed Kung Fu—our most valuable Chinese import." (Xander as they watch a Kung-Fu movie.)

Scooby

"We can have the Scooby meetings in the living room and Giles can explain the boring things over here." (Anya planning what to do in the new apartment.)

Microwave Popcorn

"Oh, there's a microwave! It would be like having hot and cold running popcorn!" (Willow when she sees that there's a microwave in Xander's new prospective apartment.)

Evil Twin

WILLOW: "Xander, you already knew he was taking over your life, and you didn't think about Anya until just now?"

XANDER: "Hey, wait until you have an evil twin. See how you handle it."

WILLOW: "I handled it fine."

※ *Episode Reference*

In the above quote, Willow is referring to her vampire self from another reality in episode 3-16, "Dopplegangland."

Klingon

LEASING AGENT: "I think someone said you're currently in your parents' basement?"

XANDER: "Right. There comes a point where you either have to move on, or just buy yourself a Klingon costume and go with it."

Peanuts, Charlie Brown, Snoopy dance

"Every Christmas we watch Charlie Brown together and I do the Snoopy dance." (Xander to Willow to prove who he is.)

※ *Episode Reference*

Willow explained in episode 2-17, "Passion," that she would watch 'A Charlie Brown Christmas' with Xander every year because her family is Jewish.

Henny Youngman

"Take my life. Please." (Xander invoking Henny Youngman's "Take my wife please" shtick as he tells Willow he thinks his replacement seems to be doing a better job at living his life than he is.)

Star Trek ('60s TV show, Episode: Whom Gods Destroy), Spock

"Kill us both Spock!" (Both Xanders in unison when Anya wonders what to do if the spell to join them doesn't work.)

※ *Episode Reference*

Standing in his parents' basement as they are packing to move him to his new apartment, Xander tells Riley, "At first it's just a place, then you start to make memories. Then you're like, that's where Spike slept. And there, that's where Anya and I drowned the separvo demon. And right there, that's where I got my heart all ripped out. I really hate this place."

Where Spike slept is a reference to the time that Spike stayed with Xander, including in episode 4-10, "Hush." Killing the separvo demon is a reference to episode 4-9, "Something Blue," and the reference to his heart getting ripped out is a reference to episode 4-22, "Restless."

Babylon 5 ('90s TV show)

ANYA: "Oh! Presents?" (Xander handed her a box to carry to help move him out.)

XANDER: "Not unless you want my collection of *Babylon 5* commemorative plates, which you cannot have."

5-4   Out of My Mind
Written by Rebecca Rand Kirshner, Directed by David Grossman

Joyce passes out in the kitchen and is put in the hospital. Spike abducts a doctor to have his chip removed, and Riley has heart problems because of what the Initiative did to him.

 Music in this Episode

"Breath" by Nickelback

Peroxide

BUFFY: "You are not going to die."

RILEY: "I bet you say that to all the boys."

BUFFY: "No. There is one peroxided pest whose number's up. When I get my hands on Spike I'm going to rip his head off."

Movie Montage

"I thought it was going to be like in the movies. You know, inspirational music, a montage, me sharpening my pencils, me reading, writing, falling asleep on a big pile of books with my glasses all crooked, 'cause in my montage I have glasses...." (Buffy to Willow on how hard it's been to keep up on her studies.)

Q, James Bond, Star Trek Next Generation ('80s TV show), Fairy Godmother, Santa Claus

"You're like my fairy godmother and Santa Claus and Q all wrapped up in one. Q from Bond, not *Star Trek*." (Buffy to the guys when she sees her new training room in the back of the Magic Box.)

Fidel Castro, CIA

"Did you know that one time the CIA tried to kill Fidel Castro with poisonous aspirin?... Another time the CIA tried to make Castro go crazy by putting itching powder in his beard." (Dawn trying and failing to contribute to the conversation.)

Peter Pan, Tinkerbell

TARA: "How'd you do that—with the light?"

WILLOW: "Oh, you know, you taught me."

TARA: "I taught you teeny Tinkerbell light."

WILLOW: "Okay. So, I tinkered with the Tinkerbell."

Bug Zapper

"Buffy. I swear I was just thinking of you. I wanted to tell you the great news. My heads all clear now. No more bug zapper in my noggin'." (Spike, mistakenly believing that the chip has been removed from his head.)

5-5   No Place Like Home

Written by Douglas Petrie, Directed by David Solomon

Giles' store has its grand opening. When he realizes how exhausting retail can be, he hires Anya to work for him. Buffy battles Glory, rescuing a captive monk, and learns the truth about Dawn.

Raves

"If you're looking for one of those rave parties, I'm afraid you're late." (Security guard when he sees Buffy in front of the abandoned warehouse.)

Iron Chef ('90s TV show)

"Who died and made you *Iron Chef*?" (Dawn after Buffy told her not to touch the breakfast tray she was making for Joyce.)

Oprah Winfrey, The Oprah Winfrey Show

"Relax all day, keep your feet up, and plenty of Oprah." (Buffy suggesting what Joyce should do that day.)

Spider-Man

"Radioactive spider bite?" (Ben on Buffy's strength.)

5-6   Family

Written and Directed by Joss Whedon

Buffy tells Giles about Dawn. Tara's family tries to take her away, insisting that she is actually a demon, but the gang steps in to help.

 Music in this Episode

"I Can't Take My Eyes Off You" by Melanie Doane

Beauty Pageants

"Any breakthroughs on the identity of Miss Congeniality?" (Buffy to Giles asking about the research on Glory.)

Scooby

WILLOW: "Well, there's Scoobyage afoot. Giles called a meeting about our spanking new menace."

TARA: "Oh. You should go. They don't need me for that. You can fill me in."

WILLOW: "No. No, you have to come. This demon-chick is supposed to be really powerful. And I was thinking, maybe we can try that spell. You know the one to find demons."

※ *Episode Reference*

When Willow mentions the spell to find the demons, this is a reference to episode 4-14, "Goodbye Iowa," in which Tara sabotaged Willow's demon-finding spell.

5-7   Fool for Love

Written by Douglas Petrie, Directed by Nick Marck

When Buffy asks Spike about the Slayers he killed before, we learn some of his backstory, and he attempts to kiss Buffy. Still reeling with headaches, Joyce checks into the hospital for observation.

❦ *Cecily becomes Halfrek*

The object of William's love, Cecily, later appears as Anya's vengeance-demon friend, Halfrek.

Cheeto

"I realize every Slayer comes with an expiration mark on the package, but I want mine to be a long time from now. Like a Cheeto." (Buffy to Giles as they look through old Watchers' diaries for information on past Slayers' deaths.)

Food chain, Discovery Channel

BUFFY: "So you traded up on the food chain. Then what?"

SPIKE: "No, please. Don't make it sound like something you'd flip past on the Discovery Channel. Becoming a vampire is a profound and powerful experience."

Picnic

DRUSILLA: "The king of cups expects a picnic. But this is not his birthday."

Scoobies

"The only reason you've lasted as long as you have is you've got ties to the world: your mum, your brat kid sister, Scoobies. They don't tie you here, but you're just putting off the inevitable. Sooner or later... you're gonna want it." (Spike explaining to Buffy that Slayers die because they have a death wish.)

※ *Episode Reference*

When Harmony says to Spike, "Okay, I'm trying to be supportive here, so don't drive a stake through my heart like last time," she is referring to episode 4-3, "The Harsh Light of Day."

5-8   Shadow

Written by David Fury, Directed by Dan Attias

Joyce's CAT scan reveals a brain tumor, or shadow, and she goes in for surgery. As the gang starts to uncover what Glory is, she sends a demon snake to find the Key.

※ *Episode Reference*

Sandy, the vampire that bites Riley, was sired by Evil Willow in episode 3-16, "Dopplegangland."

CAT Scan

"What is a CAT scan exactly? ... Where do they get the CAT scan from? I mean, do they test it on cats? Or does the machine sort of look like a cat?" (Dawn to Buffy as they wait for Joyce to finish getting a CAT scan.)

Captain America

"Yep. Captain America blowed it up real good. All by his lone wolf lonesome." (Xander, annoyed that Riley didn't wait for the gang to hit a vampire nest.)

Aleister Crowley

"*Aleister Crowley Sings*? No, I don't carry that, but I do have some very nice whale sounds." (Giles to a customer in the Magic Box.)

※ *Episode Reference*

Buffy says to Giles, "I just wanted to warn you—that thing she conjured, it's loose. It's a big snake-thing. Not Mayor-big, but it's pretty lethal looking." This is a reference to when the Mayor transformed into a giant snake demon in episode 3-22, "Graduation Day."

5-9   Listening to Fear

Written by Rebecca Rand Kirshner, Directed by David Solomon

A creature is killing seemingly insane people, including people with damage or diseases of the brain, such as Joyce. As her brain tumor progresses, Joyce asks Buffy if Dawn is really her daughter, and tells her she still has to protect her as a sister.

Jell-O

JOYCE: "There's something about food that moves by itself that gives me the heebie-jeebies."

DAWN: "It's good and wiggly. This girl at school said that gelatin is made from ground-up cow's feet and that if you eat Jell-O there's some cow out there limpin' with no feet. But, I told her I'm sure they kill 'em before they take off their feet... right?"

Santa Claus, Jewish

"I feel just like Santa Claus—only thinner and younger and female and, well, Jewish." (Willow when she brings a bag of goodies to Joyce in the hospital.)

Japanese Commercials

WILLOW: "You know what's weird?" (While stargazing on the roof of the dorm.)

TARA: "Japanese commercials are weird."

Crosswalk Signal

JOYCE: "This thing doesn't work. It's not working."

BUFFY: "I'm sure they heard you."

JOYCE: "I bet it's not even hooked up to anything. Just like the push buttons at the crosswalk that are supposed to make the signal change."

BUFFY: "I'm sure someone's on th- ... wait. The push-buttons aren't hooked up to anything?"

Piñata

ANYA: "So, we're all thinking the same thing."

XANDER: "Festive piñata? Delicious candy?"

WILLOW: "Something evil crashed to earth in this then broke out and slithered away to do badness."

GILES: "In all fairness, I don't think we know about the slithered part."

ANYA: "Oh no, I'm sure it frisked about like a fluffy lamb."

※ *Episode References*

DAWN: "No. Not just Mom. People. They keep saying weird stuff about me."

BUFFY: "Are you talking about the man in the hospital?"

DAWN: "He called me a thing too. And there was another one too. A weird guy outside the magic shop. He said I didn't belong. He said I wasn't real. Why does everybody keep doing that?"

Dawn's encounter with the man outside the Magic Box was in episode 5-2, "Real Me."

Mercury, Saturn

"Look at how teeny Mercury is compared to, like, Saturn. Whereas in contrast, the cars of the same name—" (Xander looking at a model of the solar system.)

5-10 Into the Woods

Written and Directed by Marti Noxon

Riley is allowing vampires to bite him, which Spike reveals to Buffy. When Riley gives Buffy an ultimatum, she hesitates, and he leaves Sunnydale, and her, to rejoin the military.

 In Memory: D. C. Gustafson

> This episode was dedicated to the memory of D. C. Gustafson, who worked in the show's art department.

 Music in this Episode

> "Summer Breeze" by Emilana Torrini

Moo Goo Gai Pan, Life (Game), Schnapps

XANDER: "What do you want to do now, Dawnster? Keeping in mind that I won't chase you because I'm old and I'm stuffed full of Moo Goo Gai Starch."

ANYA: "We could play that game again. Life. That was fun."

DAWN: "For you. You always win."

ANYA: "Well, we can make a wager this time. You could give me more money. That would be different."

XANDER: "And after we teach her to gamble, maybe we could all get drunk."

ANYA: "I don't think the bar would serve her, but we could bring something in. Strawberry Schnapps tastes like ice cream."

Theaters

"Okay. How about a movie? They're showing them in theaters now. I hear it's like watching a video with a bunch of strangers and a sticky floor." (Xander suggesting to Anya and Dawn that they go see a movie.)

Anton Chekhov

DAWN: "That one looks sad." (Looking at movie listings in the newspaper.)

XANDER: "The chimp playing hockey? Is that based on the Chekhov?"

Penthouse (Magazine)

XANDER: "Anya. Play nice."

ANYA: "You know, fine. Take her side instead of mine. Even though I'm the one who sleeps with you and feeds you and bathes you."

WILLOW: "She bathes you?"

XANDER: "Only in an erotic *Penthouse*-y way. Not in a sponge-bathy geriatric–"

GILES: "Please, stop! I beg of you!"

Rambo

"Yeah, when we went to deal with that vampire nest she got all Rambo and torched the place. Something seriously bad is going on with her." (Xander talking to Anya about Buffy.)

※ *Episode Reference*

Riley says, "When this started it was just some stupid immature game. I wanted to even the score after you let Dracula bite you." He is referring to episode 5-1, "Buffy vs. Dracula."

State Farm (Insurance company)

BUFFY: "I thought he was dependable."

XANDER: "Dependable? What is he—State Farm?"

5-11 Triangle

Written by Jane Espenson, Directed by Christopher Hibler

As Willow and Anya bicker, they accidentally release a troll who proceeds to smash up the magic store. Spike tries to sort out his feelings for Buffy. Overhearing Buffy, Giles, and Joyce talking, Dawn learns there is a terrible secret about her.

Music in this Episode

"There's No Other Way" by Blur
"Bohemian Like You" by The Dandy Warhols

※ *Backstory for the troll*

You learn the troll's backstory in episode 7-5, "Selfless."

Cat in the Hat (1957 book)

ANYA: "You shouldn't do things while he's gone."

WILLOW: "You're the fish! The fish in the bowl in *Cat in the Hat*. He was always saying that the cat shouldn't be there while the mother was out.... "

ANYA: "You're referencing literature I have no way to be familiar with."

Peer Pressure

"Oh. Oh! I know what this is! This is peer pressure. Any second now you're gonna make me smoke tobacco and have drugs." (Anya to Willow when she offers to teach Anya some basic magic in order to get her to stop complaining about her using ingredients from the Magic Box.)

SeaWorld

BUFFY: "The professor spit too much when he talked. It was like being at SeaWorld. 'The first five rows will get wet.'"

TARA: "That was just enthusiasm."

BUFFY: "Seemed very much like saliva."

Flowering Onion

"They have chicken wings too. Also a sort of flower-shaped thing they make from an onion. It's brilliant." (Spike to Xander on the 'onion blooms' they have at the Bronze.)

Gold Watch

"Anya, it's what you do! You spent, what, a thousand years hurting men? You got your thousand-years-of-hurting-men gold watch." (Willow to Anya on how she fears she will someday hurt Xander.)

5-12 Checkpoint

Written by Douglas Petrie & Jane Espenson, Directed by Nick Marck

The Watchers' Council threatens to deport Giles in an effort to regain control over Buffy, but she has other ideas about who is in control. Meanwhile, a new group, the Knights of Byzantium, is in town, vowing to destroy the Key and anybody protecting it.

※ *Episode Reference*

Buffy, talking about the Watcher's Council, says, "They put me through that test and almost killed me, and then when I was Faith they almost killed me again." They tested her in episode 3-12, "Helpless," and she was Faith in episode 4-16, "Who Are You"

Rasputin, Columbus, Vikings

BUFFY: "About killing him: They poisoned him and they beat him and they shot him and he didn't die.... There were reported sightings of him as late as the 1930s aren't there?"

PROFESSOR: "There is near consensus in the academic community regarding the death of Rasputin."

BUFFY: "There's also near consensus about Columbus, you know, until someone asked the Vikings what they were up to in the 1400s and they're, like, discovering this America-shaped continent."

Passions (TV show)

SPIKE: "Don't make a lot of noise. *Passions* is coming on."

JOYCE: "*Passions*? Oh, do you think Timmy is really dead?"

SPIKE: "Oh. No, no. She's just going to sew him together. He's a doll, for god's sake."

JOYCE: "What about the wedding? I mean, there's no way they're going to go through with that."

Fourth of July

ANYA: "Born on the Fourth of July. And don't think there weren't jokes about that my whole life, mister, 'cuz there were. 'Who's our little patriot?' they'd say. When I was younger, and therefore smaller and shorter than I am now."

✣ *Anya's made-up name*

Anya tells the Watchers her name is "Anya Christina Emanuella Jenkins" in this episode. Listen for another reference to this "lame-ass made-up" name (as she puts it) in episode 7-5, "Selfless."

Bangers and Mash, Blood Sausage

TARA: "Why doesn't Mr. Giles put them all out of here?"

XANDER: "Because they'd deport him. Look at them: Big, tough Council members picking on the books. If they deport him, they're not just destroying his career, they're condemning the man to a lifetime diet of blood sausage, bangers and mash."

Masterpiece Theater (TV show)

"You're Watchers. Without a Slayer you're pretty much just watching *Masterpiece Theater*." (Buffy to the Watchers' Council that they have no purpose without a Slayer.)

Ladies' Home Journal (Magazine)

"You can't do anything with the information you have except maybe publish it in the *Everyone Thinks We're Insane-o's Home Journal*." (Buffy to Watchers' Council.)

5-13 Blood Ties

Written by Steven S. DeKnight, Directed by Michael Gershman

When she and Spike break into the Magic Box, Dawn overreacts (as usual) when she discovers that she is actually a mystical energy called the Key.

Trick Candles

WILLOW: "This is exactly what you need—a 20th birthday party, with presents and funny hats and those candles that don't blow out." (Aside to Tara: "Those used to scare me.")

ABC Movie of the Week

"Geez. Don't go all *Movie of the Week*! I was just too cheap to buy a present." (Dawn to everyone when they react emotionally to the gift she made for Buffy.)

Teletubbies (TV show), Red Riding Hood

DAWN: "I'm badder than you. You're standing in the bushes hugging a bent box of chocolates and I'm—"

SPIKE: "What? Sneaking out to braid hair and watch *Teletubbies* with your mates?"

DAWN: "No. Breaking into the magic shop to steal things."

SPIKE: "Magic shop, eh? All manner of beasties there. Bet they'd go for a Red Riding Hood like you."

Ants at a Picnic

"The Knights of Byzantium are like ants. First you see one, then two, then the picnic is ruined." (Glory's minion to Ben when they spot a Knight of Byzantium in the Sunnydale Hospital psych ward.)

Gentle Ben ('60s TV show)

"What I'm trying to noodle, is what in the world was the Slayer's little sis doing here with Gentle Ben?" (Glory to Dawn in the hospital.)

Get Out of Jail Free, Monopoly

"I think you have a 'Get out of jail free' card on account of big love and drama." (Buffy to Dawn that she's not in trouble.)

5-14 Crush

Written by David Fury, Directed by Dan Attias

Buffy recoils when Spike tells her he is in love with her. Determined to put an end to his feelings, Buffy walks into what started out as a trap set by Drusilla, but ends with Spike making a choice and his ultimate proclamation of love.

 ### *Music in this Episode*

"Play It By Ear" by Summercamp
"Key" by Devics

Flowering Onion

SPIKE: "A bleedin' crime is what it is. Jackin' up the bar price to pay for fixin' up this sinkhole. Not my fault the insurance doesn't cover 'Act of Troll.'"

BUFFY: "Gee. Maybe it's time you found a new place to patronize."

SPIKE: "I've half a mind to, especially since the flowering onion got remodeled right off the soddin' menu. That's the only thing this place had going for it."

Evil Dead (1981 film)

"Hey, evil dead, you're in my seat." (Xander telling Spike to move on.)

Hunchback of Notre Dame (1831 book), Quasimodo, Charles Laughton, Disney's Hunchback of Notre Dame (1996 film), Esmerelda

WILLOW: "I just don't see why he couldn't end up with Esmerelda. They could have had their wedding right there, beneath the very bell tower where he labored thanklessly for all those years."

TARA: "No, see, it can't end like that. Because all of Quasimodo's actions were selfishly motivated. He had no moral compass, no understanding of right. Everything he did, he did out of love for a woman who would never be able to love him back. Also, you can tell it's not going to have a happy ending when the main guy's all bumpy."

WILLOW: "What did you think, Buffy?"

BUFFY: "This test isn't until tomorrow, right? I don't have an opinion until then."

WILLOW: "But you read it, right?"

BUFFY: "Kind of not. I rented the movie."

TARA: "Oh. With Charles Laughton?"

BUFFY: "I don't know. Was he one of the singing gargoyles?"

I Wanna Be Sedated (1978 song), The Ramones

This is the song that Spike began to sing in the car during the stakeout.

※ *"Angel" Episode Cross Reference*

Spike says to Drusilla: "So, let me get this straight. Darla got mojo'd back from the beyond, you vamped her, and now she and you are working on turning Angel into his old bad self again. Sounds fun." This is a reference to "Angel" episodes 2-5, "Dear Boy," 2-9, "The Trial," and 2-10, "Reunion."

Tinkertoy

"You were born to slash and bash and... bleed like beautiful poetry. No little Tinkertoy could ever stop you from flowing." (Drusilla telling Spike that his chip can't control him.)

Charlize Theron, Threesome

"No threesomes unless it's boy, boy, girl—or Charlize Theron." (Harmony to Spike when she sees him with Drusilla.)

Addams Family ('60s TV show), Morticia

"It's no use you crawling back to him, 'cause Spikey doesn't play that game any more—Morticia!" (Harmony to Drusilla.)

Chips Ahoy (Cookies)

JOYCE: "He could become dangerous."

BUFFY: "Not really. As long it's still 'Chips Ahoy' in Spike's head, he can't hurt me, or any of us."

Musical Chairs, Chains

"Not nice to change the game mid-play, Spike. You've taken my chair and the music hasn't stopped." (Drusilla to Spike when he chains her up and professes his love to Buffy.)

※ "Angel" Episode Cross Reference

After this episode, Harmony goes to Los Angeles to visit Cordelia. This is shown in "Angel" episode 2-17, "Disharmony."

5-15 I Was Made to Love You

Written by Jane Espenson, Directed by James A. Contner

Buffy learns that a perky girl in town looking for Warren is a robot, built and programmed to be the perfect girlfriend. Seeing a way to quench his thirst for the Slayer, Spike has Warren build him a BuffyBot.

Lutherans

"Oh. Well, at first it was confusing. Just the idea of computers was, like—Whoa, I'm eleven-hundred years old. I had trouble adjusting to the idea of Lutherans." (Anya, telling Tara about when she started using computers.)

Online Trading

"You have to try online trading. It's great. The secret is avoiding the tech companies everyone was jumping on and going with the smaller firms that supply the basic components." (Anya to Tara on her success with online trading.)

Warren Beatty, Warren Harding

"It's an unusual name. There's hardly any, except Warren Beatty and, you know, president Harding. It's probably not either of them." (Willow on the Warren that the robot is looking for.)

Chex Cereal

ANYA: "Look at these little grain patties! They're woven. That's craftsmanship."

XANDER: "They're not hand-woven, you know."

※ Episode Reference

When Dawn says, "A robot? Really? Was it Ted?," she is referring to her mother's brief relationship with a robot in episode 2-11, "Ted."

Avengers (Marvel comic series)

WILLOW: "I want to be there for Buffy."

XANDER: "You're right. The Avengers gotta get with the assembling. We'll go. We'll deal. We'll help. That's what we do. We help Buffy."

5-16 The Body

Written and Directed by Joss Whedon

Buffy comes home to find that Joyce has died on the couch.

 Nebula nomination for The Body

This episode was nominated for an Nebula award in 2002.

Santa Claus, Christmas, Menorah

DAWN: "My nog tastes funny. I think I got one with rum in it."

XANDER: "Now Santa's gonna pass you right by, naughty booze-hound."

WILLOW: "Santa always passes me by. Something puts him off. Could be the big honkin' menorah."

TARA: (To Dawn) "Oh, did you write him a letter?"

XANDER: "What did you ask for?"

DAWN: "Um, guys. Hello. Puberty? Sort of figured out the whole no-Santa thing."

ANYA: "That's a myth."

DAWN: "Yeah."

ANYA: "No. I mean, it's a myth that it's a myth. There is a Santa Claus."

XANDER: "The advantage of having a thousand-year-old girlfriend. Inside scoop."

TARA: "There's a Santa Claus?"

ANYA: "Been around since like the 1500s. He wasn't always called Santa, but you know. Christmas night, flying reindeer, coming down the chimney—all true. Well, he doesn't traditionally bring presents so much as, you know, disembowel children. But otherwise...."

※ *Episode Reference*

GILES: "Shall I open another?" (Holding a bottle of wine.)

JOYCE: "Do you think we dare?"

BUFFY: "As long as you two stay away from the band candy, I'm cool with anything."

This is a reference to Giles and Joyce's behavior in episode 3-6, "Band Candy."

5-17 Forever

Written and Directed by Marti Noxon

Dawn tries to resurrect Joyce. Ben accidentally reveals to one of Glory's minions that the Key is a person, so Glory targets anybody in Buffy's life who is new or who the Slayer seems to be protecting the most.

Sex

> ANYA: "She got me thinking about how people die all the time, and how they get born too, and how you kind of need one to have the other. When I think of it that way, it makes death a little less sad and sex a little more exciting... I think I understand sex more now. It's not just about two bodies smooshing together. It's about life. It's about making life.

Star Wars (1977 film), Jawa

> BEN: "Tell my sister I'm sick of running into her Jawa rejects."

> JINX: "The news of your relationship with the Slayer—"

> BEN: "We don't have a relationship."

> JINX: "But you attempted to court her, did you not?"

※ Episode Reference

Ben's gave his phone number to Buffy and was flirting with her at a party in episode 5-15, "I Was Made to Love You." Glory knows about Ben and Buffy because she heard a phone message from Buffy at the end of the same episode.

Peter and the Wolf

> Doc hums the theme to *Peter and the Wolf* as he looks for the book with the resurrection spell.

5-18 Intervention

Written by Jane Espenson, Directed by Michael Gershman

Wanting answers about her powers, Buffy goes with Giles to the desert where she encounters the First Slayer. Meanwhile, Spike is spotted by Xander being amorous in the cemetery with his new BuffyBot. When Glory's minions also see this, they assume he must be the Key, and kidnap Spike and take him to Glory.

Holy Grail

> GILES: "There is something in the Watchers' Diaries—a quest."

> BUFFY: "A quest? Like finding a grail or something?"

> GILES: "Not a grail. Maybe answers."

Hokey Pokey (Dance/song)

BUFFY: "Ancient shamans were called upon to do the hokey pokey and turn themselves around."

GILES: (Jumps in, jumps out, and shakes his gourd.)

BUFFY: "That's what it's all about."

Hello Kitty

This is what Buffy says when she sees her animal guide in the desert.

Salem Witch Trials, Discovery Channel

WILLOW: "Those darn Salem judges with their less-satanic-than-thou attitudes."

TARA: "Oh Honey, let's change it. The Discovery Channel has koala bears."

The Hobbit (1937 book), Leprosy

"Those guys that work for Glory, you said they're like Hobbits with leprosy? Well this is a whole flock of Hobbits." (Spike to Buffy about Glory's minions.)

Price Is Right (TV game show), Bob Barker

SPIKE: (Resisting Glory's torture.) "That price show, where they guess what stuff costs."

MINIONS: "Bob Barker? We will bring you the limp and beaten body of Bob Barker."

※ *Episode Reference*

WILL: (Seeing the BuffyBot) "There's two of them!"

XANDER: "I know this! They're both Buffy!"

Xander is referring to when he was split into two distinct selves in episode 5-3, "The Replacement."

5-19 Tough Love
Written by Rebecca Rand Kirshner, Directed by David Grossman

Struggling with the loss of her mother, Buffy tries to push her responsibilities on Giles. Still looking for the Key among those in the Slayer's life, Glory attacks Tara and sucks her brain. Infuriated beyond reason, Willow evokes very dark magic against Glory.

Capitalism, Democracy, American

ANYA: "I've recently come to realize that there's more to me than just being human. I'm also an American."

GILES: "Yes, I suppose you are, in a manner of speaking. You were born here—your mortal self."

ANYA: "Well that's right, foreigner. So I've been reading a lot about the good ol' Us of A, embracing the extraordinarily precious ideology that's helped to shape and define it."

WILLOW: "Democracy?"

ANYA: "Capitalism."

Frankenstein

WILLOW: "I took Psych 101. I mean, I took it from an evil government scientist who was skewered by her Frankenstein-like creation before the final, but I know what a Freudian slip is."

※ *Episode Reference*

In the above quote, Willow is referring to studying psychology under Dr. Maggie Walsh, who was murdered by her creation, Adam, in episode 4-14, "Goodbye Iowa."

Twinkie Defense, My dog ate my homework

"You can also tell me the dog ate your homework, or maybe eating Twinkies made you do it." (Ben's boss, after telling Ben that he's been fired.)

Don Giovanni (Opera)

"Hey, what's up? It's Dawn Giovanni and the Buffster." (Xander when Dawn and Buffy walk into the Magic Box.)

The Little Princess (1939 film), Miss Minchin's Select Seminary for Girls

TARA: "It's understandable about Buffy. She has to look after Dawn now."

WILLOW: "Yeah, but not in a 'Miss Minchin's Select Seminary for Girls' way."

Communism

GILES: "It's dreadful."

ANYA: "It's like Communism."

(They are commiserating about how much they hate the hospital.)

5-20 Spiral

Written by Steven S. DeKnight, Directed by James A. Contner

When Glory finally identifies Dawn as the Key, the gang flees in an old RV. After being attacked by the Knights of Byzantium, their RV is wrecked and they hide in an abandoned garage. They call Ben to come take care of wounded Giles, but when he turns into Glory, she finally gets her Key.

Bugs Bunny, Elmer Fudd, Piano

ANYA: "Piano!"

XANDER: "Because that's what we used to kill that big demon that one time. No, wait. That was a rocket launcher. An, what are you talking about?"

ANYA: "We should drop a piano on her. That works for that creepy cartoon rabbit when he's running from that nice man with the speech impediment."

XANDER: "Yes, or we can just paint a convincing tunnel on the side of a mountain."

※ Episode Reference

In the above quote, when Xander mentioned a rocket launcher, he was referring to how they defeated The Judge in episode 2-14, "Innocence."

Later, Buffy says, "We're not going to win this with stakes or spells or pulling out some uranium power core." Her comment about a uranium power core is a reference to how they defeated Adam in episode 4-21, "Primeval."

Florence Nightengale

BUFFY: "Are you sure you're okay?"

DAWN: "Yeah. But Spike's hurt."

BUFFY: (Looks at Spike's hands) "They'll heal."

SPIKE: "Florence bloody Nightengale to the rescue."

Swiss Army Knife

"Handier than a Swiss knife. Look, the door to my crypt's got this nasty squeak. Maybe you could...." (Spike to Willow when she uses magic to get an old pay phone working.)

Sgt. Rock (Comic character)

"Hey, we gotta be like Sgt. Rock—cool and collected in the face of overwhelming odds." (Xander as they are waiting for Buffy, preparing to leave town to run from Glory.)

Dead Man Walking (1995 film)

"You can give it a rest or you can be undead man walking. See how fast you can hitch a ride with a flaming thumb." (Xander to Spike in the getaway RV.)

Heckel and Jeckel (Cartoon characters)

"... or until Heckel and Jeckel punch a hole through it." (Willow about the Byzantium clerics in dark robes who are trying to bring her wall down.)

Outer Limits ('60s TV show)

"I know this must look extra *Outer Limits*-ey to you...." (Buffy to Ben as he helps deal with Giles' wound in their abandoned garage hideout.)

Renaissance faire

"It's nothing compared to the little bits we're gonna get chopped into when the Renaissance faire kicks the door down." (Spike to Xander as they wait for the Knights of Byzantium to break through Willow's protective spell and kill them.)

5-21 The Weight of the World

Written by Douglas Petrie, Directed by David Solomon

Buffy is traumatized by the loss of Dawn. Consumed by guilt, she retreats into a dream state. Willow uses magic to reach Buffy's subconscious to attempt to bring her back to the world to get back in the fight to save Dawn.

※ *Episode Reference*

Doc says to Spike, "That girl you brought here. Sweet little thing. How did things work out with her mom? Changed her mind, didn't she?" He is referring to when Spike brought Dawn to him for help in resurrecting her mom in episode 5-17, "Forever."

In the kingdom of the blind..., Desiderius Erasmus

"I'm crazy? Honey, I'm the original one-eyed chicklet in the kingdom of the blind, cuz at least I admit the world makes me nuts." (Glory to Dawn, talking about how she doesn't understand how humans can stand living in the world.)

5-22 The Gift

Written and Directed by Joss Whedon

When the gang goes into the final battle with Glory, Buffy sacrifices herself to prevent Glory from using Dawn to open the gates between the Hell dimensions and Earth.

St. Crispin's Day

SPIKE: "Not exactly the St. Crispin's Day speech, was it?"

GILES: "We few. We happy few."

SPIKE: "We band of buggered."

Cannibal: the Musical (1993 film), Shpadoinkle

"Shpadoinkle." (Xander when he sees Glory's tower.)

Season Five: Minion-speak

Glory's toady minions had many ways to express their reverence for their god, and they never used the same one twice.

- Most Beauteous and Supremely Magnificent One
- Most Tingly and Wonderful Glorificus
- Shiny Special One
- Your Elaborate Marvelousness
- Your Terrifically Smooth One
- Your Creamy Coolness
- Your Extremeness
- Perturbed, Yet Ultimately Merciful One
- Most Silky and Effervescent Glorificus
- Your Most Fresh-and-cleanness
- Your Inconceivableness
- Great One
- Your Eminence
- The Magnificent Glory
- The Beauteous Glory
- Her Magnificently-scented Glorificus
- Your New-and-improvedness
- Most... Highest You
- Good One
- Most Glamorous, Yet Tasteful One
- Oh... Thou
- Your Unholiness
- Stunning One
- Oh Glittering, Glistening Glorificus
- Your Scrumptiousness. We bathe in your splendiferous radiance.
- Her Magnificent Incandescence
- Her blindingly scrumptious luminescence
- Perfect all-encompassing light
- Your Magnificence
- Your Holiness
- Oh Groove-tastic One
- O Most Sweaty, Naughty Feelings-Causing One

And from Ben:
- The Most Unstable One

Season Six:
Buffy Grows Up

Aired: 2001-2002

Big-bad: The Trio, Evil Willow

(Episode Table starts on page 246)

"A vampire with a soul? Oh my God. How lame is that?"

— *Joan/Buffy*

*"I pictured something cooler.
More ILM, less Ed Wood."*

— *Andrew (Tucker's brother)*

*"This is a special kind of angel called a 'Charlie.'
We don't have wings. We just skate around
with perfect hair and fight crime."*

— *Anya*

*"You know what they say:
Those of us who fail history—doomed to
repeat it in summer school."*

— *Buffy*

Season Six:
Buffy Grows Up

Having conquered death, now it's time for Buffy to conquer life.

With the use of Spike's re-engineered Buffybot, the gang has kept news of Buffy's death a secret from the world, both to keep Dawn out of foster care and to show the demon world that Sunnydale is still protected by the Slayer. Convinced that her friend is trapped in a hell dimension, Willow and the gang work the ultimate magic to bring Buffy back to life.

Brought back not from hell, but rather from a heavenly dimension, Buffy struggles to adjust to life on earth. She feels so disconnected from her life that, when a demon's venom blurs reality, she cannot be sure if her life is real or if she is actually a long-term patient in an asylum. Feeling completely alone and convinced that she has come back somehow "wrong," Buffy succumbs to Spike's advances. She entangles herself in a sexually violent relationship that shocks and shames her, just as she knows that she needs it. Spike indeed loves her, but for Buffy it is just an attempt to reach through her numbness to feel something.

Season six is about facing life and living it instead of hiding from it in fear or just getting by. It's about taking responsibility and doing what needs to be done. Everything makes sense when she is fighting evil, but now Buffy's battles are not just against demons and vampires, but against telephone bills, social services workers, and loan officers. Working at a fast-food place just to make ends meet, Buffy doesn't feel that she belongs anywhere. Just as she said to Dawn before she died, she finds that the hardest thing in this life is living it.

Meanwhile, the others are having their own challenges. Willow's expertise and ease with magic has surpassed everyone's comfort zone, with Tara and Giles suspecting that she is in danger. Dawn is stealing and ditching classes at school, Giles is unsure if he is helping or hindering Buffy, and Xander is terrified about getting married, finally breaking Anya's heart at the altar and sending her reeling back into her gig as a vengeance demon.

While life itself is the season's big-bad, Buffy must also deal with the Trio of Nerds. Their antics start out as a mere annoyance, but they escalate into killing Tara and pushing Willow over the edge into a dark magic that will change her life forever. In the end it is Willow herself that threatens the very world, and it is only the pure heart of Xander that stops her.

Season Six Episodes and Pop Culture References

6-1,2 Bargaining (Parts 1 & 2)
Written by Marti Noxon & David Fury, Directed by David Grossman

Trying to hide Buffy's death from the human authorities and from the demon world, the gang takes over patrol duties and has the BuffyBot pose as the Slayer. The very day that Giles returns to England, Willow leads the others in bringing Buffy back from the dead.

\

❯❯ *Mutant Enemy finger puppet:*
When Tara gives her gift to Giles at the airport, watch for the Mutant Enemy trademark reference.

Great Googly Moogly (from 1970 song Nanook Rubs It, by Frank Zappa)

"Great googly moogly, Willow! Would you quit doing that?" (Xander to telepathic-Willow when her sudden voice in their heads startle him and Anya.)

The Fury (1978 film)

"I know, I know. I don't have to talk when I answer you. But I saw *The Fury*, and that way lies spooky carnival death." (Xander to telepathic-Willow.)

Dada , Marzipan

BUFFYBOT: "That'll put marzipan in your pie plate, Bingo!"

SPIKE: "What's with the Dadaism, Red?"

TARA: "Yeah. She says that pie thing every time she stakes a vamp now."

eBay, Backstreet Boys (Band)

TARA: "You found the last known Urn of Osiris on eBay?"

ANYA: "Yeah. From a desert gnome in Cairo. He drove a really hard bargain, but I got him to throw in a limited-edition Backstreet Boys lunch box for a (Xander interrupts with a cough) … a friend."

Discovery Channel

"Tomorrow?... Discovery Channel has monkeys, and our tape machine's all wonky." (Anya coming up with an excuse not to follow through with their plans.)

Boss

WILLOW: "Nobody's changing their minds. Period."

XANDER: "'Scuse me? Who made you boss of the group?"

ANYA: "You did."

TARA: "You said Willow should be boss."

ANYA: "Then you said 'Let's vote,' and it was unanimous."

TARA: "And you made her this little plaque that said 'Boss of us,' and you put the sparkles on it."

Zombies

XANDER: "Scenario: We raise Buffy from the grave. She tries to eat our brains..."

WILLOW: "Xander, this isn't zombies."

ANYA: "And zombies don't eat brains anyway, unless instructed to by their zombie masters. A lot of people get that wrong."

※ *Episode Reference*

When Willow says, "This isn't like Dawn trying to bring Mrs. Summers back," she is referring to events in episode 5-17, "Forever."

411

"I know you guys don't usually let vampires join the gang, we've got that whole sunlight issue—but I was thinking. As thanks for the 411 you could let me throw in with your—" (Vampire to the evil demon gang leader right before being decapitated.)

The Music Man (1962 film)

"We've got trouble right here in Hellmouth City." (Xander to Willow about the demon motorcycle gang in Sunnydale.)

Cirrhosis

XANDER: "Will, the Urn of Cirrhosis—"

WILLOW: "Osiris?"

Peter Pan, Tinkerbell

"And how long have you known that your girlfriend's Tinkerbell?" (Xander to Willow when she tells him the fluttery light in the forest is really Tara.)

NORAD, DEFCON

"Maybe they're on their way here. I mean, this place is NORAD and we're at DEFCON 1." (Xander on how Spike and Dawn may be on their way to the Magic Box during a demon invasion.)

Radio Shack, The Wild Bunch (1969 film)

TARA: "It's the BuffyBot."

XANDER: "Oh peachy. No doubt to lead the Wild Bunch to us again. Hey Will, next time this thing's damaged, couldn't you program it to find the nearest Radio Shack?" (Xander, mistaking Buffy for the BuffyBot.)

Red Riding Hood

"The better to cut you down to size, Grandma." (Xander to the demon when told he has a big axe.)

6-3   After Life

Written by Jane Espenson, Directed by David Solomon

Buffy is struggling to adapt to life when the gang realizes that *something* came back to this world when Buffy did. Buffy confides in Spike that she had been in heaven, and that everything in the world seems like hell to her now.

Jet Lag

"Jet lag from hell must be—you know. Jet lag from hell." (Anya when Buffy, newly risen from the dead, says that she is tired.)

※ *Episode Reference*

Willow, concerned about Buffy's condition, says, "When Angel came back, Buffy said he was wild—like an animal." This is a reference to Angel's inexplicable return from a hell dimension in episode 3-4, "Beauty and the Beasts."

Summer School

"You better go. You've been out of school since... I got back. And you know what they say: Those of us who fail history—doomed to repeat it in summer school." (Buffy to Dawn on how much school she's missed.)

Pig Latin

XANDER: "I was possessed. The demon used me to eavesdrop on our conversation."

ANYA: "Great. So now what? We have to talk in some kind of anti-demon secret code?"

XANDER: "ood-gay idea-ay, An-yay."

DAWN: "Stop talking wrong in Pig Latin and drive!"

6-4   Flooded

Written by Jane Espenson, Directed by Douglas Petrie

Learning that she has no money and many accumulated bills, Buffy tries to get a loan from the bank. Turned down by the bank, everything seems to go wrong. But she begins to feel hope when Giles returns from England.

Clown Cars, Circus

"It's like little clown cars at the circus." (Willow when Dawn comments on how much water can be held in the pipes.)

Spider-Man

DAWN: "You can't charge innocent people for saving their lives."

ANYA: "Spider-Man does."

DAWN: "Does not. Xander?"

XANDER: "Action is his reward."

Star Wars (1977 film), Jedi, The Force

ANDREW: "What are you—some kind of Jedi?" (When Warren convinces M'Fashnik to leave.)

WARREN: "The Force sometimes has great power on the weak minded."

Christina Ricci

ANDREW: "Don't trust him. Robo pimp-daddy's all mouth."

WARREN: "Shut up, Andrew! You're just mad I wouldn't build you Christina Ricci."

ANDREW: "You owe me, man!"

WARREN: "Or else what? You'll train another pack of devil-dogs to ruin my prom? Graduated!"

ANDREW: "That wasn't me. How many times do I have to say it? The prom thing was my lame-o brother Tucker."

※ Episode Reference

In the above quote, when Andrew calls Warren "Robo pimp-daddy," this is a reference to Warren building himself a robot girlfriend in episode 5-15, "I Was Made to Love You," and building the BuffyBot for Spike in episode 5-18, "Intervention." The episode with the pack of devil dogs is episode 3-20, "The Prom."

Star Trek, Pig Latin, Vulcan

ANDREW: "Ix-nay on the urder-may."

WARREN: "Vote."

JONATHAN: "Who's for *not* killing Buffy?"

(Andrew and Jonathan vote by raising their hands, both with their fingers in the traditional Vulcan "live long and prosper" position.)

Blair Witch Project (1999 film)

"So scary the Blair Witch would have had to watch like this." (Willow puts her hands over her eyes and peeks through her fingers as she describes the resurrection spell to Giles.)

※ "Angel" Episode Cross Reference

At the end of this episode, Buffy gets a call from Angel and she announces that she must go to see him. This meeting is not shown, but it takes place just before "Angel" episode 3-5, "Fredless."

6-5   Life Serial

Written by David Fury & Jane Espenson, Directed by Nick Marck

Buffy tries to remain positive and look for a job, just as the Trio of Nerds subjects her to a battery of tests to see how she performs and to load data about her into their computer for analysis.

Life Cereal

The title pun.

Star Wars (1977 film), Return of the Jedi (1983 film), Death Star

Andrew paints the Death Star on the side of their van, and the horn plays the first bar of the *Star Wars* theme.

Spongebob Squarepants

"... once, Willow and I were watching *Spongebob Squarepants*...." (Tara starting to chat right before Buffy time-slips because of Warren's test.)

Gidget

BUFFY: "Excuse me, but—"

TONY: "Hang on, Gidget."

(Tony, the construction foreman, is complaining that Xander has brought Buffy to be on his crew.)

Star Trek Next Generation ('80s TV show, Episode: Cause and Effect), Mr. Data, X-Files ('90s TV show, Episode: Monday), Scully

ANDREW: "I hope she solves it faster than Data did in the ep of *TNG* when the Enterprise kept blowing up."

WARREN: "Or Mulder in that *X-Files* when the bank kept exploding."

ANDREW: "Scully wants me so bad."

(The Nerds discussing how fast Buffy may figure out she is in a time loop while she works in the Magic Box.)

Bob Dole

"Yes, and then I'm going to marry Bob Dole and raise penguins in Guam." (Buffy testing to see if Giles is listening to her.)

Monty Python: Dead Parrot

WARREN: "This mummy-hand has ceased to be."

ANDREW: "It is an ex-mummy-hand."

Jeopardy (Game show)

WARREN: "The Double Jeopardy—where Buffy's the one in Jeopardy."

※ *Episode Reference*

GILES: "Besides, it's Halloween. The one time of the year that supernatural threats give it a well-deserved rest. As should you."

BUFFY: "Yeah but what about costumes that take over your personality? Or wee little Irish fear-demon-ey thingies?"

Buffy is referring to the costume debacle in episode 2-6 "Halloween," and the miniature yet potent demon in episode 4-4 "Fear, Itself."

James Bond, Sean Connery, Roger Moore, Timothy Dalton, Dr. No (1962 film), Moonraker (1979 film), License to Kill (1989 film), Living Daylights (1987 film)

ANDREW: "We're really super villains now—like Dr. No."

WARREN: "Yes, back when Bond was Connery and movies decent."

JONATHAN: "Who even remembers Connery? I mean, Roger Moore was smooth."

ANDREW: "I like Timothy Dalton."

WARREN: "Connery is Bond. He had style."

JONATHAN: "Yeah, but Roger Moore was funny."

WARREN: "*Moonraker*? The gondola turns into a hovercraft? It's retarded. Besides, the guy had no edge."

ANDREW: "Dalton had edge. In *License to Kill* he was a rogue agent. That's edgy. And he was amazing in *Living Daylights*."

JONATHAN: "Yeah, which was written for Roger Moore, not Timothy Dalton."

Timothy Dalton, Sean Connery, Oscar

WARREN: "Connery is the only actor of the bunch!"

ANDREW: "Timothy Dalton should get an Oscar and beat Sean Connery over the head with it!"

6-6   All the Way

Written by Rebecca Rand Kirshner, Directed by David Solomon

Dawn lies to Buffy and goes on a risky Halloween date. After a long day helping out at the Halloween holiday sale at the Magic Box, Xander and Anya finally announce their engagement. Giles is becoming more and more concerned about Buffy depending too much on him.

 Music in this Episode

"Even If" by Lift

Charlie's Angels ('70s TV show)

DAWN: "So what are you supposed to be?" (About Anya's Halloween costume.)

ANYA: "An angel."

DAWN: "Oh. Shouldn't you have wings?"

ANYA: "Oh no. This is a special kind of angel called a 'Charlie.' We don't have wings. We just skate around with perfect hair and fight crime."

Episode Reference

When Spike asks Buffy why she is working at the Magic Shop, she says, "One-time deal to help out, and I mean straight time. No loop-de-loop mummy-hand repeat-o vision." She is referring to the time-loop sequence in episode 6-5, "Life Serial."

It's the Great Pumpkin, Charlie Brown (1966 TV special)

"It's not like I don't already have plans. *The Great Pumpkin* is on in 20." (Spike to Buffy when she turns down his offer to go on patrol.)

Fantasia (1940 film), Mickey Mouse, The Sorcerer's Apprentice

WILLOW: "I can whip up a jaunty self-cleaning incantation. It'd be like *Fantasia*."

GILES: "We all know how splendidly that turned out for Mickey."

WILLOW: "I think I'm a little more adept than a cartoon mouse."

TARA: "And have more fingers. Which is good, 'cuz then there's no need to wear those big white gloves to overcompensate."

Crimes and Misdemeanors (1989 film)

"I had to stop for crimes and misdemeanors." (Dawn's friend Janice to the boys at the park when they ask what took her so long.)

Pop Goes the Weasel

This is the tune that old man Kaltenback hummed to himself.

Santa Claus

"I say we get the funk out of here before Satan Claus tries to stuff us up the chimney." (Dawn's friend about leaving the house.)

Lunchables

"So what do you think—Lunchable? Or should we go all the way and turn them?" (Vampire Zach asking Justin whether they should just snack on Dawn and her friend or go further.)

Lunch Money

GILES: "Rupert is an exceptionally strong name." (Suggesting a name for Anya and Xander's future children.)

ANYA: "Yeah, if we want our progeny to eat paste and have their lunch money stolen."

Superman

JUSTIN: "Nah. Cold doesn't bother me."

DAWN: "What are you, Superman?"

Star Wars (1977 film), Luke Skywalker, Princess Leia

"Do they know they're brother and sister?" (Willow about two dancers at the bronze who are dressed as Leia and Luke.)

Mamma Yamma, Kids' Canada (CBC TV show)

"Hard to believe such a hot mama-yamma came from humble, geek-infested roots." (Willow to Tara that she was a geek when she was a kid.)

Harry Houdini

"Dawn and her friend pulled a Houdini." (Spike to Buffy on how Dawn lied about where she was going to be.)

6-7   Once More, with Feeling

Written and Directed by Joss Whedon

Everyone reveals their secrets and fears in song. Buffy yearns to feel alive again, and spike burns with passion for Buffy. Xander and Anya admit their insecurities about marriage, Tara discovers Willow is using magic to make her forget their arguments, and Giles realizes that he must leave if Buffy is ever to strike out on her own.

❧ *Emmy nomination for Music Direction*

This episode was nominated for an Emmy for Outstanding Music Direction.

❧ *Mutant Enemy Monster sings*

After the credits at the end of this musical episode, the Mutant Enemy monster sings his "Grr, Argh" line.

Magnolia (1999 film)

"Respect the cruller and tame the doughnut!" (Xander playing with pastries in an homage to Tom Cruise's genitalia-laden line from *Magnolia*.)

❋ *Episode Reference*

Anya sings, "His penis got diseases from the Chumash tribe." This is a reference to Xander's illness in episode 4-8, "Pangs."

David Brinkley

XANDER: "Will our lives become too stressful if I'm never that successful?"

ANYA: "When I get so worn and wrinkly that I look like David Brinkley."

Yma Sumac (Opera singer soprano)

"A 600-pound Chirago demon making like Yma Sumac." (Spike on the oddities he's seen since the singing started.)

Michael Flatley, Lord of the Dance

"Willow said they have a lead on the whole musical extravaganza evil. This demon that can be summoned—some sort of lord of the dance. But not the scary one. Just a demon." (Tara about the possible cause of the singing.)

❧ *The singing producers*

The characters Mustard Man and Parking Ticket Woman are played by series directors/producers David Fury and Marti Noxon. (Also watch for them in another musical Joss Whedon project, "Dr. Horrible's Sing-along Blog.")

Twist and Shout (1962 song)

"I'm the heart of swing. I'm the twist and shout." (The demon Sweet signing about how he is the embodiment of music and dance.)

Nero

"I bought Nero his very first fiddle." (The demon Sweet signing about how he has been evil for a long time.)

Movie Montage

BUFFY: "I'm just worried this whole session's gonna turn into some training montage from an '80s movie."

GILES: "Well, if we hear any inspirational power chords we'll just lie down until they go away."

※ *Episode Reference*

Tara sings: "I'm under your spell. God how can this be—playing with my memory. You know I've been through hell, Willow don't you see, there'll be nothing left of me." This is a reference to what Glory did to her in episode 5-19, "Tough Love."

Pinocchio

"Strong. Someday he'll be a real boy." (Spike about the puppet demon.)

※ *Episode Reference*

Dawn says, "The hardest thing in this world is to live in it." This is exactly what Buffy said to Dawn before she gave her life to close the rift to the hell dimensions in episode 5-22, "The Gift."

Kumbaya (song)

"You should go back inside. Finish the big group sing, get your kumbayayas out." (Spike to Buffy when she leaves the group mid-song to join Spike outside.)

Seventy-six Trombones, The Music Man (1962 film)

"The day you suss out what you do want there'll probably be a parade. Seventy-six bloody trombones." (Spike to Buffy.)

6-8   Tabula Rasa

Written by Rebecca Rand Kirshner, Directed by David Grossman

Desperate to keep Tara from leaving, Willow casts a memory spell. When the spell goes awry, the entire Scooby gang has complete amnesia. When the spell is broken, Tara breaks up with Willow and moves out.

 Music in this Episode

"Goodbye To You" by Michelle Branch

Gone With the Wind (1939 film)

"We kissed. You and me. All *Gone With the Wind*, with the rising music, and the rising... music." (Spike trying to get Buffy to talk with him about their kiss.)

Birkenstocks

"Do you think she walked around on clouds wearing, like, Birkenstocks and played a harp? Because that's just not flattering. You know, the clunky sandals." (Anya wondering what Buffy may have been like in heaven.)

✳ *Episode Reference*

WILLOW: "I didn't mean to—"

TARA: "To what? To violate my mind like that? How could you Willow? How could you after what Glory did to me?"

This is a reference to what Glory did to Anya in episode 5-19, "Tough Love."

Creature Feature ('60s film genre)

"Hurry up. You don't want to miss the lowdown on our latest feature creature." (Dawn telling Willow to hurry and join them at the Magic Box.)

Psychology Test

"Why was I on the ground? Why are you all staring at me? Is this some kind of psych test? Am I getting paid for this?" (Xander—not remembering who he is—upon waking up on the floor of the Magic Box.)

Candid Camera ('40s TV show), Alan Funt

GILES: "Maybe we got terribly drunk and this was some sort of blackout."

DAWN: "I don't think I drink."

ANYA: "I don't see any booze. I don't feel any head-bumps. And I don't see Alan Funt."

Mary Poppins (1964 film)

"Oh, listen to Mary Poppins. He's got his crust all stiff and upper with that nancy-boy accent." (Spike scoffing at Giles' positive outlook and English accent.)

Angel (1999-2004 TV show)

RANDY/SPIKE: "I must be a noble vampire. A good guy on a mission of redemption. I help the hopeless. I'm a vampire with a soul."

JOAN/BUFFY: "A vampire with a soul? Oh my God. How lame is that?"

Jason and the Argonauts (1963 film)

Giles sword-fights with a skeleton, looking much like a scene from *Jason and the Argonauts*.

King Ralph (1991 film)

Xander laughs after they regain their memories. "Sorry. I just got back the memory of seeing *King Ralph*."

6-9   Smashed

Written by Drew Z. Greenberg, Directed by Turi Meyer

Spike discovers that he can hurt Buffy, and they finally come to violent terms with how they feel for each other. Meanwhile, Willow turns Amy back into human form and they party with the magic, crossing a line into magic addiction. At the end of this episode, Buffy and Spike consummate their strange relationship, smashing an abandoned house and Buffy's self-esteem in the process.

 Music in this Episode

"Vermillion Borders" and "Parachute" by Virgil

Murder, She Wrote ('80s TV show), Jessica Fletcher

"Way to go with the keen observiness, Jessica Fletcher." (Buffy to Spike when he attacks a human thinking it's a demon.)

Langley

"We're not breaking into Langley here, it's Sunnydale." (Jonathan, when Andrew takes their museum heist too seriously.)

Disneyland

"We love the learning, Rusty. Museums, libraries, Disney Hall of Presidents—not boring. But more to the point, Goodbye." (Warren to Rusty the museum guard, right before zapping him with the freeze-ray.)

※ *Episode Reference*

Willow says, "Amy, three things we have to talk about. One, Larry's gay; two, Larry's dead; and three, high school's kinda over." Larry came out in episode 2-15, "Phases," and he is killed in episode 3-22, "Graduation Day."

Gatorade, Tom Cruise, Nicole Kidman

AMY: "It's crazy all the things that have happened since I went away. Snyder got eaten by a snake, high school got destroyed."

BUFFY: "Oh, Gatorade has a new flavor... blue."

AMY: "People getting frozen, Willow's dating girls. And did you hear about Tom and Nicole?"

❋ *Episode reference*

In Amy's quote above, Principal Snyder being eaten by a snake and the high school being destroyed happened in episode 3-22, "Graduation Day."

Raisinettes, Gummy Bears

TARA: "Good god, that's a lot of shake. I mean, I know, part of our big milkshake and movie fun-day, but good god, that's a lot of shake!"

DAWN: "Helps to wash down the Raisinettes."

TARA: "Promise me that you will eat something green tonight. Leafy green, not gummy green."

Holodeck, Star Trek Next Generation ('80s TV show)

"You can play holodeck another time, but right now, I'm in charge." (Spike forcing the Trio of Nerds to look at the chip in his head.)

Boba Fett, Star Wars (1977 film)

SPIKE: "Examine my chip, or Mr. Fett here is the first to die."

JONATHAN: "Hey all right—let's not do anything crazy here."

ANDREW: "That's a limited edition 1979 mint condition Boba Fett."

WARREN: "All right Dude. Chill. You can still make it right. You know you don't want to do this."

Dr. Who, Red Dwarf (BBC TV shows)

"You're English, right? I've seen every episode of *Dr. Who*. Not *Red Dwarf* though, because it's not out yet on DVD." (Andrew to Spike, because Spike is British.)

Star Trek ('60s TV show), Spock

"Help me out here Spock. I don't speak loser." (Spike to Warren, that he should explain the situation with his chip rather than asking him to read complicated printouts.)

Ellen DeGeneres

"Well nobody asked you, Ellen." (Creepy guy at the bar to Willow, when she points out that Amy said she didn't want to dance with him.)

Dungeons & Dragons

XANDER: "Aha! I got it! Here's our villain right here."

ANYA: "That's a D&D manual, Sweetie."

Peroxide

"So, what did Captain Peroxide want?" (Xander asking Buffy why Spike called her at the Magic Box.)

※ *Episode Reference*

Buffy says, "After all the things that have happened: the bank robbery, the jewelry heist—" and Xander says, "Exploding lint." They are referring to things that have happened since the Evil Trio of Nerds came on the scene. The bank robbery was in episode 6-4, "Flooded," and the exploding lint was in episode 6-5 "Life Serial."

6-10 Wrecked

Written by Marti Noxon, Directed by David Solomon

Buffy feels guilty and shocked by her behavior with Spike, vowing it will never happen again. Willow's magic addiction puts Dawn in danger, and Buffy realizes she needs to pay more attention to what's going on at home.

In Memory: J. D. Peralta

This episode was dedicated to the memory of J.D. Peralta, who was Marti Noxon's assistant since midway through the show's fourth season.

Music in this Episode

"Black Cat Bone" by Laika

Martha Stewart, Decoupage

XANDER: "Anya has a theory. She thinks that Martha Stewart froze that guy."

ANYA: "Don't be ridiculous. Martha Stewart isn't a demon, she's a witch."

XANDER: "Really?"

ANYA: "Of course. Nobody could do that much decoupage without calling on the powers of darkness."

Mommy Dearest (1981 film), Joan Crawford

"I think she's feeling all Joan Crawford." (Dawn about Buffy's residual guilt over staying out all night.)

Lojack

"Again? Ever think about a Lojack for the girl?" (Spike when Buffy says she needs him to help her look for Dawn, who has gone missing again.)

6-11 Gone

Written by David Fury, Directed by David Fury

When the Nerds accidentally hit Buffy with an invisibility ray, she enjoys the opportunity to take a vacation from real life.

 Music in this Episode

"I Know" by Trespassers William

Bongs

"Yeah, you know, to you and me they're just candles. But to witches, they're like bongs." (Buffy when Dawn complains about having to get rid of all the candles.)

✳ Episode Reference

Xander asks, "How did this hap— Wait a sec, have you been feeling ignored lately?" Buffy answers, "Yeah, ignored. I wish. No, this isn't a Marcie deal. I don't know what happened." This is a reference to the invisible girl in episode 1-11, "Out of Mind, Out of Sight."

Industrial Light & Magic (ILM), Ed Wood

"I pictured something cooler. More ILM, less Ed Wood." (Andrew on Warren's invisibility ray gun.)

Frodo, Lord of the Rings ('50s book trilogy by J.R.R. Tolkien)

"Oh cheer up Frodo!" (Warren to Jonathan when he complains about Warren firing the invisibility ray gun at the chair.)

Star Trek: The Wrath of Khan (1982 film)

"I deserve the wrath of Dawn." (Willow to Buffy about the icy treatment she is getting from Dawn.)

Godfrey Cambridge (Comedian), Goldilocks

SPIKE: "What should I call you then? Pet? Sweetheart? Or Goldilocks? You know I love this hair, the way it bounces around when—"

XANDER: (Walking in on Spike and Buffy) "Good Godfrey Cambridge!"

Yahtzee (Game)

"Yahtzee!" (Buffy when she finds what she was looking for.)

Lex Luthor, Superman, Metropolis

"Yeah, Lex Luthor. He's always trying to take over Metropolis, but he doesn't try to kill Superman." (Andrew protesting Warren's willingness to kill the Slayer.)

Bizarro (DC Comics supervillain who is the mirror image of Superman)

"Did I fall into some backward dimension here? Is this Bizarro world?" (Buffy wondering aloud how it can be that Spike kicked her out of his crypt.)

X-Files ('90s TV show), Mulder

"Working on it. Anya and Xander are Muldering out what happened." (Buffy to Dawn that they are investigating what may have caused her invisibility.)

※ *Episode Reference*

After tormenting Doris the social worker, invisible Buffy leaves the social services office whistling the tune "I Just Want to Be Alive," from the musical episode 6-7, "Once More With Feeling."

6-12 Double Meat Palace

Written by Jane Espenson, Directed by Nick Marck

With her finances in disarray, Buffy gets a job at a fast food restaurant that may be using dubious ingredients, and naturally there's a demon to fight.

※ *Episode Reference*

Xander says, "Now, I get Warren being a supervillain-ey type, but I thought Jonathan completely learned that lesson. I've never even heard of this other guy." The comment about Jonathan is a reference to episode 4-17, "Superstar."

Star Trek: Enterprise (2001 TV show), Vulcan

"... and pictures of the Vulcan woman on *Enterprise*." (Willow on what Buffy found at the Nerds' place.)

Sleepless in Seattle (1993 film), Tom Hanks, Meg Ryan

"Like how the cow and the chicken come together even though they've never met. It's like *Sleepless in Seattle* if Tom and Meg were, like, minced." (Buffy on the chicken and beef at Double Meat Palace.)

Soylent Green (1973 film)

"It's people!" (Buffy about the Double Meat burgers.)

Disneyland

"It was like a trip to Disneyland without the lines." (Amy to Willow about the spell she cast.)

6-13 Dead Things

Written by Jane Espenson, Directed by James A. Contner

The Nerds' annoyances cross the line when they accidentally kill a girl and try to frame Buffy with the murder. Buffy realizes that she didn't "come back wrong," so has to deal with the reasons she is carrying on with Spike.

 Music in this Episode

"Out of This World" by Bush

Episode Reference

When she gets home from work, Buffy says, "Is there singing? Are we singing again?" She is referring the musical episode 6-7, "Once More With Feeling."

New Kids on the Block

"I think the New Kids on the Block posters are starting to date me." (Buffy to Spike on interior decorating.)

Shake Your Groove Thing (1978 song), Soul Train (TV show)

ANYA: "Come share in the joy of our groove thang." (Anya inviting Buffy and Willow to join them on the dance floor at the Bronze.)

BUFFY: "I think I'll catch the next Soul Train out."

David Lynch

"So that's why time went all David Lynch?" (Buffy asking Anya if the demon she identified is what caused the time shifts.)

6-14 Older and Far Away

Written by Drew Z. Greenberg & Rebecca Rand Kirshner, Directed by Michael Gershman

Dawn, tired of feeling alone, wishes that everyone would hang out with her and just stay put. When everyone gathers at the house for Buffy's birthday party, her wish is granted and everyone is compelled to stay—along with a lethal demon.

 Music in this Episode

"Clouds Like These" by Aberdeen

 An homage to "Exterminating Angel"

This episode is a modern reimagining of Luis Buñuel's 1962 masterpiece "Exterminating Angel," in which a group of socialites are compelled not to leave the house after a dinner party.

✻ *Episode Reference*

When asked if they should set out candles for the party, Xander says, "Not if they're that horrible slug kind you're trying to unload." The slug candles were first introduced in episode 6-5, "Life Serial."

Twilight Zone episode: It's a Good Life (1961)

"The only thing missing is a cornfield. There isn't a cornfield, is there?" (Xander when they're magically trapped in the house.)

✻ *Episode Reference*

Xander says, "Well, 'cuz you know, sometimes we do something that seems like a good idea at the time, like, say, invoke the power of a musical amulet. And it turns out, you know, not so much." He is referring to episode 6-7, "Once More With Feeling."

✻ *Episode Reference*

HALFREK: "William?"

SPIKE: "Hey, wait a minute."

BUFFY: "You guys know each other?"

HALFREK: "Uh, no."

SPIKE: "Not really."

Spike and Halfrek knew each other when they were humans William and Cecily, as shown in Spike's backstory in episode 5-7, "Fool For Love."

6-15 As You Were

Written by Douglas Petrie, Directed by Douglas Petrie

Riley returns to Sunnydale and asks Buffy to help him and his wife Sam track a spawning demon and hunt down the underworld-type who is selling its eggs. After the battle, Buffy finally breaks up with Spike.

Doritos

XANDER: "Cool Ranch?"

ANYA: "Cajun Fiesta."

(The couple is munching Doritos as they drive to the airport to pick up relatives at the airport for their wedding.)

James Bond

"You still carry around all that James Bond stuff. It's so cute." (Buffy when she sees Riley again.)

※ *Episode Reference*

RILEY: "I have some big stories to tell you too, when we get half a second."

BUFFY: "Did you die?"

RILEY: "No."

BUFFY: "I'm gonna win."

Buffy is referring to her death in episode 5-22, "The Gift."

Heartbreaker (1979 song), Pat Benatar

"Hey there's the man. Life taker. Heart breaker. You know, figuratively speaking." (Xander, greeting Riley.)

Star Trek ('60s TV show), Tribbles

"So, they're like really mean Tribbles? Sorry—I've been dealing with these geeks...." (Buffy to Riley about Suvolte demons.)

Nick Fury (Comics)

"I have a hard time imagining Nick and Nora Fury hiding from their own relatives in the bathroom." (Xander to Anya in the bathroom as they quietly hide from their relatives who have gathered for the wedding.)

6-16 Hell's Bells

Written by Rebecca Rand Kirshner, Directed by David Solomon

As Xander and Anya prepare to walk down the aisle, the families bicker and Xander's father shows the ugly side of marriage. A mysterious visitor gives Xander a faux vision of his future which convinces him that the marriage must not go on. He leaves Anya at the altar, changing both their lives.

※ *Episode Reference*

Willow tells Xander, "It's a good thing I realized I was gay, otherwise, you and me in formal wear...." She is referring to their mutual attraction in episode 3-20, "The Prom."

Marlene Dietrich, Bridesmaid

WILLOW: "I'm supposed to be best man. Shouldn't I be all Marlene Dietrich-ey in a dashing tuxedo number?"

BUFFY: "No. That would be totally unfair. We must share equally in the cosmic joke that is bridesmaidsdom."

Circus, Bat Mitzvah

BUFFY: "I just can't believe everyone bought that story about Anya's people being circus-folk. Did you see the guy with the tentacles? What's he supposed to be? Inky the Squid-Boy?"

WILLOW: "And Xander's family. I haven't seem them that bad since my Bat Mitzvah. Did you see how much they drank?"

BUFFY: "Kinda. Mr. Harris threw up in my purse."

Episcopalians

"The Harrises are very broad-minded. We're Episcopalians." (Xander's cousin when Anya's demon friend asks if Xander and Anya should raise their children in ignorance of Anya's family's ways.)

Mary Kay (Cosmetics)

"I hope you crash your stupid pink car!" (Xander to Anya in his vision of their possible future.)

6-17 Normal Again

Written by Diego Gutierrez, Directed by Rick Rosenthal

When the sting of a demon causes Buffy to fade in and out of reality, she begins to question which world is real: the demon-inhabited world of Sunnydale, or the psychiatric hospital where she has been a patient for the last six years.

The Shining (1980 film), Jack Torrence

"I'm going Jack Torrence in here." (Jonathan to Warren on how he's tired of hiding in the basement.)

Legion of Doom (Comics)

ANDREW: "We're on the lam. We have to lay low. Underground."

JONATHAN: "It's figurative, Doofus! Did you even read *Legion of Doom*?"

DSL

"How come you're all home, hearth, and DSL anyway?" (Buffy asking Willow why she's staying home on the computer instead of going out to see Tara.)

Ken Russell

"Got her trippin' like a Ken Russell film festival." (Warren about Buffy and how she is hallucinating.)

Spanky, Little Rascals ('50s TV show)

"What do you think, Spanky. Do you think we're plotting against you?" (Warren when Jonathan asks what Warren and Andrew have been up to.)

Ocean's Eleven (2001 film)

WARREN: (Looking at diagram on the computer.) "Ah. There's the vault."

ANDREW: "I still say we're going to need eight other guys to pull this off."

WARREN: "Never should've let you see that movie."

One Flew Over the Cuckoo's Nest (1975 film)

"No more cuckoo's nest?" (Willow asking Buffy if she's feeling better after taking the antidote.)

※ *Episode Reference*

When the doctor tells Buffy, "Last summer when you had a momentary awakening, it was them who pulled you back in," he is referring to her resurrection in episode 6-1, "Bargaining."

Friends, Romans..., Shakespeare, Julius Caesar

"Friends? Romans? Anyone?" (Xander calling out at Buffy's house to see who's around.)

6-18 Entropy

Written by Drew Z. Greenberg, Directed by James A. Contner

Anya returns after having been left at the altar, and she is seeking vengeance on Xander. When she seeks solace with Spike, she has no idea that the Nerds' camera in the Magic Box reveals the liaison to the rest of the gang.

Music in this Episode

"That Kind Of Love" by Allison Krauss

Star Wars (1977 film), Padawan

WARREN: "I'm not impressed, Padawan. When do we hit pay dirt?"

JONATHAN: "If something goes wrong we're gonna surge, and we'll be deader than an ex-girlfriend."

※ *Episode Reference*

In the quote above, Jonathan is referring to episode 6-13, "Dead Things," in which Warren kills his ex-girlfriend.

Indiana Jones and the Temple of Doom (1984 film), Short Round

"Cheer up, Short Round." (Warren to Jonathan.)

✳ *Episode Reference*

Buffy says to Spike, "I tried to kill my friends, my sister last week. Guess how much they hate me. Zero. Zero much. So I'm thinkin', sleeping with you: they'll deal." She is referring to episode 6-17, "Normal Again."

Babylon 5 ('90s TV show)

"He's got that look he had that time I highlighted in his *Babylon 5* novels." (Andrew to Warren about Jonathan.)

✳ *Episode Reference*

TARA: "Okay, wait—it was under her wig?"

WILLOW: "Well, it was this thing. It just came out from inside her head."

TARA: "Oh, that's disgusting! What did it look like?"

WILLOW: "Well, let's put it this way: if I wasn't gay before…."

Filling Tara in on the things she has missed since she's been gone, Willow is referring to events in episode 6-12, "Double Meat Palace."

International House of Pancakes

"Uh, did we open a chain? Are we the International House of something?" (Dawn to Buffy when she sees the big breakfast she made.)

✳ *Episode Reference*

DAWN: "I don't use that word any more."

ANYA: "Coagulate?"

DAWN: "W - i - s - h."

ANYA: "Oh, Wish. As in: 'I wish Xander–'"

DAWN: "Right. That word. There are vengeance demons out there that are still active, remember?"

Dawn's reluctance to say the word 'wish' is due to the events in episode 6-14, "Older and Far Away," in which Dawn's wish wreaked havoc.

Scooby Doo

"I saved the Scoobies, how many times? And I can't stand the lot." (Spike complaining with Anya about the gang.)

6-19 Seeing Red

Written by Rebecca Rand Kirshner, Directed by Michael Gershman

Willow and Tara are happily back together. Buffy foils the Nerds' latest heist, getting Jonathan and Andrew arrested and infuriating the escaping Warren. Having reached his limit of the Slayer's interference, Warren comes to Buffy's house with a gun, putting Buffy in the hospital and killing Tara.

 Music in this Episode

"Displaced" by Azure Ray

Sherlock Holmes

"We should go back. Tara and I can Sherlock around." (Willow about looking for clues at the Nerds' house.)

H.R. Pufnstuf (1969 TV show)

"Want a piece of this, huh? Not so tough, are ya now, Pufnstuf!" (Andrew, as he zaps a demon with a mega cattle prod.)

Siegfried and Roy

"You can't Siegfried and Roy the barrier. It's got to be the real deal." (Andrew to Jonathan that the demon's barrier cannot be breached with magic.)

Hair gel, Blade Runner (1982 film)

ANDREW: "Dude. Unholy hair gel."

JONATHAN: "Get off!"

ANDREW: "Make me, skin job!"

Gandhi

"Mahatma!" (Jonathan's exclamation when Warren, with the help of the orbs, defeats a demon.)

Charles Atlas

"We're risking everything so that Charles Atlas can get a date." (Jonathan in dismay that they stopped at a bar so Warren can pick up on women.)

Star Trek Next Generation ('80s TV show), Betazoid, Deanna Troi, Picard

"Warren's the boss. He's Picard. You're Deanna Troi. Get used to the feeling, Betazoid." (Andrew to Jonathan.)

Star Trek ('60s TV show), Klingon

WILLOW: "We were able to decipher pretty much everything except these."

TARA: "It isn't written in any ancient language we could identify."

XANDER: "It's Klingon. They're love poems. Which doesn't have anything to do with the insidious scheme you're about to describe."

BUFFY: "What have you got that doesn't rhyme?"

Mighty Mouse

"Be careful. Warren's gone all Mighty Mouse. Emphasis on the Might." (Xander to Buffy about how Warren has somehow become freakishly strong.)

Knight Rider ('80s TV show), Hot wings

"Uh, Knock knock. I was just in the neighborhood so I thought, you know- there's a *Knight Rider* marathon on the TV. So, I got hot wings!" (Clem when he shows up at Spike's place with a bucket of hot wings.)

Uno (Game), Rocket Man (1972 song)

XANDER: "Time for the spring poking already?"

BUFFY: "Just making sure there are no more evil trio cameras. Or, Evil uno."

XANDER: "The sinister, yet addictive card game?"

BUFFY: "Warren. Jonathan and Andrew got clinked, but Warren pulled a rocket man."

6-20 Villains

Written by Marti Noxon, Directed by David Solomon

Willow fully succumbs to dark magic when Tara is murdered before her eyes. After storming the hospital and saving Buffy, she goes on the hunt for Warren. She flays him in the woods, then turns her attention to the other two nerds.

※ *Episode Reference*

Willow appeals to the god Osiris to bring Tara back—the same being to whom she appealed to bring Buffy back in episode 6-1, "Bargaining." Osiris is the Egyptian god of afterlife.

Dragnet ('60s TV show), Sony Discman

ANDREW: "Do you think they'll let my aunt bring me my Discman?"

JONATHAN: "That's what you're worried about? In-flight entertainment? We're in jail!"

ANDREW: "We're in custody. We're not in jail yet."

JONATHAN: "Thank you, *Dragnet*."

Oz ('90s TV show), Mayberry R.F.D. ('60s TV show)

"You have got to chill out. This isn't *Oz*, it's like Mayberry." (Andrew to Jonathan when Jonathan worries about being in jail.)

Matthew Broderick, WarGames (1983 film), Ferris Bueller's Day Off (1986 film)

"... like *WarGames*. Remember that decoder that Matthew Broderick used? I miss Ferris-Matthew. Broadway-Matthew, I find him cold." (Andrew to Jonathan.)

⁂ *Episode Reference*

When Buffy awakens in the hospital after Warren shoots her, Xander says, "You've got to stop doing this. This dying thing's funny once, maybe twice." This is a reference to Buffy's deaths in episode 1-12, "Prophecy Girl," and episode 5-22, "The Gift."

Nostradamus

RACK: "The girl is running on pure fury. I've never felt anything like it."

WARREN: "Thank you for the tip, Nostradamus. Just load me up, okay?"

Puppet Master (1989 film)

"Fine, fine! Puppet Master wants to drive? Go right ahead!" (Xander when Willow magically takes control of the car and makes it turn off the road into the desert.)

Country Time (Drink mix), Bugles, Liverwurst

"Can I get you ladies something? I was about to mix up some Country Time… I've got Bugles and liverwurst." (Clem to Dawn and Buffy when they find him in Spike's crypt.)

Parcheesi (Game), The Wedding Planner (2001 film)

"Do you Parcheesi? Or we could rent videos. I've been dying to see *The Wedding Planner*." (Clem to Dawn.)

⁂ *Episode Reference*

Buffy says to Willow, "What did you do?" and Willow answers, "One down." This is a reference to the title of the following episode, 6-21, "Two to Go."

6-21 Two to Go (Part 1)

Written by Douglas Petrie, Directed by Bill L. Norton

Willow goes after Jonathan and Andrew, who are in the Sunnydale police station. Buffy rescues them and brings them to the Magic Box to protect them. Just when it seems there is no way to stop her, Giles appears to confront Willow.

Star Wars (1977 film)

"Laugh it up, Fuzzball!" (Andrew when Jonathan scoffs at Andrew's belief that Warren will rescue them.)

Superman, Spider-Man, Lex Luthor, Santa Claus

JONATHAN: "You're checking for implants?"

ANDREW: "Lex Luthor had a false epidermis escape kit in *Superman vs. the Amazing Spider-Man, Treasury Edition*."

JONATHAN: "First of all, those were sonic disrupters. Second of all, you are sadness personified. Waiting for Warren? Yeah, maybe he'll come bust us out of here on Santa's magic sleigh."

Star Wars (1977 film)

"You were out of the Trio a long time ago... in a galaxy far, far away." (Andrew to Jonathan.)

Circus

ANYA: "Please stop looking at me like this is your first trip to the circus and do your job. Let them out!" (Telling the guard to release Andrew and Warren.)

Dark Phoenix, X-Men (comic)

BUFFY: "We're going to have to make a run for it."

ANDREW: "Are you kidding? She's like Dark Phoenix up there. You expect us to just outrun her?"

Cheese-It (snack crackers)

ANDREW: "Jeez It!"

Doritos

CLEM: "Not that I'm knocking the Nacho Cheese ones. It's not the taste, it's the texture I can't deal with. So gritty. Kind of hurts my tongue. So, I give 'em a 7. Maybe a 7.5. And you think this is dumb, don't you?"

DAWN: "No. As taste tests go, this is definitely one of the better ones I've been to."

PG-13

"Let me get my hat and my coat. I'll take you to a movie. We'll go nuts! PG-13." (Clem trying to cheer up Dawn.)

No. 2 Pencil

"This is a test. And since your pad is decked out gladiator-style and no number-two pencils have been provided, I guess we're not starting with the written." (Spike to the demon on the test he must pass.)

Smells Like Teen Spirit (1991 song), Nirvana

"Here we are now, entertain us." (Spike to the opponent he must battle to the death.)

Star Wars (1977 film), Jawa, Midichlorians, Darth Vader

ANDREW: "You saw her. She's a truck-driving magic mama, and we've got maybe seconds before Darth Rosenberg grinds everybody into Jawa burgers. And not one of you bunch has the midichlorians to stop her."

XANDER: "You've never had any tiny bit of sex, have you?"

ANYA: "The annoying virgin has a point."

※ *Episode Reference*

ANYA: "There is nothing in this world that would give me greater or more lasting satisfaction than to wreak bloody vengeance upon you, Xander Harris. But I can't. Not officially. Not magically. So smile. It's your lucky day. You got away with it. I can't hurt you."

XANDER: "Right. 'Cause you varnishing the table with Spike, how could that possibly have hurt. It may have chafed."

ANYA: "That wasn't vengeance. It was solace."

Xander is referring to when Spike and Anya had sex in the Magic Box in episode 6-8, "Entropy."

※ *Episode Reference*

Willow says to Buffy, "You're trying to sell me on the world? The one where you lie to your friends when you're not trying to kill them? You screw a vampire just to feel? And insane asylums are comfy alternatives? This world?" Willow is referring to episode 6-17, "Normal Again."

Sabrina the Teenage Witch (Comic, '90s TV show)

"We're supposed to wait around for Sabrina to come along and disembowel us?" (Andrew when Xander says they just need to find a place to hide until Buffy finishes battling Willow.)

6-22 Grave (Part 2)

Written by David Fury, Directed by James A. Contner

Buffy realizes that she can bring Dawn into the world instead of constantly protecting her from it. When the powerful magic Giles transfers to Willow makes her realize the extent of universal suffering, she turns her focus on bringing it to an end, and Xander uses his simple power of affection and love to stop Willow and save the world.

 Music in this Episode

"Prayer of St. Francis" by Sarah McLachlan

※ *Episode Reference*

Buffy says, "It was like, when I clawed my way out of that grave, I left something behind—part of me. I just, I don't understand why I'm back." This is a reference to Buffy's resurrection in episode 6-1, "Bargaining."

Duct Tape

GILES: (Laughing) "Duct tape?"

BUFFY: "On their mouths. So the demon could eat them."

GILES: "Because they were figments."

BUFFY: "All of it. You, Sunnydale. And I was just some nut-case in L.A. Of course. Why didn't we see it before?"

※ *Episode Reference*

In the above quote, Buffy is telling Giles about what happened in episode 6-17, "Normal Again."

Dead Man Walking, (1995 film)

"You're always saving everyone. It's kinda pesky. You probably even think you're buying time for Jonathan and the other one. But I got a little secret for ya. I can kill them from anywhere I want... with this. It'll find them. It'll bury them, along with anyone else helping those dead men walking." (Willow sending Buffy off to save Xander and Dawn.)

Brown-eyed Girl (1967 song)

"Hey black-eyed girl." (Xander to witchy-Willow.)

Cartoons

WILLOW: "Is this the master plan? You're gonna stop me by telling me you love me?"

XANDER: "Well, I was gonna walk you off a cliff and hand you an anvil but, it seemed kinda cartoon-ey."

Yellow Crayon

XANDER: "The first day of Kindergarten, you cried because you broke the yellow crayon, and you were too afraid to tell anyone. You've come pretty far. Ending the world, not a terrific notion. But the thing is: Yeah. I love you. I love crayon-break-ey Willow, and I love scary vein-ey Willow."

Season Seven: Buffy Changes the World

Aired: 2002-2003

Bid Bad: The First

(Episode Table starts on page 248)

"We're all at death's door repeatedly ringing the doorbell like maniacal Girl Scouts trying to make quota."

— *Anya*

"Knowledge comes from crafted bindings and pages, Buffy, not ones and zeros."

— *Giles*

"Who're you gonna call?
God, that phrase is never gonna be usable again, is it?"

— *Spike*

"Okay, I got my tumbleweed, my eggs.
I got my chrysalises... chrysali?
My butterfly transformer pods."

— *Willow*

Season Seven:
Buffy Changes the World

Buffy is understandably paranoid when Dawn starts at the newly rebuilt Sunnydale high school. Looking for danger around every corner, she senses something suspicious about the new principal. With the warning "From beneath you it devours" ringing in her ears, Buffy finds Spike living in the school basement—clearly insane, and sporting a shiny new soul.

Willow returns from England, still recovering from her experience with dark magic, but aware that possibly the greatest evil Buffy will ever face is about to appear in Sunnydale, and that she needs to be there to help fight it.

The First is the ultimate, original source of evil, aided by Übervamps that are nearly impossible to defeat. Taking the appearance of Warren, The First lures Jonathan and Andrew back to Sunnydale to unleash the Übervamps into the world. Willow captures the repentant Andrew and brings him into the gang, first as a prisoner, but later as a willing member.

Against this desperate backdrop, Anya struggles to get back to her old self and find solace in the vengeance game. Having spent some time as a human, she finds her heart is no longer into vengeance when a wish she grants has particularly gruesome results. Buffy sets out to slay her, and Anya offers her life in exchange to reverse her spell.

Meanwhile, girls are being hunted and killed around the world, and soon they start traveling to Sunnydale for the protection of the Slayer. These are the Potentials—the girls in the line to be Slayers when their predecessors die. With the systematic hunting of the Potentials, Buffy and Faith know that the goal of The First is the elimination of the Slayer line.

Season seven brings Buffy up against the greatest possible challenges. No evil is greater, and for much of the time she is sure that she cannot win. But the tide is turned when she retrieves a special scythe, a sure weapon against The First's army. With Willow's magic and her band of Potentials, Buffy's team fights the battle. But it is the final gift from her champion, Spike, that destroys The First's army and wipes Sunnydale off the map.

When you can't win the game, change the rules. When Buffy's plan turns all the world's Potentials into Slayers, she changes the rules, and the world, forever.

Season Seven Episodes and Pop Culture References

7-1 Lessons

Written by Joss Whedon, Directed by David Solomon

Dawn starts school at the newly rebuilt Sunnydale High. In the school basement, Buffy finds an insane Spike, and Dawn encounters ghosts. Meanwhile, Willow is in England with Giles, working on controlling the magic that is now permanently a part of her.

❦ *Shooting scenes at Anthony's place*

The scenes with Willow and Giles in the yard and house in England were filmed at Anthony Head's home.

Synchronized Swimming

WILLOW: "Is there anything you don't know everything about?" (When Giles identifies an obscure flower that Willow caused to grow and bloom.)

GILES: "Synchronized swimming. Complete mystery to me."

Bangers and Mash

"… but there's this look that they get, like I'm gonna turn them all into bangers and mash or something—which I'm not even really sure what that is." (Willow to Giles on how the other women in the coven are afraid of her.)

Dumbledore, Harry Potter (1997-2007 books)

"When you brought me here, I thought it was to kill me or to lock me in a mystical dungeon for all eternity…. Instead you go all Dumbledore on me." (Willow to Giles on her experience with him in England.)

Food Channel (Cable channel), Cereal Box

XANDER: "How exactly do you make cereal?"

BUFFY: "Ah. You put the box near the milk. I saw it on the Food Channel."

James Bond, 007

"Hey. Check out Double-Oh Xander." (Dawn on how nice Xander looks in his suit.)

※ *Episode Reference*

Xander says, "The last two principals were eaten. Who would even apply for that job?" Principal Flutie was eaten by students possessed by hyena demons in episode 1-6, "The Pack," and Principal Snyder was eaten by the newly-ascended Mayor in Episode 3-22, "Graduation Day."

※ *Episode Reference*

Warning Dawn to be careful at high school, Buffy says, "And stay away from Hyena people. Or any loser-type athletes, you know, or if you see anyone that's invisible...." Hyena people is a reference to episode 1-6, "The Pack." Loser-type athletes is a reference to episode 2-20, "Go Fish." Invisibility is a reference to episode 1-11, "Out of Mind, Out of Sight."

The Silver Chair (1953 book), Chronicles of Narnia, To Serve Man

"I know! You never know what's coming. The stake is not the power. *To Serve Man* is a cookbook. I love you. Go away!" (Dawn to Buffy that she knows all the warnings.)

Britney Spears

"I'm very into Britney Spears' early work before she sold out. So, mostly her finger painting and macaroni art. Very underrated." (Dawn introducing herself to her new high school class.)

Intervention

"What is this, an intervention? Shouldn't all my demon friends be here?" (Anya when Halfrek tells her that everyone is noticing that she hasn't been very evil.)

Zombie

"It's great! If you're a zombie-ghost thing." (Buffy when Xander asks if the new school passed her inspection.)

Alice in Wonderland (1951 film)

"Curiouser and curiouser." (Principal Wood to Buffy when he sees how she is able to get some anti-social kids together.)

7-2   Beneath You

Written by Douglas Petrie, Directed by Nick Marck

The consequences of Anya's return to the vengeance biz is a giant, toothy worm under Sunnydale. Buffy learns that Spike has regained his soul, and Willow, sensing that something evil is brewing at the Hellmouth, begins her journey home.

※ *Episode Reference*

Buffy says to Dawn, "Wasn't that having a smoochathon with teen-vampire last Halloween?" She is referring to events in episode 6-6, "All the Way."

Bastinado

PRINCIPAL WOOD: "'There're only three things these kids understand: the boot, the bat, and the bastinado'. Heh heh. That joke... It's a bad joke. It's the bastinado. Nobody ever knows what that thing is."

BUFFY: "Wooden rod to slap the soles of the feet in Turkish prisons. But if made with the correct wood makes an *awesome* billy club."

PRINCIPAL WOOD: "I think you're going to fit in just fine."

Vegetarian

BUFFY: "Is it my sparkling personality? Or maybe you enjoyed my work at the Double Meat Palace."

PRINCIPAL WOOD: "I'm a vegetarian."

※ *Episode Reference*

Buffy's work at the fast-food restaurant Double Meat Palace that she mentions in the above quote began in episode 6-12, "Double Meat Palace," and ended in episode 6-15, "As You Were."

※ *Episode Reference*

Xander says, "In the biggest way, I am not loving this plan. I'm not loving Spike. He tried to rape you." This is a reference to Spike's actions in episode 6-19, "Seeing Red."

Yorkshire Terrier

BUFFY: "Anya, that thing you created burst through solid pavement and ate her dog!"

ANYA: "Oh, puppy!"

XANDER: "Wait. That gets your sad noise? People's lives are in danger and you give it up for the Yorkie?"

※ *Episode Reference*

When Anya says, "Spike, you don't get to go there again," he says, "Please, I've already forgotten about our little time together." This is a reference to their brief tryst in the Magic Box in episode 6-18, "Entropy."

Batman

"Is that it? A little touchy-feely and you're off to the batpoles?" (Spike to Buffy as she leaves.)

7-3   Same Time, Same Place

Written by Jane Espenson, Directed by James A. Contner

Worried and unsure if her friends will welcome her home, Willow's subconscious magic creates a minor dimensional shift, rendering her invisible and making her friends invisible to her. When a Sunnydale demon leaves its flayed victim at a construction site, Xander and Buffy wonder if perhaps Willow is in town after all.

Yellow crayon

XANDER: "I used yellow crayon. It was a thing from when I talked to Willow on the bluff. I hope she gets it." (When asked why his sign was so hard to read.)

※ *Episode Reference*

The above quote is a reference to Xander's intervention with Willow in episode 6-22, "Grave."

※ *Episode Reference*

In the school basement, Spike says to Buffy, "Look at you. You're glowing. What's a word means 'Glowing'? Got a rhyme." This is a very touching reference to episode, 5-7, "Fool For Love,"where we see Spike when he was a mortal named William with a penchant for poetry. In his poem about the lovely Cecily, he was struggling to find a word that rhymed with "gleaming," and instead used the word "effulgent," which is a synonym for "glowing."

Sherlock Holmes ("It's elementary")

"It's smellementary! Also, I'm sure there's tons of stuff like this. You know, procedures we can use that don't involve magic spells. Just good solid detective work." (Dawn on how she can contribute to the gang's efforts with her detective work—and hopefully wear high heels more often while she's at it.)

Limbo (dance)

XANDER: "It'll be all right. We'll get you fixed up. You'll be doing the limbo in no time."

DAWN: (Paralyzed.) "Yeah, as a pole."

Meditation

BUFFY: "I didn't realize meditating was such hard work."

WILLOW: "I'm healing. Growing new skin."

BUFFY: "Wow. That's magic right? I mean, when most people meditate, they don't get extra skin, right? 'Cause Clem should like, cut back."

7-4   Help

Written by Rebecca Rand Kirshner, Directed by Rick Rosenthal

When a girl is sent to School Counselor Buffy for not turning in her homework, the girl, Cassie, reveals that she knows she will die on Friday. Buffy does everything she can to save her.

I Like Ike, Milk—it does a body good (Advertising slogan)

XANDER: "'From beneath you it devours.' It's not the friendliest jingle, is it? It's no 'I Like Ike' or 'Milk—it does a body good'."

 Rocks on the tombstone?

When Willow visits Tara's grave for the first time, she places several small rocks on the tombstone. This is a Jewish tradition that speaks to the permanence of remembering the lost loved one.

Google

WILLOW: "Have you googled her yet?"

XANDER: "Willow! She's 17!"

(Xander misunderstands what googling is when Willow asks if he has used it to learn more about Cassie.)

Doogie Howser, MD (1989 TV show)

"You join chat rooms. You write poetry. You post *Doogie Howser* fan fic." (Willow on what normal teens do online, thereby revealing her inner nerd.)

Blue Oyster Cult

"Do you know how lame this is? Four teenage boys trying to raise up a demon? Sorry it didn't show. I bet it's because you forgot the boom box playing some heavy metal thing, like Blue Clam Cult. I think that's the key to the raising of lame demons." (Buffy to the teens trying to raise a demon.)

※ *Episode Reference*

Near the end of the episode, Cassie turns to Spike and says "She'll tell you. Someday she'll tell you." This promise comes true in episode 7-22, "Chosen," when, right before the very end, Buffy tells Spike that she loves him.

7-5 Selfless

Written by Drew Goddard, Directed by David Solomon

Buffy must finally slay demon Anya who goes too far with her vengeance, killing twelve frat boys by granting a single wish. Xander and Willow interfere, and Anya makes a painful, selfless choice. We see Anya's backstory, including scenes of happier times.

Montresor, The Cask of Amontillado (1846 book by Edgar Allen Poe)

> BUFFY. "Spike, this basement is killing you. This is the Hellmouth. There is something bad down here. Possibly everything bad."
>
> SPIKE: (Laughing) "Can't hear you. Can't hear you."
>
> BUFFY: "You have a soul? Fine. Show me."
>
> SPIKE: "Scream Montresor all you like, pet."
>
> BUFFY: "Get up and get out of this basement."

Spider-Man

> "This isn't springy, high-flying fun!" (Xander when he encounters the spider demon's sticky web.)

Water cooler

> "The flaying of Warren Meers. Truly inspired. That was 'water-cooler vengeance.'" (D'Hoffryn complimenting Willow's vengeance work when she summons him.)

※ *Episode Reference*

In the above quote, D'Hoffryn refers to events in episode 6-20, "Villains."

※ *Episode Reference*

Anya says, "This is getting to be a pattern with you, Buffy. Are there any friends of yours left you haven't tried to kill?" This is a reference to events in episode 6-17, "Normal Again."

Pop Culture Reference

> ANYA: "You're apologizing to me? What fight are you watching? Or is this like one of your little pop culture references I don't get because I'm a vengeance demon?"

※ *Episode Reference*

The neighbors sing, "On no! Mustard on my shirt. Mustard! We'll never get it out. My favorite red shirt. Dry clean it. How could you sir? Mustard!" This is the backstory for the Mustard Man in episode 6-7, "Once More With Feeling."

※ *Episode Reference*

In Anya's song, she sings "... Mrs. Anya Christina Emanuella lame-ass-made-up maiden-name Harris." This is a reference to episode 5-12, "Checkpoint," in which Anya makes up a last name for fear that the Watcher's Council would realize that she was an ex-demon.

※ *Episode Reference*

After pulling a sword from her chest, Anya says, "You know better than that, Buffy. It takes a lot more to kill a vengeance demon." We learned from Halfrek that a sword through the heart cannot kill a vengeance demon in episode 6-14, "Older and Far Away."

Abercrombie & Fitch

"Oh! Breathtaking. It's like somebody slaughtered an Abercrombie & Fitch catalog." (D'Hoffryn on Anya's work in the frat house.)

7-6   Him

Written by Drew Z. Greenberg, Directed by Michael Gershman

The girls in the gang compete when they fall for the school quarterback because of his magic letterman's jacket.

Music in this Episode

"Theme From A Summer Place" by Percy Faith
"Handsome Drink" by Aberdeen
"New Slang" by The Shins
"Little Fury" by The Breeders

L.A. Lakers, Laker Girls

"I could use a chair, or we all could, like the Laker Girls." (Cheerleader with a broken leg on how she can still participate with the team.)

Anna Nicole Smith

"Anna Nicole Smith thinks you look tacky." (Buffy to Dawn on how revealingly she's dressed.)

※ Episode Reference

ANYA: "They're crazy little lust puppies, aren't they."

XANDER: "Well at least the yelling went away. Starting to sound like Christmas morning with my family."

WILLOW: "Love spells. People forget how dangerous they can be."

XANDER: "Hey. Been there." (Flashback to a scene of mayhem.) "Good times."

This is a reference to episode 2-16, "Bewitched, Bothered, and Bewildered."

Model U.N.

"I gotta tell you. There was a time I was worried about R.J. He used to be all into comic books, model U.N. Geek stuff. No offense Harris." (Lance, R.J.'s brother, talking about what R.J. was like before he started wearing the family jacket.)

Box of Raisins

"Lance, do you have guests down there? There's little boxes of raisins if you want snacks." (Lance's mom calling down from upstairs, further cementing the little box of raisins as the snack of nerds.)

7-7   Conversations with Dead People
Written by Drew Goddard & Jane Espenson, Directed by Nick Marck

Buffy, Dawn, and Willow interact with dead people, or actually, The First, using its knowledge of the girls to deceive them. Meanwhile, Andrew and Jonathan return to Sunnydale from their hideout in Mexico, hoping to redeem themselves and find acceptance from Buffy. Manipulated by The First posing as Warren, Andrew kills Jonathan so his blood will activate the Seal of Danzalthar.

Music in this Episode

"Blue" by Angie Hart, Splendid, and Joss Whedon
"The Never Never" by Scout

What happened to Scott Hope?

In this episode we will learn that Scott Hope, the boy who was Buffy's interest in episode 3-3, "Faith, Hope & Trick," later came out as gay.

Klingon

JONATHAN: "We should have stayed in Mexico."

ANDREW: "I didn't like it there. Everyone spoke Mexicoan."

JONATHAN: "We could have learned it. We learned the entire Klingon dictionary in two and half weeks."

ANDREW: "That had much clearer transitive and intransitive rules, okay?"

Anchovies

DAWN: "Anchovies, anchovies! You're so delicious! I love you more than all the other fishes!

Pippen

"Junior year, spring production of *Pippen*... I did the lighting design." (Holden Webster, the vampire Buffy's fighting, when they realize they knew each other in high school.)

Back to the Future (1985 film), McFly

"Think, McFly. Why would she believe us without any proof?" (Andrew to Jonathan when he suggests going to Buffy.)

※ *Episode Reference*

The First, as Cassie, says, "Remember that time on the bridge when you sang to each other? Well, she says even though you can't hear it, she still sings to you." This is a reference to the song that Tara sang to Willow in episode 6-7, "Once More With Feeling." She also says "You're strong, like an Amazon. Remember?" This is a reference to episode 5-16, "The Body."

Indiana Jones and the Temple of Doom (1984 film), Short Round, Star Wars (1977 film)

WARREN: "Come on: If you strike me down..."

ANDREW: "'I shall become more powerful than you could possibly imagine.' Of course.... Do you think maybe Willow could kill me too?"

WARREN: "Hey, don't worry. When Short Round pulls off his end of the bargain then we become gods."

ANDREW: (looking after Jonathan) "That boy is our last hope."

WARREN: "No, there is another."

ANDREW: "Wait, really? Who's our last hope?"

WARREN: "No, I was just going with it. It was a thing. No. He's our last hope."

※ *Episode Reference*

When the vampire Holden Webster says, "Hey, wouldn't it be cool if we became nemeses?" Buffy asks, "Is that how you say that word?" This is a reference to episode 6-11, "Gone," when the trio couldn't figure out the plural of nemesis.

Hellraiser (1987 film), Pinhead

"Everything is shifting around—I feel like we're in *Hellraiser*. I hate Pinhead." (Andrew to Jonathan as they try to find their way in the high school basement.)

Indigo Girls

"I can see it now. Candlelight. The Indigo Girls playing. Picture of your dead girlfriend in your lap." (The First, as Cassie, trying to convince Willow to commit suicide.)

7-8   Sleeper

Written by David Fury & Jane Espenson, Directed by Alan J. Levi

Buffy suspects Spike may be killing again when a vampire she slays tells her Spike sired him. Spike suspects himself too, and they discover that he is a "sleeper." Knowing that he is a danger, Spike is willingly held captive at Buffy's house.

 Music in this Episode

"This Is How It Goes" and "Pavlov's Bell" by Aimee Mann

CSI (TV show)

"Okay. Let's look at this objectively. Figure it out in a cold, impersonal *CSI*-like manner. 'Cause we're a couple of carpet fibers away from a case." (Xander to Buffy on if Spike is killing again.)

Oscar, Academy Award

BUFFY: "You think it's an act?" (On Spike's claim he has no memory of killing.)

XANDER: "I don't really know. And neither do you."

BUFFY: "No. There's something. I can feel it. He's different. He's changed. And if it is an act, then the Oscar goes to—"

❋ **Episode Reference**

Xander says to Anya, "You didn't mind being alone with him before." He is talking about her tryst with Spike in episode 6-18, "Entropy." This episode is referred to again when Anya says to Spike (as an excuse for being in his room), "I can't help it. I can't stop thinking about you and us and our brief, but unforgettable time together."

Billy Idol

BOUNCER: "Billy Idol wannabe?" (When asked if he has seen Spike.)

BUFFY: "Actually, Billy Idol stole his look from him."

❧ **Musicians can act, too**

When Aimee Mann says, "Man, I hate playing vampire towns," this is the only time in the show that one of the actual musicians has a line.

Cool Whip

"Cool as Cool Whip. What's up with that?" (Xander on how Spike didn't seem to react when Buffy mentioned the name of the vamp she staked—a vamp who claimed to have been sired by Spike.)

7-9   Never Leave Me

Written by Drew Goddard, Directed by David Solomon

Willow encounters Andrew at the butcher shop where he is buying blood for the Seal. She brings him to Buffy's house where he is held captive and questioned. When Bringers attack, they kidnap Spike, and the Potentials are puzzled by Buffy's insistence that they must save him.

Star Wars (1977 film)

WARREN: "We've got work to do."

ANDREW: "Do we have to do work right now? Can't I just walk around for a while in my coat?"

WARREN: "Don't go soft on me now. We're right in the trench and the exhaust port is in sight."

Obi Wan Kenobi, Star Wars (1977 film), Patrick Swayze, Ghost (1990 film)

WARREN: "I can't take corporeal form. Feel me... I'm like Obi Wan."

ANDREW: "Or Patrick Swayze."

Babe 2 (1995 film), Conan the Destroyer (1984 film)

ANDREW: "*Babe 2: Pig in the City* was underrated."

WARREN: "Don't think about Babe."

ANDREW: "Right."

WARREN: "You're Conan. You're the destroyer. It's you against nature, You're the hunter. You're primal. You live off the land. You're Andrew. Everyone knows you. You play by your own rules. It's kill or be killed!"

ANDREW: "That'll do pig!"

The Matrix (1999 film)

"This is a butcher's shop, Neo. We don't sell toothpaste." (Butcher to Andrew who is wearing a black leather trench coat.)

※ *Episode Reference*

When Andrew says to Willow, "Hey, your hair's not even black any more," this is a reference to episode 6-21, "Two To Go."

※ *Episode Reference*

When Buffy said that Spike had been singing, Anya said, "Maybe it's another musical... a much crappier musical." This is a reference to episode 6-7, "Once More With Feeling."

Trigger, Lone Ranger ('40s TV show)

XANDER: "Trigger."

ANDREW: "The horse?"

XANDER: "No. In his head. It's a trigger. It's a brainwashing term. It's how the military makes sleeper agents. They brainwash operatives and condition them with a specific trigger, like a song that makes them drastically change at a moment's notice."

WILLOW: "Is this left over from your days in the army?"

XANDER: "No, this is left over from every army movie I've ever seen."

※ Episode Reference

When Willow mentions Xander's days in the army, this is a reference to episode 2-6, "Halloween."

7-10 Bring on the Night
Written by Douglas Petrie & Marti Noxon, Directed by David Grossman

After the Watcher's Council is destroyed, Giles arrives in Sunnydale with three potential Slayers, who are being hunted around the world. Buffy fights the Übervamp and is badly beaten.

※ Episode Reference

As he sweeps up glass from the broken windows which he had just replaced, Xander says, "It's a loop. Like the mummy hand. I'm doomed to replace these windows for all eternity." This is a reference to episode 6-5, "Life Serial."

Cliff Notes

"Nothing and nothing. *Cliff Notes* to nothing. Nothing abridged." (Anya on how her research is not turning up anything.)

※ Episode Reference

Buffy, describing the evil power they are up against, says, "When I came up against this thing, it—I felt it. It was ancient, and enormous. It nearly got Angel to kill himself." She is referring to her encounter with The First in episode 3-10, "Amends."

Sleeping Beauty

"I wish Sleeping Ugly would come to. He's been out all night." (Xander talking about Andrew, who is unconscious (unless he's faking it) and tied to a chair.)

Lex Luthor, Superman, Voldermort, Harry Potter (1997-2007 books)

ANDREW: "Not very ominous sounding."

DAWN: "It is if you understand the context."

ANDREW. "No. Evil names should be like Lex or Voldermort."

Wonder Woman (Comic)

ANDREW: "It's like Wonder Woman issue 297-299."

XANDER: "*Catacombs*. Yeah with the skeletons."

BOTH: "That was cool."

The Exorcist (1973 film), Blair Witch Project (1999 film), Rob Schneider

BUFFY: "Love those evil, evil movies... like *Exorcist, Blair Witch*...."

PRINCIPAL WOOD: "As opposed to, say, Rob Schneider's oeuvre."

Red Bull, Jackass (2002 film)

"Hello people of the future! Kids today like Red Bull and... *Jackass*!" (Dawn to Principal Wood when Buffy says they were in the school basement with a shovel because they were burying a time capsule.)

Signs (2002 film), M. Night Shymalan

XANDER: "Now all we have to do is trap the Übervamp in the pantry and it's Game Over."

WILLOW: "Xander. Newbies. Let's ease them into the whole 'jokes in the face of death' thing."

XANDER: "Who's joking? That pantry thing could work. You saying M. Night Shymalan lied to us?"

Spider-Man, Spider Sense

"I've got a bad feeling about this. My spider sense is tingling. This is gonna get hairy. I'm talkin' weird with a beard." (Still tied to a chair, Andrew is nervous as the gang prepares for an attack on Buffy's house.)

Dr. Doom, Apocalypse, Riddler, Darth Vader, Dark Side, Return of the Jedi (1983 film)

"You think I'm a supervillain like Dr. Doom, or Apocalypse, or the Riddler. I admit I went over to the dark side... but just to pick up a few things, and now I'm back. I've learned. I'm good again... I'm like Vader in the last 5 minutes of *Jedi*...." (Andrew saying that Buffy may think he's a villain, but he's not.)

7-11 Showtime

Written by David Fury, Directed by Michael Grossman

Hopelessness, fear, and low morale are becoming an issue with the Potentials. To combat this, Willow and Xander help Buffy stage a cage-fight-style battle with the Übervamp to show the Potentials that they can prevail. With the Übervamp defeated, Buffy rescues Spike from The First.

The Land Time Forgot (1975 film)

BUF: "What about the Turak-Han?"

XANDER: "The vampire time forgot?"

BUFFY: "Time might have forgotten him, but I sure as hell won't."

Botox

GILES: "There is one avenue that we haven't tried yet… Beljoxa's Eye."

BUFFY: "What is Botox's eye?"

Misery (1990 film, 1987 book), Kathy Bates

BUFFY: "Did you ever see the movie *Misery*?" (Threatening Andrew to behave when they untie him.)

ANDREW: "Six times. But the book was scarier than the movie, cause instead of crushing his foot with a sledgehammer, Kathy Bates chops it off with– I'll be good."

Albert Broccoli and Barbara Broccoli (James Bond franchise producers), James Bond, Timothy Dalton, License to Kill (1989 film)

DAWN: "Buffy said if you talked too much I'm allowed to kill you."

ANDREW: "Not even."

DAWN: "Even."

ANDREW: "License to kill, huh? Pretty cool. You know, Timothy Dalton never got his props, because he came in at the end of an old regime. But he had it going on. He went rogue. But the Broccolis were just treading water, stylistically."

Six Degrees of Kevin Bacon

"Do you wanna play Kevin Bacon?" (Andrew to Dawn, after commenting on how alone he is.)

Justice League (Comics), Imperium

BUFFY: "We need to stick together. We're stronger that way. We cannot afford to fall apart now."

ANDREW: "She's right. Where would the Justice League have been if they hadn't put their differences aside to stop the Imperium and his shape-shifting alien horde?"

Star Trek, Deflector Shield

"Deflector shields up!" (Andrew as Willow attempts to do a shielding spell to stop the Übervamp.)

Mad Max Beyond Thunderdome (1985 film)

BUFFY: "Welcome to Thunderdome."

ANDREW: "Two men enter, one man leaves."

7-12 Potential

Written by Rebecca Rand Kirshner, Directed by James A. Contner

The coven in England calls Willow, saying they have discovered that another Potential is living in Sunnydale. Buffy and Spike take the Potentials out for training as Xander, Willow, and Dawn stay home to cast a spell to try to locate the new Potential—who they learn might be Dawn.

Chaka Khan

"It was putting a lot of stock in that Übervamp... the... chaka kahn." (Buffy, mispronouncing Turak-Han, saying that The First was going to be scarce for a while now that the Übervamp is dead.)

Snausages

"You're like a small dog dancing for Snausages." (Buffy to Andrew as he begs to go on a training mission with the Potentials.)

Dragonball Z (Anime), Vegeta, Goku

"But I'm reformed. I'm like Vegeta on *Dragonball Z*. I used to be a pure saiyon, and now I fight on the side of Goku." (Andrew to Buffy that he's not evil.)

Chrysalis

"Okay, I got my tumbleweed, my eggs. I got my chrysalises... chrysali? My butterfly tranformer pods." (Willow, smoothly recovering from not quite knowing the right word.)

The Pope, Catholic

"It's a lot like being the Pope in that way—except you don't have to be some old Catholic." (Anya on how a Potential only becomes a Slayer when the current Slayer dies.)

Microwave Popcorn, Orville Redenbacher

"Are we going to replace the microwave? Because I was thinking some Orville Redenbacher with fresh butter flavor...." (Andrew.)

History Channel, Tivo

"I saw this great show on the History Channel the other night that I knew you would love—then something went all flooie with my Tivo." (Clem when he sees Buffy and the Potentials in Willy's bar.)

 An homage to "Beetleguise"

When Clem startles the girls in the demon bar, this uses the same set-up and sound effects that were used in a similar scenario in the 1988 film "Beetleguise."

Star Wars (1977 film), Luke Skywalker

ANDREW: "Plucked from an ordinary life, handed a destiny?" (When they learn that Dawn may be a Potential.)

XANDER: "Say 'Skywalker' and I smack you."

7-13 The Killer in Me

Written by Drew Z. Greenberg, Directed by David Solomon

Willow and Kennedy are getting closer when Willow turns into Warren, due to a curse cast by a bitter Amy. Meanwhile, Spike's malfunctioning chip is threatening his life—or rather, his existence—so Buffy contacts the government to request help.

 Music in this Episode

"Sink or Float" and "Cities and Buses" by Aberdeen

Hokey Pokey

"Apparently someone told them that the vision quest consists of me driving them to the desert, doing the hokey pokey, until a spooky Rasta-mama-Slayer arrives and speaks to them in riddles." (Giles on what Buffy told the Potentials about what's in store for them.)

S'mores

"She says she wants you to meditate extra hard for her and bring her back some s'mores!" (Willow to Giles about Kennedy, who is staying back while Giles and the Potentials go to the desert.)

Gaydar

WILLOW: "What, you think you have some sort of 'lesbidar' or something?"

KENNEDY: "Okay, you know there's a better word for that, right?"

Robert Parker, Skate punk

"And we like the same things: Italian, skate punk, Robert Parker mysteries...." (Kennedy telling Willow why she likes her.)

Ghostbusters (1984 film)

"Who're you gonna' call? God, that phrase is never gonna be usable again, is it?" (Spike when Buffy says she will call someone.)

Scarlett O'Hara, Gone With the Wind (1939 film)

"It was *Gone With the Wind*. I saw that and I knew I wanted to sweep Scarlet off her feet." (Kennedy telling Willow how she realized she was gay.)

Moulan Rouge (2001 film)

"I love the way you always turn off the *Moulan Rouge* DVD at chapter 32 so it has a happy ending." (Kennedy to Willow.)

Underoos, Aquaman, Yellow crayon

"There are other stories from Kindergarten. Non-yellow crayon stories in which you don't come out in such a good light. An incident involving Aquaman Underoos, for example." (Willow, looking like Warren, proving to Xander that she is who she says she is.)

❋ *Episode Reference*

The comment about "yellow crayon stories" in the above quote is a reference to the events at the end of episode 6-22, "Grave."

League of Extraordinary Gentlemen (2003 film)

"I'm supposed to get a call when the new *League of Extraordinary Gentlemen* comes in." (Andrew on why he is taking calls at Buffy's house.)

7-14 First Date

Written by Jane Espenson, Directed by David Grossman

Much to Giles' chagrin, Buffy goes on a dinner date with Principal Robin Wood. When Buffy and Robin encounter vampires on the way to dinner, Buffy learns that he is the son of a former Slayer. Meanwhile Xander meets a woman whom he asks on a date, but naturally she turns out to be a demon, and she uses his blood to re-open the Seal.

Google

"I've googled till I just can't google no more. He's not in there." (Willow about not finding anything online about Principal Wood.)

❋ *Episode Reference*

The First, as Jonathan, says, "You don't need a manual, it's intuitive. There's a button marked 'clock-set' for pity's sake. What kind of nerd are you? No wonder you crashed your jet pack." The mention of a jet pack is a reference to episode 6-19, "Seeing Red."

Pizza

BUFFY: "I chose a top that says, you know, I'm comfortable in a stodgy office or a swinging casual setting, or killing, you know, if you're a demon."

ANYA: "It also says 'I sometimes get blood on my shoulder.' Or it might be pizza. I don't think I can fix it."

※ *Episode Reference*

The shirt discussed in the above quote is the one which Dawn got pizza on in episode 7-7, "Conversations With Dead People."

Superman, Kryptonite

"Do you have any weaknesses I should know about—like kryptonite, or allergies?" (Andrew to The First—who looks like Jonathan.)

Star Trek: Enterprise (2001 TV show), Scott Bakula, Captain Archer

XANDER: "I'm mentally undressing Scott Bakula."

ANDREW: "Captain Archer."

(Xander has said he's going to "go gay" because he's fed up that all the women he's attracted to turn out to be demons.)

7-15 Get It Done

Written by Douglas Petrie, Directed by Douglas Petrie

Buffy takes a hard stance with the Potentials, saying it's time for them to stop waiting for the battle to come to them. Using the materials Robin gives her from his mother's bag, Buffy visits another dimension where she confronts the men who created the First Slayer. She is given a vision of what is to come, and is horrified to learn of the multitude of Übervamps awaiting them in the Hellmouth.

Bring It On (2001 film)

WILLOW: "Well Buffy, I see that our preparations for the school pep-dance-cheer-drill contest are coming along. Bring it on!"

BUFFY: "It's okay. I filled him in on everything."

WILLOW: "Oh, thank god. If I had to explain all these weapons... I had nothing."

Winnie the Pooh, TTFN, Tigger

"Ta-ta for now. It's what Tigger says when he leaves. Chloe loved Winnie the Pooh." (Rona explaining TTFN.)

Muppets, Kermit, Fozzie Bear, Miss Piggy

"Now if we could just airlift Kermit, Fozzie Bear, and Miss Piggy into town, The First would be a-runnin'." (Xander saying maybe The First is afraid of puppets when he sees the shadow casters.)

Twinkies

"... Although, Twinkies and kisses—also peachy motivational tools." (Willow when Buffy apologizes for coming down so hard on everyone.)

7-16 Storyteller

Written by Jane Espenson, Directed by Marita Grabiak

Andrew turns his camera on Buffy and the gang to document the coming battle. As he shows his gentleviewers his somewhat skewed view of the world around him, Buffy takes the chance that he may be the key to closing the Seal.

Mutant Enemy Monster changes his line

Instead of hearing the Mutant Enemy monster say "Grr, Argh" after the credits at the end of the episode, we hear Jonathan sing "We are as gods!"

Masterpiece Theater (TV show)

The opening of this episode is a take-off on *Masterpiece Theater*.

Zima

"But it tickles and I'm all tense. Can't I have a cool, refreshing Zima?" (Andrew wanting a break from the hypnosis-aided interrogation.)

Episode Reference

When Principal *Wood asks Buffy if she has seen strange things at the high school before, she answers: "Sure. You know, swim-team monsters, or killer prom-dogs." Swim-team monsters is a reference to episode 2-20, "Go Fish," and killer prom-dogs is a reference to episode 3-20, "The Prom."*

7-17 Lies My Parents Told Me
Written by David Fury & Drew Goddard, Directed by David Fury

In an attempt to diffuse The First's control over Spike, Giles helps him relive his earliest days as a vampire, revealing more of the tragedy in Spike's backstory. The gang discovers that the trigger that forces Spike to turn is a specific song from his past. Meanwhile, Giles and Robin conspire to deal with Spike permanently.

 Music in this Episode

"Early One Morning" performed by Nana Mouskouri

Episode Reference / William's love poem

When Spike sees visions of his past, we hear him reading this poem to his mother, which he wrote to proclaim his love for Cecily:

> *"Yet the smell, it doth linger, painting pictures in my mind / Her eyes, bowls of honey, Angel's harps her laugh / Oh lark, grant a sign / If crooked be Cupid's shaft. / Hark! The lark, her name it hath spake. / Cecily, it discharges, from 'twixt its wee beak."*

This may be the continuance of his poem of which we heard the beginning in Episode 5-7, "Fool for Love:"

> *"My heart expands. 'Tas grown ebulgent. / Inspired by your beauty effulgent."*

"Angel" Episode Cross Reference

When Willow gets a call from Fred, this correlates to episode 4-15 of "Angel," "Orpheus," in which Willow goes to Los Angeles to help return Angel's soul.

Pink, Get the Party Started (2001 song), Yul Brynner

"It's not like it had a catchy hook or anything. You know, like 'I'm coming up so you'd better get this party started.'... It was boring, old, and English. Just like you—ul. Brynner. Yul Brynner." (Buffy telling Giles about the song Spike hummed before he turned.)

Get out of Jail Free, Monopoly

KENNEDY: "So Spike's trigger's been active all this time."

RONA: "How could Buffy take this for granted? I mean, he lives in our house. We train with him."

ANYA: "Don't waste your time down that road. Spike's got some sort of Get out of Jail Free card that doesn't apply to the rest of us. I mean, he could slaughter a hundred frat boys, and.... Forgiveness makes us human. Blahdy blah blah blah."

Episode Reference

In the above quote, Anya is referring to her slaughter in episode 7-5, "Selfless."

7-18 Dirty Girls

Written by Drew Goddard, Directed by Michael Gershman

A lone Potential making her way to Sunnydale is picked up by Caleb, who tells her to let the Slayer know that he has something of hers. We learn Caleb is not only an agent of The First, but is the organizer behind the army of Bringers. Faith returns to Sunnydale to join in the fight. Buffy, Faith, Xander, and the Potentials go to meet Caleb in battle, only to be badly beaten. Several Potentials are killed, and Xander loses an eye.

※ *"Angel" Episode Cross Reference*

Faith is with Willow because they were working together in Los Angeles to help Wesley with Angel. This is shown in "Angel" episode 4-15, "Orpheus."

※ *Episode Reference*

SPIKE: "Let me guess: Leather pants, nice right cross, doe-eyes, holier-than-thou glower. You must be Faith."

FAITH: "Oh goody. I'm famous."

SPIKE: "Told you were coming. Bit of a misunderstanding here. I'm—"

FAITH: "Spike. We've met before."

Faith met Spike when she swapped bodies with Buffy in episode 4-16, "Who Are You?" This episode is referred to again when Faith and Spike talk on the front porch and Faith says, "I was kind of wearing a different body."

Ray Charles

"All the work I've done for you... organizing the Ray Charles brigade...." (Caleb on organizing the Bringers.)

Star Trek ('60s TV show), Vulcan

AMANDA: "What the hell are you talking about. I thought Faith killed a 'vulcanologist.'"

ANDREW: "Silly, silly Amanda. Why would Faith kill someone who studied Vulcans?"

※ *Episode Reference*

Andrew is telling the girls about Faith's background, including when she killed a vulcanologist who may have had information about the type of demon the Mayor was going to become after his ascension. This happened in episode 3-21, "Graduation Day, Part 1."

Starbucks

"No more Starbucks for the wannabees, man. They've been spazzin' for, like, hours." (Faith to Spike in the basement when they hear a crashing sound from upstairs.)

Glitter (2001 film)

FAITH: (Describing jail.) "… movie every third Sunday, it could have been worse."

SPIKE: "What movie?"

FAITH: "*Glitter*. I guess it couldn't get worse."

Godzilla (1998 film), Matthew Broderick

KENNEDY: "I don't care if it's Godzilla. I want to get in this thing." (Speculating about what The First has sent to guard the vineyard.)

ANDREW: "Godzilla's Tokyo-based so he's probably gonna be a no-show."

AMANDA: "Besides, if Matthew Broderick can kill Godzilla, how tough is he?"

ANDREW: "Xander?!"

XANDER: "Matthew Broderick did not kill Godzilla. He killed a big, dumb lizard. That was *not* the real Godzilla."

Little Bus

"You're scared: that's smart. You've got questions: you should. But you doubt her motives, you think Buffy is all about the kill, then you take the little bus to battle. I've seen her heart, and this time, not literally. And I'm telling you right now, she cares more about your lives than you will ever know. You gotta trust her. She's earned it." (Xander telling the Potentials to trust Buffy.)

Falconcrest (1981 TV show)

KENNEDY: "Evil vineyard, huh?" (Entering Caleb's vineyard to do battle.)

SPIKE: "Like *Falconcrest*."

※ *"Angel" Episode Cross Reference*

Willow told Buffy that Faith had been in Los Angeles helping Angel. When Buffy asks how Angel is doing, Faith says, "Better. Had to do this whole magical mind-walk with him." This is a reference to events in "Angel" episode 4-15, "Orpheus."

7-19 Empty Places

Written by Drew Z. Greenberg, Directed by James A. Contner

Sunnydale empties of its residents—human and demon. Buffy is sure that their next step is another offense against Caleb, but the rest of the gang won't hear of it. While Spike and Andrew are off researching information about Caleb, there is a standoff and confrontation and Buffy is rejected as the leader. She leaves the house, and Faith is put in charge.

 Music in this Episode

"Rock City News" by Nerf Herder

7-Eleven

"What about you? You just going for a quick spin to 7-Eleven… in Nebraska?" (Buffy to Clem when she sees him among the people evacuating Sunnydale.)

Interpol

"Thank you, Inspector. We don't get a lot of contact with Interpol, so we're happy to help with anything you need." (Police officer to Giles and Willow, who have glamored him into believing that they are from Interpol so he will give them police files about Caleb.)

Jaws 3D (1983 film)

"You know what the best is? Nobody will ever make me watch *Jaws 3D* again." (Xander to Willow about his losing an eye.)

Scotch Guard

"Holy Water runs off these guys like they've been Scotch Guarded." (Anya instructing the Potentials about the Übervamps.)

Harry Potter (1997-2007 books), Hogwarts

"Shouldn't you be down at Hogwarts?" (Faith to Kennedy, referring to Anya's lessons to the Potentials in the basement.)

※ *Episode Reference*

AMANDA: "Do you think there are gonna be questions about her sex life on the test? 'Cause I really hope I don't have to study all that."

FAITH. "Yeah, whenever she starts talking about getting all sweaty with Xander like that, I just remind her I had him first. Shuts her right the hell up."

Faith is referring to her encounter with Xander in episode 3-13, "The Zeppo."

Hot Pocket, Post-It

ANDREW: "Mr. Giles! Faith stole the last meatball mozzarella-flavored Hot Pocket out of the freezer even though I called dibs on it…. Yup, see. The Post-It's still here: *Andrew's–Please do not eat*. But the box is empty."

Cartoon Birdies

"Still able to make me see cartoon birdies all around my head? You betcha." (Buffy to Giles on what Caleb can do.)

7-Up (Soft drink)

FAITH: "Hey, how old are you?"

AMANDA: "17."

FAITH: "Yeah, we're gonna get you a real nice 7-Up, okay?"

Flowering Onion

ANDREW: (On the back of Spike's motorcycle.) "You sure you don't want to stop and pick up some burgers or something, you know, road trip food?"

SPIKE: "It's not a road trip. It's a covert operation."

ANDREW: "I bet even covert operatives eat curly fries. They're really good."

SPIKE: "Not as good as those onion blossom things."

ANDREW: "Ooh, I love those…. It's an onion and it's a flower. I-I don't understand how such a thing is possible."

SPIKE: "Well, you see, the genius of it is, you soak it in ice water for an hour so it holds its shape. Then you deep-fry it root-side up for about five minutes…. Tell anyone we had this conversation, and I'll bite you."

Wizard of Oz (1939 film), Ding Dong the Witch is Dead (Song)

"Ding dong the witch is dead." (Rona when Buffy leaves.)

7-20 Touched

Written by Rebecca Rand Kirshner, Directed by David Solomon

Everyone is nervous as they prepare to follow Faith in battle to capture the Bringers' weapons cache. Meanwhile Spike has found Buffy and goes with her to the vineyard to confront Caleb and take what belongs to Buffy.

 Music in this Episode

"It's Only Love" by Heather Nova

Girl Scouts

"We're all at death's door repeatedly ringing the doorbell like maniacal Girl Scouts trying to make quota." (Anya about the danger they are all in.)

Model U.N., Parliamentary Procedure

"When I was involved with the Model U.N. we found the parliamentary procedure to be a total lifesaver." (Amanda on how they should organize their discussion.)

Tab (Soft drink)

"Got any Tab?" (Buffy to the departing homeowner as she looks in his refrigerator.)

I Spy (Game)

"I Spy with my little eye something that begins with a 'T'." (Andrew fighting boredom as he and Spike await sundown so they can leave the mission.)

Steroids

"There's the 'roid-rage vamps…." (Dawn contributing to their list of bad guys.)

Rhodes Scholar

"You were expecting what, a Rhodes Scholar?" (Anya to Giles when he said the Bringers were dumb, not understanding that he meant they were mute.)

Moon Pie, Little Women (1880 book)

"Ask me a question only I would know the answer to. Something like, where did I hide the moon pies in my office? Or, who was my favorite character in *Little Women*? Meg. I know. I know, most people guess Beth. But Meg, she's such a proper young lady. Remember when Jo burned her hair—" (The First, as the Mayor, convincing Faith that he really is the Mayor.)

Monty Python: Comfy Chair

"That diabolical old torture device, the comfy chair." (Spike readying to stay the night in a chair by Buffy's bed.)

Achilles' Heel

ROBIN: "That's exactly what The First does. Find your Achilles' heel."

FAITH: "No, it just talked to me. It does a heel thing too?"

Jack Daniel's (Whiskey)

"Hittin' things and a whole lot of Jack D dulls it some." (Faith to Principal Wood about dealing with loneliness.)

7-21 End of Days
Written by Douglas Petrie & Jane Espenson, Directed by Marita Grabiak

The tide is turned when Buffy outwits Caleb and takes an ancient weapon from him which is mystically intended only for the Slayer.

❧ *What happened to Miss Kitty Fantastico?*

> *In this episode we get a hint at what happened to Tara and Willow's kitten when Dawn says she doesn't leave crossbows laying around, "Not since that time with Miss Kitty Fantastico."*

Funkytown (1980 song), Jaffa Cakes

ANDREW: "The produce was on its way to Funky Town."

GILES: "Jaffa Cakes!"

(Andrew brings supplies to the house after looting the grocery store.)

King Arthur, Sword in the Stone

GILES: "In addition to being ancient, it's clearly mystical."

BUFFY: "I figured that one out when I King-Arthured it out of the stone."

Monty Python and the Holy Grail (1975 film), Holy Hand Grenade

"You did it. Fulfilled your mission. Found the Holy Grail, or the Holy Hand Grenade, or whatever the hell that is." (Spike about Buffy's new scythe.)

Carrot Top

"Have you gone completely Carrot Top?" (Spike after Buffy calls him a dope.)

Jaws (1975 film), Roy Scheider

"They would only be useful if something big was attacking. Then we could shove one down their throat and blow 'em up like Roy Scheider did with that shark in *Jaws*." (Anya to Andrew when they see oxygen tanks while they are robbing the hospital.)

※ *Episode Reference*

> *When Andrew asks why she is staying with the gang despite the danger, Anya says, "Well, there was this other apocalypse this one time, and well, I took off. But this time, I don't know." She is referring to the apocalypse that the Mayor attempted to cause in episode 3-22, "Graduation Day."*

Luxor Casino

"Hence the Luxor Casino theme." (Buffy commenting on the ancient look of the temple.)

I, Claudius (1976 TV miniseries)

"I mean, give me some 'eye of the beholder' jokes, you know? Or some 'eye for eye' jokes. Or maybe even a post-modern '*I, Claudius*' joke, you know?" (Xander to Dawn, riffing on the better-quality jokes he expects to hear now that he has only one eye.)

Colorforms

XANDER: "It was chloroform." (Explaining what happened and why they were driving away from Sunnydale.)

DAWN: "Colorforms—what?"

7-22 Chosen

Written and Directed by Joss Whedon

Buffy decides the time for waiting is over, and plans an ingenious attack that not only defeats The First's army of Übervamps, but wipes Sunnydale off the map, and changes the world.

❧ *Mutant Enemy Monster turns his head*

In addition to his usual shuffle across the screen after the credits, the Mutant Enemy monster turns his head when he delivers his "Grr, Argh" line.

Scrubbing Bubbles (advertising slogan)

"Is it a purifying power or cleansing power—possibly scrubbing bubbles. The translation is… eugh. Anyway, it bestows strength to the right person who wears it." (Angel on the power of the champion's amulet.)

✳ *"Angel" Episode Cross Reference*

Angel was given the amulet by Lila of Wolfram and Hart in "Angel" episode 4-22, "Home."

Peroxide, Dawson's Creek ('90s TV show)

ANGEL: "I'm getting the brush-off for Captain Peroxide. That doesn't necessarily bring out the champion in me."

BUFFY: "You're not getting the brush-off. Are you just gonna come here and go all *Dawson* on me every time I have a boyfriend?"

✳ *Episode Reference*

When Buffy says "What was the highlight of our relationship? When you broke up with me, or when I killed you?" Angel broke up with Buffy in episode 3-20, "The Prom," and she killed him in episode 2-22, "Becoming."

Cookie Dough

BUFFY: "I'm cookie dough. I'm not done baking. I'm not finished becoming whoever the hell it is I'm gonna turn out to be. I make it through this and the next thing and the next thing, and maybe one day I turn around and realize, I'm ready. I'm cookies. And then, you know, if I want someone to eat me– or enjoy warm, delicious, cookie me, then that's fine. That'll be then. When I'm done."

Pierced Tongue

"It's a total loss of control, and not in a nice, wholesome, 'my-girlfriend-has-a-pierced-tongue' kind of way." (Willow on how she is unsure if she can cast the spell that Buffy needs.)

Rock 'em Sock 'em Robots

"You're trippin'. That was rock 'em sock 'em!" (Faith when Principal Wood gives a not-so-glowing appraisal of their sexual encounter.)

Trogdor the Burninator, Homestar Runner, Dungeons & Dragons

"You go through the door and are confronted by Trogdor the Burninator." (Andrew as a Dungeons and Dragons dungeon master playing with Giles, Xander, and Amanda the Potential.)

Dungeon Master

"So that leaves me and the Dungeon Master in the north hall?" (Anya about Andrew.)

Miniature Golf, Nicotine Patch

BUFFY: "So what do you guys want to do tomorrow?" (Easing the tension before the battle.)

WILLOW: "Nothing strenuous."

XANDER: "Well, mini-golf is always the first thing that comes to mind."

...

BUFFY: "I want to go shopping.... I'm having a wicked shoe craving."

XANDER: "Aren't you on the patch?"

Elizabeth Taylor

"Not to be a buzz-kill, luv. But my fabulous accessory isn't exactly tingling with power. I'm getting zero juice here, and I look like Elizabeth Taylor." (Spike about his champion's amulet.)

Greenhouse Effect

"We call it the greenhouse effect. Very dangerous." (Xander after killing a group of vampires by exposing them to sunlight.)

✳ *Episode Reference*

Anya's death was foreshadowed in episode 7-5, "Selfless," in which Anya said to D'Hoffryn, "You should have killed me." He replied, "Oh I wouldn't worry about that. From beneath you it devours. Be patient. All good things in time."

School's Out For the Summer (1972 song), Alice Cooper

"Gotta move, lamb. I think it's fair to say, school's out for bloody summer." (Spike telling Buffy that her battle is won and she must leave so he can finish the job.)

The Gap, Starbucks, Toys R Us

DAWN: "We destroyed the mall? I fought on the wrong side."

XANDER: "All those shops gone—the Gap, Starbucks, Toys R Us. Who will remember all those landmarks unless we tell the world about them."

✳ *Episode Reference*

Cleveland as a location of another Hellmouth was first mentioned in the alternate reality episode 3-9, "The Wish."

Episode Tables

Reading the Tables

The tables in this guide show the character participation in each episode as well as other details.

Character Categories: Along the left

The tables place the characters into two categories:

- **Scoobies**: Our core characters.
- **Friends, Enemies, & Others**: Family, friends, enemies, and other characters.

Episode Watchability Key: Along the top

If I learned anything from the reaction to the Episode Watchability Key in the first edition of this book, it's that opinions differ. Those episodes that I may think are so-so and eminently skippable may be the very episodes that you love and have near the top of your list of favorites.

The tables in this edition still include a two-part Watchability row. The top part of the row has blank spaces for you to mark your own rating of the episodes. Use a numeric scale or Tolkien-esque runes, or get out your crayons and devise your own color coding to indicate which episodes are your favorites, which can be missed, or which feature your favorite quotes involving puppies. Or leave the spaces blank. Whatever you want.

In the second part of the row, I use this mark (♀) to indicate which episodes I think are important to the overall story arc, a circled star (⊛) to indicate what I think are the very greatest episodes, and a star (★) to indicate the episodes which I think are very good, as shown in the example below.

Why don't more episodes show a ★ or ⊛? Honestly, there are so many excellent episodes that it would be easy to nearly fill the row with stars. But that wouldn't be very helpful, so I judged as critically as possible and used this row to call your attention to the very best. Of course, our opinions may differ.

Character Participation Key: In the tables

The character's row is shown as white (or lightly shaded) when the character exists in the season, even if the character is not present in many episodes.

The row is gray before a character's beginning and after the character's final appearance in the show.

X — Character is present in this episode.

O — Character is in this episode only in a dream or hallucination, or as a spirit or a visage borrowed by another entity.

B — Character begins or is introduced in this episode.

E — Character ends—dies or is otherwise terminated.

BE — Character begins and ends in this one episode.

M — Character otherwise absent from the season is mentioned.

I admit there is some amount of the ridiculous to have an X in every column in the rows for the Scoobies. However the alternative, to leave Buffy, Giles, Willow, and Xander out of the tables, just didn't seem right. Our four heroes are in every episode through Season Five, after which Giles returns to England a few times. The remaining three Scoobies are in every episode, except Willow and Xander miss one episode each in Season Seven.

Credits: Writers and Directors: The final rows

The last two rows list the initials of the writers and directors of the episodes. Refer to the Writers and Directors tables at the end of this guide for their names, starting on page 257.

Bands in the Bronze: Left of the episode names

To the left of the episode names I list the bands that perform in Sunnydale's only live music venue: the Bronze. The numbers before the band names are the episodes in which they appear.

Season One Table (Episodes 1-12)

Bronze Bands
1-1: Spring Monkey
1-4: Superfine
1-5: Velvet Chain

		Welcome to the Hellmouth	The Harvest	Witch	Teacher's Pet	Never Kill a Boy on the First Date	The Pack	Angel	I, Robot... You, Jane	The Puppet Show	Nightmares	Out of Mind, Out of Sight	Prophecy Girl
	Page:	33	35	36	37	39	41	42	44	44	45	47	48
	Watchability:	♟	♟	♟		★		♟					♟
	Episode :	1-1	1-2	1-3	1-4	1-5	1-6	1-7	1-8	1-9	1-10	1-11	1-12
SCOOBIES	Buffy Summers	B	x	x	x	x	x	x	x	x	x	x	x
	Rupert Giles	B	x	x	x	x	x	x	x	x	x	x	x
	Willow Rosenberg	B	x	x	x	x	x	x	x	x	x	x	x
	Xander Harris	B	x	x	x	x	x	x	x	x	x	x	x
FRIENDS, ENEMIES, & OTHERS	Cordelia Chase	B	x	x	x	x		x		x	x	x	x
	Joyce Summers (Mom)	B	x	x				x		x	x		x
	Angel (Angelus)	B	x		x	x		x				x	x
	Jenny Calendar								B				x
	Hank Summers (Dad)										x		
	Amy			B									
	Harmony Kendall		B									x	
	Master	B	x		x			x		x			E
	Anointed One (Colin)					B		x			x		x
	Principal Flutie	B			x	x	x	E					
	Principal Snyder										B	x	
	Darla	B	x					E					
	Jesse	B	E										
	Luke	B	E										
	Episode :	1-1	1-2	1-3	1-4	1-5	1-6	1-7	1-8	1-9	1-10	1-11	1-12
CREDITS	Writers	JW	JW	DR	DG	RDH, DB	MK, JR	DG	AG, TAS	RDH, DB	JW	JW	JW
	Director(s)	CMS	JTK	SC	BSG	DSe	BSG	SB	SP	ESP	BSG	RB	JW

KEY: **Watchability**: ♟: *Key episode.* ★: *Great episode.* ⊛: *One of the best episodes.*
Characters: **X**: *Present.* **M**: *Mentioned.* **O**: *Visage or dream only.* **B**: *Begins.* **E**: *Ends.* **BE**: *Begins and ends.*
Credits: *See key for Writer initials starting on page 257, and Director initials starting on page 263.*

Season Two Table (Episodes 1-11)

Bronze Bands
2-1: Cibo Matto
2-3: Nickel
2-4: Dingoes Ate My Baby
2-19: Splendid

	When She Was Bad	Some Assembly Required	School Hard	Inca Mummy Girl	Reptile Boy	Halloween	Lie to Me	The Dark Age	What's My Line (Part 1)	What's My Line (Part 2)	Ted
Page:	53	55	56	57	59	59	60	62	63	65	67
Watchability:	🕴★		🕴⊗			🕴★			🕴	🕴	
Episode:	2-1	2-2	2-3	2-4	2-5	2-6	2-7	2-8	2-9	2-10	2-11
SCOOBIES Buffy Summers	x	x	x	x	x	x	x	x	x	x	x
Rupert Giles	x	x	x	x	x	x	x	x	x	x	x
Willow Rosenberg	x	x	x	x	x	x	x	x	x	x	x
Xander Harris	x	x	x	x	x	x	x	x	x	x	x
FRIENDS, ENEMIES, & OTHERS Cordelia Chase	x	x		x	x	x		x	x	x	x
Joyce Summers (Mom)	x		x	x							x
Angel (Angelus)	x	x	x		x	x	x	x	x	x	x
Jenny Calendar	x		x				x	x			x
Hank Summers (Dad)	x										
Oz (Daniel Osborne)				B		x			x	x	
Kendra									B	x	
Larry						B					
Chanterelle/Lily							B				
Willy the Snitch									B	x	
Spike (William the Bloody)			B			x	x		x	x	
Drusilla			B			x	x		x	x	
Amy											
Harmony Kendall											
Master	x										
Anointed One (Colin)	x		E								
Darla											
Principal Snyder	x		x			x			x		
Ethan Rayne						B		x			
Mayor Richard Wilkins III											
Ted											BE
Jonathan Levinson				B	x					x	
The Judge											
Episode:	2-1	2-2	2-3	2-4	2-5	2-6	2-7	2-8	2-9	2-10	2-11
CREDITS Writers	JW	TK	JW, DG	MK, JR	DG	CE	JW	RDH, DB	HG, MN	MN	JW, DG
Directors	JW	BSG	JTK	ESP	DG	BSG	JW	BSG	DSO	DSe	BSG

KEY: **Watchability:** 🕴: *Key episode.* ★: *Great episode.* ⊗: *One of the best episodes.*
Characters: X: *Present.* M: *Mentioned.* O: *Visage or dream only.* B: *Begins.* E: *Ends.* BE: *Begins and ends.*
Credits: *See key for Writer initials starting on page 257, and Director initials starting on page 263.*

Season Two Table (Episodes 12-22)

	Bad Eggs	Surprise (Part 1)	Innocence (Part 2)	Phases	Bewitched, Bothered, and Bewildered	Passion	Killed by Death	I Only Have Eyes for You	Go Fish	Becoming (Part 1)	Becoming (Part 2)
Page:	68	69	70	71	72	73	74	75	77	79	80
Watchability:		♟	♟★	♟★		♟⊛				♟⊛	♟★
Episode :	2-12	2-13	2-14	2-15	2-16	2-17	2-18	2-19	2-20	2-21	2-22

SCOOBIES

	Bad Eggs	Surprise (Part 1)	Innocence (Part 2)	Phases	Bewitched, Bothered, and Bewildered	Passion	Killed by Death	I Only Have Eyes for You	Go Fish	Becoming (Part 1)	Becoming (Part 2)
Buffy Summers	x	x	x	x	x	x	x	x	x	x	x
Rupert Giles	x	x	x	x	x	x	x	x	x	x	x
Willow Rosenberg	x	x	x	x	x	x	x	x	x	x	x
Xander Harris	x	x	x	x	x	x	x	x	x	x	x

FRIENDS, ENEMIES, & OTHERS

	Bad Eggs	Surprise (Part 1)	Innocence (Part 2)	Phases	Bewitched, Bothered, and Bewildered	Passion	Killed by Death	I Only Have Eyes for You	Go Fish	Becoming (Part 1)	Becoming (Part 2)
Cordelia Chase	x	x	x	x	x	x	x	x	x	x	x
Joyce Summers (Mom)	x	x			x	x	x			x	x
Angel (Angelus)	x	x	x	x	x	x	x	x		x	x
Jenny Calendar		x	x		x	E					O
Hank Summers (Dad)											
Oz (Daniel Osborne)		x	x	x	x					x	x
Kendra			x							E	
Larry				x							
Chanterelle/Lily											
Willy the Snitch											
Spike (William the Bloody)		x	x		x	x		x		x	
Drusilla		x	x		x	x		x		x	
Amy						x					
Harmony Kendall						x					
Master											
Anointed One (Colin)											
Darla										x	
Principal Snyder								x			
Ethan Rayne											
Mayor Richard Wilkins III								M			M
Ted											
Jonathan Levinson	x					x			x		
The Judge		B	E								

CREDITS

	Episode :	2-12	2-13	2-14	2-15	2-16	2-17	2-18	2-19	2-20	2-21	2-22
	Writers	MN	MN	JW	RDH, DB	MN	TK	RDH, DB	MN	DF, EH	JW	JW
	Directors	DG	ML	JW	BSG	JAC	MGe	DSa	JWJ	DSe	JW	JW

KEY: **Watchability**: ♟: *Key episode.* ★: *Great episode.* ⊛: *One of the best episodes.*
Characters: X: *Present.* M: *Mentioned.* O: *Visage or dream only.* B: *Begins.* E: *Ends.* BE: *Begins and ends.*
Credits: *See key for Writer initials starting on page 257, and Director initials starting on page 263.*

Season Three Table (Episodes 1-11)

Bronze Bands
3-1: Belly Love
3-16: k's Choice

	Anne	Dead Man's Party	Faith, Hope & Trick	Beauty & the Beasts	Homecoming	Band Candy	Revelations	Lovers Walk	The Wish	Amends	Gingerbread
Page:	83	84	85	88	89	90	92	93	94	95	96
Watchability:	🯄		🯄★			⊛		🯄	🯄⊛		
Episode :	3-1	3-2	3-3	3-4	3-5	3-6	3-7	3-8	3-9	3-10	3-11
SCOOBIES											
Buffy Summers	x	x	x	x	x	x	x	x	x	x	x
Rupert Giles	x	x	x	x	x	x	x	x	x	x	x
Willow Rosenberg	x	x	x	x	x	x	x	x	x	x	x
Xander Harris	x	x	x	x	x	x	x	x	x	x	x
FRIENDS, ENEMIES, & OTHERS											
Cordelia Chase	x	x	x	x	x	x	x	x	x	x	x
Joyce Summers (Mom)	x	x	x			x		x		x	x
Angel (Angelus)	x	x	x	x			x	x	x	x	x
Jenny Calendar										O	
Oz (Daniel Osborne)	x	x	x	x	x		x	x	x	x	x
Anya									B		
Wesley Wyndam-Pryce											
Faith			B		x		x			x	
Larry	x								x		
Chanterelle/Lily	E										
Willy the Snitch										B	
Spike (William the Bloody)								x			
Drusilla								x			
Amy											x
Harmony Kendall									x		
Master									x		
Principal Snyder		x	x								
Mr. Trick					B	x		x			
Watchers' Council			M								
Mayor Richard Wilkins III					B	x					
Allan (Mayor's Assistant)					B			x			
Jonathan Levinson		x			x			x			
The Bringers										x	
Evil Willow									B		
D'Hoffryn											
Ethan Rayne						x					
The 1st Evil										x	
Episode :	3-1	3-2	3-3	3-4	3-5	3-6	3-7	3-8	3-9	3-10	3-11
CREDITS											
Writers	JW	MN	DG	MN	DG	JE	DP	DV	MN	JW	TSJ, JE
Directors	JW	JWJ	JAC	JWJ	DG	ML	JAC	DSe	DG	JW	JWJ

KEY: **Watchability:** 🯄: *Key episode.* ★: *Great episode.* ⊛: *One of the best episodes.*
Characters: **X**: *Present.* **M**: *Mentioned.* **O**: *Visage or dream only.* **B**: *Begins.* **E**: *Ends.* **BE**: *Begins and ends.*
Credits: *See key for Writer initials starting on page 257, and Director initials starting on page 263.*

Season Three Table (Episodes 12-22)

		Helpless	The Zeppo	Bad Girls	Consequences	Dopplegangland	Enemies	Earshot	Choices	The Prom	Graduation Day (1)	Graduation Day (2)
	Page:	97	99	101	102	103	105	106	106	108	110	111
	Watchability:	♊★	⊛	♊	♊★	⊛					♊	♊
	Episode:	3-12	3-13	3-14	3-15	3-16	3-17	3-18	3-19	3-20	3-21	3-22
SCOOBIES	Buffy Summers	x	x	x	x	x	x	x	x	x	x	x
	Rupert Giles	x	x	x	x	x	x	x	x	x	x	x
	Willow Rosenberg	x	x	x	x	x	x	x	x	x	x	x
	Xander Harris	x	x	x	x	x	x	x	x	x	x	x
FRIENDS, ENEMIES, & OTHERS	Cordelia Chase	x	x	x	x	x	x	x	x	x	x	x
	Joyce Summers (Mom)	x		x	x		x	x	x	x	x	
	Angel (Angelus)	x	x	x	x		x	x	x	x	x	
	Jenny Calendar											
	Oz (Daniel Osborne)	x	x	x		x	x	x	x	x	x	x
	Anya					x			x	x		
	Wesley Wyndam-Pryce			B	x	x	x	x		x	x	x
	Faith		x	x	x	x	x		x		x	x
	Larry							x	x			E
	Chanterelle/Lily											
	Willy the Snitch		x									
	Spike (William the Bloody)											
	Drusilla											
	Amy/Rat	M									x	
	Harmony Kendall										x	x
	Master											
	Principal Snyder										x	E
	Mr. Trick			x	E							
	Watchers' Council	x										
	Mayor Richard Wilkins III			x	x		x		x		x	E
	Allan (Mayor's Assistant)			E								
	Jonathan Levinson							x	x			x
	The Bringers											
	Evil Willow					E						
	D'Hoffryn					B						
	Ethan Rayne											
	The 1st Evil											
CREDITS	Episode:	3-12	3-13	3-14	3-15	3-16	3-17	3-18	3-19	3-20	3-21	3-22
	Writers	DF	DV	DP	MN	JW	DP	JE	DF	MN	JW	JW
	Directors	JAC	JWJ	ML	MGe	JW	DGr	RK	JAC	DSO	JW	JW

KEY: **Watchability:** ♊: *Key episode.* ★: *Great episode.* ⊛: *One of the best episodes.*
Characters: X: *Present.* M: *Mentioned.* O: *Visage or dream only.* B: *Begins.* E: *Ends.* BE: *Begins and ends.*
Credits: *See key for Writer initials starting on page 257, and Director initials starting on page 263.*

Season Four Table (Episodes 1-11)

Bronze Bands
4-1: Splendid
4-3: Bif Naked
4-5: Thc (as Shy)
4-6: Thc (as Shy)
4-17: Royal Crown Revue

		The Freshmen	Living Conditions	The Harsh Light of Day	Fear, Itself	Beer Bad	Wild at Heart	The Initiative	Pangs	Something Blue	Hush	Doomed
	Page:	115	117	118	120	122	123	124	126	128	129	131
	Watchability:	♟					♟	♟		⊛	⊛	♟
	Episode :	4-1	4-2	4-3	4-4	4-5	4-6	4-7	4-8	4-9	4-10	4-11
SCOOBIES	Buffy Summers	x	x	x	x	x	x	x	x	x	x	x
	Rupert Giles	x	x	x	x	x	x	x	x	x	x	x
	Willow Rosenberg	x	x	x	x	x	x	x	x	x	x	x
	Xander Harris	x	x	x	x	x	x	x	x	x	x	x
FRIENDS, ENEMIES, & OTHERS	Joyce Summers (Mom)	x			x							
	Angel (Angelus)									x		
	Oz (Daniel Osborne)	x	x	x	x	x	x					
	Anya			x	x				x	x	x	
	Riley Finn	B			x	x	x	x	x	x	x	x
	Tara										B	
	Faith											
	Percy											x
	Olivia (Giles' girlfriend)	B									x	
	Willy the Snitch											
	Spike (William the Bloody)						x	x	x	x	x	x
	Amy / Amy the Rat									x		x
	Harmony Kendall		x					x	x			
	Principal Snyder											
	Ethan Rayne											
	Watchers' Council											
	Mayor Richard Wilkins III											
	Sunday	BE										
	Jonathan Levinson											
	Maggie Walsh	B			x	x	x	x				
	Veruca		B			x	E					
	Parker		B	x	x	x			x			
	Adam											
	D'Hoffryn									x		
	The Initiative	B			x	x	x	x	x		x	x
	The 1st Slayer											
	Episode :	4-1	4-2	4-3	4-4	4-5	4-6	4-7	4-8	4-9	4-10	4-11
CREDITS	Writers	JW	MN	JE	DF	TF	MN	DP	JE	TF	JW	MN, JE, DF
	Directors	JW	DGr	JAC	TG	DSO	DGr	JAC	ML	NM	JW	JAC

KEY: **Watchability:** ♟: *Key episode.* ★: *Great episode.* ⊛: *One of the best episodes.*
Characters: **X**: *Present.* **M**: *Mentioned.* **O**: *Visage or dream only.* **B**: *Begins.* **E**: *Ends.* **BE**: *Begins and ends.*
Credits: *See key for Writer initials starting on page 257, and Director initials starting on page 263.*

	A New Man	The I in Team	Goodbye Iowa	This Year's Girl (Part 1)	Who Are You (Part 2)	Superstar	Where the Wild Things Are	New Moon Rising	The Yoko Factor (Part 1)	Primeval (Part 2)	Restless
Page:	132	133	135	136	137	138	139	140	141	143	144
Watchability:	★	♙		♙⊛	♙⊛	★		♙★	♙★	♙	★
Episode:	4-12	4-13	4-14	4-15	4-16	4-17	4-18	4-19	4-20	4-21	4-22
SCOOBIES											
Buffy Summers	x	x	x	x	x	x	x	x	x	x	x
Rupert Giles	x	x	x	x	x	x	x	x	x	x	x
Willow Rosenberg	x	x	x	x	x	x	x	x	x	x	x
Xander Harris	x	x	x	x	x	x	x	x	x	x	x
FRIENDS, ENEMIES, & OTHERS											
Joyce Summers (Mom)				x	x						x
Angel (Angelus)										x	
Oz (Daniel Osborne)								x			O
Anya	x	x	x		x	x	x	x	x	x	O
Riley Finn	x	x	x	x	x	x	x	x	x	x	x
Tara	x	x	x	x	x	x	x	x	x	x	O
Faith				x	x						
Percy											
Olivia (Giles' girlfriend)											
Willy the Snitch			x								
Spike (William the Bloody)	x	x	x	x	x	x	x	x	x	x	O
Amy / Amy the Rat											
Harmony Kendall											O
Principal Snyder											O
Ethan Rayne	x										
Watchers' Council				x	x						
Mayor Richard Wilkins III				x							
Sunday											
Jonathan Levinson							x				
Maggie Walsh	x	x	x							E	
Veruca											
Parker											
Adam	B	x	x		x			x	x	E	O
D'Hoffryn											
The Initiative	x	x	x					x	x	E	
The 1st Slayer											B
Episode:	4-12	4-13	4-14	4-15	4-16	4-17	4-18	4-19	4-20	4-21	4-22
CREDITS Writers	JE	DF	MN	DP	JW	JE	TF	MN	DP	DF	JW
Directors	MGe	JAC	DSO	MGe	JW	DGr	DSO	JAC	DGr	JAC	JW

KEY: **Watchability:** ♙: *Key episode.* ★: *Great episode.* ⊛: *One of the best episodes.*
Characters: **X**: *Present.* **M**: *Mentioned.* **O**: *Visage or dream only.* **B**: *Begins.* **E**: *Ends.* **BE**: *Begins and ends.*
Credits: *See key for Writer initials starting on page 257, and Director initials starting on page 263.*

Season Five Table (Episodes 1-11)

Bronze Bands
5-14: Summer Camp
5-14: Devics

		Buffy vs. Dracula	Real Me	The Replacement	Out of My Mind	No Place Like Home	Family	Fool for Love	Shadow	Listening to Fear	Into the Woods	Triangle
	Page:	149	150	152	154	155	155	156	157	157	159	160
	Watchability:		👤	★		👤★	★	👤⊗	👤★		👤	★
	Episode:	5-1	5-2	5-3	5-4	5-5	5-6	5-7	5-8	5-9	5-10	5-11
SCOOBIES	Buffy Summers	x	x	x	x	x	x	x	x	x	x	x
	Rupert Giles	x	x	x	x	x	x	x	x	x	x	x
	Willow Rosenberg	x	x	x	x	x	x	x	x	x	x	x
	Xander Harris	x	x	x	x	x	x	x	x	x	x	x
FRIENDS, ENEMIES, & OTHERS	Joyce Summers (Mom)	x	x	x	x	x		x	x	x	x	x
	Angel (Angelus)							x				
	Dawn Summers	B	x	x	x	x	x	x	x	x	x	x
	Anya	x	x	x	x	x	x	x	x	x	x	x
	Riley Finn	x	x	x	x	x	x	x	x	x	x	
	Tara	x	x		x		x		x	x		x
	Hank Summers (Dad)											
	Spike (William the Bloody)	x	x	x	x	x	x	x	x	x	x	x
	Drusilla							x				
	Harmony Kendall		x		x							
	Darla							x				
	Watchers' Council											
	Knights of Byzantium											
	Ben and Glory					B	x		x	x		
	Warren Mears											
	Troll Olaf											x
	The 1st Slayer											
	BuffyBot											
	Halfrek/Cecily							B				
	Katrina											
	Doc (Evil Joel Gray)											
	Episode:	5-1	5-2	5-3	5-4	5-5	5-6	5-7	5-8	5-9	5-10	5-11
CREDITS	Writers	MN	DF	JE	RBK	DP	JW	DP	DF	RBK	MN	JE
	Directors	DSO	DGr	JAC	DGr	DSO	JW	NM	DA	DSO	MN	CH

KEY: **Watchability:** 👤: *Key episode.* ★: *Great episode.* ⊗: *One of the best episodes.*
Characters: **X**: *Present.* **M**: *Mentioned.* **O**: *Visage or dream only.* **B**: *Begins.* **E**: *Ends.* **BE**: *Begins and ends.*
Credits: *See key for Writer initials starting on page 257, and Director initials starting on page 263.*

244

Season Five Table (Episodes 12-22)

	Checkpoint	Blood Ties	Crush	I Was Made to Love You	The Body	Forever	Intervention	Tough Love	Spiral	The Weight of the World	The Gift
Page:	161	162	163	165	166	167	167	169	170	171	171
Watchability:	👤⊗			★	👤⊗		👤★	👤	👤	★	👤⊗
Episode:	5-12	5-13	5-14	5-15	5-16	5-17	5-18	5-19	5-20	5-21	5-22

SCOOBIES

	Checkpoint	Blood Ties	Crush	I Was Made to Love You	The Body	Forever	Intervention	Tough Love	Spiral	The Weight of the World	The Gift
Buffy Summers	x	x	x	x	x	x	x	x	x	x	x
Rupert Giles	x	x	x	x	x	x	x	x	x	x	x
Willow Rosenberg	x	x	x	x	x	x	x	x	x	x	x
Xander Harris	x	x	x	x	x	x	x	x	x	x	x

FRIENDS, ENEMIES, & OTHERS

	Checkpoint	Blood Ties	Crush	I Was Made to Love You	The Body	Forever	Intervention	Tough Love	Spiral	The Weight of the World	The Gift
Joyce Summers (Mom)		x	x	x	E						
Angel (Angelus)						x					
Dawn Summers	x	x	x	x	x	x	x	x	x	x	x
Anya	x	x	x	x	x	x	x	x	x	x	x
Riley Finn											
Tara	x	x	x	x	x	x	x	x	x	x	x
Hank Summers (Dad)									x		
Spike (William the Bloody)	x	x	x	x	x	x	x	x	x	x	x
Drusilla			E								
Harmony Kendall			x								
Darla											
Watchers' Council	x										
Knights of Byzantium	B	x								E	
Ben and Glory	x	x	x	x		x	x	x	x	x	E
Warren Mears				B			x				
Troll Olaf											
The 1st Slayer							x			x	
BuffyBot							B				x
Halfrek/Cecily											
Katrina				B							
Doc (Evil Joel Gray)						B				x	E

CREDITS

	Checkpoint	Blood Ties	Crush	I Was Made to Love You	The Body	Forever	Intervention	Tough Love	Spiral	The Weight of the World	The Gift
Episode:	5-12	5-13	5-14	5-15	5-16	5-17	5-18	5-19	5-20	5-21	5-22
Writers	DP, JE	SSD	DF	JE	JW	MN	JE	RRK	SSD	DP	JW
Directors	NM	MGe	DA	JAC	JW	MN	MGe	DGr	JAC	DSO	JW

KEY: **Watchability:** 👤: *Key episode.* ★: *Great episode.* ⊗: *One of the best episodes.*
Characters: **X**: *Present.* **M**: *Mentioned.* **O**: *Visage or dream only.* **B**: *Begins.* **E**: *Ends.* **BE**: *Begins and ends.*
Credits: *See key for Writer initials starting on page 257, and Director initials starting on page 263.*

Season Six Table (Episodes 1-11)

Bronze Bands
6-6: Man of the Year
6-8: Michelle Branch
6-9: Virgil
6-9: Halo Friendlies

		Bargaining (Parts 1,2)	After Life	Flooded	Life Serial	All the Way	Once More, with Feeling	Tabula Rasa	Smashed	Wrecked	Gone
	Page:	175	177	178	179	181	183	185	186	188	189
	Watchability:	♟⊗	♟		♟★		♟⊗	♟★	♟★		
	Episode:	6-1,2	6-3	6-4	6-5	6-6	6-7	6-8	6-9	6-10	6-11
SCOOBIES	Buffy Summers	x	x	x	x	x	x	x	x	x	x
	Rupert Giles	x		x	x	x	x	x			
	Willow Rosenberg	x	x	x	x	x	x	x	x	x	x
	Xander Harris	x	x	x	x	x	x	x	x	x	x
FRIENDS, ENEMIES, & OTHERS	Joyce Summers (Mom)										
	Dawn Summers	x	x	x	x	x	x	x	x	x	x
	Anya	x	x	x	x	x	x	x	x	x	x
	Riley Finn										
	Tara	x	x	x	x	x	x	x			x
	Hank Summers (Dad)										
	Spike (William the Bloody)	x	x	x	x	x	x	x	x	x	x
	Amy / Amy Rat								x	x	x
	Rack (Warlock)										B
	Jonathan Levinson										
	Andrew			B							
	Warren Mears										
	Nerds			B	x				x	x	
	D'Hoffryn										
	BuffyBot	E									
	Halfrek										
	Katrina										
	Clem				B						
	Sam (Mrs. Riley)										
	Episode:	6-1,2	6-3	6-4	6-5	6-6	6-7	6-8	6-9	6-10	6-11
CREDITS	Writers	MN, DF	JE	JE, DP	DF, JE	SSD	JW	RRK	DZG	MN	DF
	Directors	DGr	DSO	DP	NM	DSO	JW	DGr	TM	DSO	DF

KEY: **Watchability:** ♟: *Key episode.* ★: *Great episode.* ⊗: *One of the best episodes.*
Characters: X: *Present.* M: *Mentioned.* O: *Visage or dream only.* B: *Begins.* E: *Ends.* BE: *Begins and ends.*
Credits: *See key for Writer initials starting on page 257, and Director initials starting on page 263.*

Season Six Table (Episodes 12-22)

	Double Meat Palace	Dead Things	Older and Far Away	As You Were	Hell's Bells	Normal Again	Entropy	Seeing Red	Villains	Two to Go (Part 1)	Grave (Part 2)
Page:	190	191	191	192	193	194	195	197	198	199	201
Watchability:		♟			♟★	⊛		♟★	♟⊛	♟⊛	♟★
Episode:	6-12	6-13	6-14	6-15	6-16	6-17	6-18	6-19	6-20	6-21	6-22
SCOOBIES											
Buffy Summers	x	x	x	x	x	x	x	x	x	x	x
Rupert Giles											x
Willow Rosenberg	x	x	x	x	x	x	x	x	x	x	x
Xander Harris	x	x	x	x	x	x	x	x	x	x	x
FRIENDS, ENEMIES, & OTHERS											
Joyce Summers (Mom)						x					
Dawn Summers	x	x	x	x	x	x	x	x	x	x	x
Anya	x	x	x	x	x		x	x	x	x	x
Riley Finn				x							
Tara		x	x		x	x	x	E			
Hank Summers (Dad)						x					
Spike (William the Bloody)	x	x	x	x	x	x	x	x	x	x	x
Amy / Amy Rat											
Rack (Warlock)									x	E	
Jonathan Levinson									x	x	x
Andrew									x	x	x
Warren Mears								x	E		
Nerds		x	x			x	x	E			
D'Hoffryn					x						
BuffyBot											
Halfrek	x		x	x	x	x	x	x			
Katrina		E									
Clem			x		x				x	x	
Sam (Mrs. Riley)					x						
Episode:	6-12	6-13	6-14	6-15	6-16	6-17	6-18	6-19	6-20	6-21	6-22
CREDITS — Writers	JE	SSD	DZG	DP	RRK	DiG	DZG	SSD	MN	DP	DF
Directors	NM	JAC	MGe	DP	DSO	RR	JAC	MGe	DSO	BLN	JAC

KEY: **Watchability**: ♟: *Key episode.*   ★: *Great episode.*   ⊛: *One of the best episodes.*
Characters: **X**: *Present.*   **M**: *Mentioned.*   **O**: *Visage or dream only.*   **B**: *Begins.*   **E**: *Ends.*   **BE**: *Begins and ends.*
Credits: *See key for Writer initials starting on page 257, and Director initials starting on page 263.*

Season Seven Table (Episodes 1-11)

Bronze Bands
7-6: The Breeders
7-7: Angie Hart
7-8: Aimee Mann
7-9, 7-13: Aberdeen
7-10, 7-19: Nerf Herder

		Lessons	Beneath You	Same Time, Same Place	Help	Selfless	Him	Conversations with Dead People	Sleeper	Never Leave Me	Bring on the Night	Showtime
	Page:	205	206	208	209	210	211	212	214	215	216	218
	Watchability:	👤★	👤★	★		⊛		👤★	👤	👤★	👤	👤★
	Episode:	7-1	7-2	7-3	7-4	7-5	7-6	7-7	7-8	7-9	7-10	7-11
SCOOBIES	Buffy Summers	x	x	x	x	x	x	x	x	x	x	x
	Rupert Giles	x							x		x	x
	Willow Rosenberg	x		x	x	x	x	x	x	x	x	x
	Xander Harris	x	x	x	x	x	x		x	x	x	x
FRIENDS, ENEMIES, & OTHERS	Joyce Summers (Mom)							O		O		
	Angel (Angelus)											
	Dawn Summers	x	x	x	x	x	x		x	x	x	x
	Anya	x				x	x		x	x	x	x
	Faith											
	Principal Robin Wood	B	x		x		x			x	x	
	Potential Slayers	B	x	x		x					x	x
	Spike (William the Bloody)	x	x	x	x		x	x	x	x	x	x
	Drusilla	O									O	
	Amy											
	Cassie Newton				BE			O				
	Master	O										
	Watchers' Council									x	E	
	Mayor Richard Wilkins III	O										
	Ben and Glory	O										
	Jonathan Levinson							E		O		
	Andrew						x	x	x	x	x	x
	Warren Mears	O						O		O		
	Troll (Olaf)					x						
	Adam	O										
	Bringers	x	x							x	x	x	x
	Übervamps									x	x	x
	D'Hoffryn					x						
	The 1st Evil							x			x	
	First Slayer											
	Halfrek	x				E						
	Clem			M								
	Episode:	7-1	7-2	7-3	7-4	7-5	7-6	7-7	7-8	7-9	7-10	7-11
CREDITS	Writers	JW	DP	JE	RRK	DrG	DZG	JE, DrG	DF, JE	DrG	MN, DP	DF
	Directors	DSO	NM	JAC	RR	DSO	MGe	NM	AJL	DSO	DGr	MGm

KEY: **Watchability:** 👤: *Key episode.* ★: *Great episode.* ⊛: *One of the best episodes.*
Characters: **X**: *Present.* **M**: *Mentioned.* **O**: *Visage or dream only.* **B**: *Begins.* **E**: *Ends.* **BE**: *Begins and ends.*
Credits: *See key for Writer initials starting on page 257, and Director initials starting on page 263.*

Season Seven Table (Episodes 12-22)

		Potential	The Killer in Me	First Date	Get It Done	Storyteller	Lies My Parents Told Me	Dirty Girls	Empty Places	Touched	End of Days	Chosen
	Page:	219	220	221	222	223	224	225	227	228	230	231
	Watchability:			♟		⊛		♟★	♟★	♟	♟★	♟⊛
	Episode:	7-12	7-13	7-14	7-15	7-16	7-17	7-18	7-19	7-20	7-21	7-22
SCOOBIES	Buffy Summers	x	x	x	x	x	x	x	x	x	x	x
	Rupert Giles		x	x			x	x	x	x	x	x
	Willow Rosenberg	x	x	x	x	x	x	x	x	x	x	x
	Xander Harris	x	x	x	x	x	x	x	x	x	x	x
FRIENDS, ENEMIES, & OTHERS	Joyce Summers (Mom)											
	Angel (Angelus)										x	x
	Dawn Summers	x	x		x	x	x	x	x	x	x	x
	Anya	x	x	x	x	x	x	x	x	x	x	E
	Faith							x	x	x	x	x
	Principal Robin Wood		x	x	x	x	x	x	x	x		x
	Potential Slayers	x		x	x	x	x	x	x	x	x	x
	Spike (William the Bloody)	x	x	x	x	x	x	x	x	x	x	E
	Drusilla											
	Amy		x									
	Cassie Newton											
	Master											
	Watchers' Council											
	Mayor Richard Wilkins III									O		
	Ben and Glory											
	Jonathan Levinson			O		x						
	Andrew	x	x		x	x	x	x	x	x	x	x
	Warren Mears		O			x						
	Troll (Olaf)											
	Adam											
	Bringers					x		x		x		
	Übervamps				x						x	E
	D'Hoffryn											
	The 1st Evil									x		
	First Slayer					x						
	Halfrek											
	Clem	x							x			
	Episode:	7-12	7-13	7-14	7-15	7-16	7-17	7-18	7-19	7-20	7-21	7-22
CREDITS	Writers	RRK	DZG	JE	DP	JE	DF, DrG	DrG	DZG	RRK	DP, JE	JW
	Directors	JAC	DSO	DGr	DP	MGr	DF	MGe	JAC	DSO	MGr	JW

KEY: **Watchability**: ♟: *Key episode.*   ★: *Great episode.*   ⊛: *One of the best episodes.*
Characters: **X**: *Present.*   **M**: *Mentioned.*   **O**: *Visage or dream only.*   **B**: *Begins.*   **E**: *Ends.*   **BE**: *Begins and ends.*
Credits: *See key for Writer initials starting on page 257, and Director initials starting on page 263.*

Episode Tables

Characters and Cast

For most of the characters who appeared in the show, this table shows the character, actor, and the seasons in which the character appeared, sorted by first name. Even if the character had only a cameo appearance in one episode, that season is included in the final column.

There are many actors not included in this list who played smaller roles or walk-on parts. They may not be in this list, but they played an important part in the success of the show.

Characters and Actors	Appear in Seasons:						
1st Slayer (played by Sharon Ferguson)				4	5		
Abraham Benrubi (as character Olaf / Olaf the Troll)					5		7
Adam (played by George Hertzberg)				4			7
Adam Busch (as character Warren Meers)					5	6	7
Adam Kaufman (as character Parker Abrams)				4			
Alexandra Johnes (as character Sheila Martini)		2					
Alexis Denisof (as character Wesley Wyndam-Pryce)			3				
Allan Finch (Deputy Mayor) (played by Jack Plotnick)			3				
Alyson Hannigan (as character Evil Willow)			3				
Alyson Hannigan (as character Willow Rosenberg)	1	2	3	4	5	6	7
Amber Benson (as character Tara Maclay)				4	5	6	
Amelinda Smith (as character Katrina (Warren's girlfriend))					5	6	
Ampata Gutierrez (Inca Mummy) (played by Ara Celi)		2					
Amy Madison (played by Elizabeth Anne Allen)	1	2	3	4		6	7
Andrew J. Ferchland (as character Collin (Anointed One))	1	2					
Andrew Wells (Tucker's brother) (played by Tom Lenk)						6	7
Andy Umberger (as character D'Hoffryn)			3	4		6	7
Angel / Angelus / Liam (played by David Boreanaz)	1	2	3	4	5		7
Dr. Angelman (of the Initiative) (played by Jack Stehlin)							7
Anne (Spike's mother) (played by Caroline Lagerfelt)							7
Anthony Head (as character Giles, Rupert)	1	2	3	4	5	6	7
Anthony Head (as character Rupert Giles)	1	2	3	4	5	6	7
Anya / Anyanka / Aud (played by Emma Caulfield)			3	4	5	6	7
April (the robot) (played by Shonda Farr)					5		

Characters and Actors	1	2	3	4	5	6	7
Ara Celi (played Ampata Gutierrez (Inca Mummy))		2					
Armin Shimerman (as character Principal Snyder)	1	2	3	4			
Azura Skye (as character Cassie Newton)							7
Bailey Chase (as character Graham Miller (Riley's friend))				4			
Ben (played by Charlie Weber)					5		
Bianca Lawson (as character Kendra)		2					
Billy 'Ford' Fordham (played by Jason Behr)		2					
Billy Palmer (played by Jeremy Foley)	1						
Brad Kane (as character Tucker Wells)			3				
Brian Thompson (as character Luke)	1						
Brian Thompson (as character The Judge)		2					
Buffy Summers (played by Sarah Michelle Gellar)	1	2	3	4	5	6	7
BuffyBot (played by Sarah Michelle Gellar)					5	6	
Caleb (played by Nathan Fillion)							7
Camden Toy (as characters Turaok-Han, *Hush* Gentleman, Gnarl				4			7
Caroline Lagerfelt (as character Anne (Spike's mother))							7
Cassie Newton (played by Azura Skye)							7
Cecily (played by Kali Rocha)					5		
Channon Roe (as character Jack O'Toole)			3				
Chanterelle/Lily (played by Julia Lee)		2	3				
Chao-Ahn (Potential) (played by Kristy Wu)							7
Charisma Carpenter (as character Cordelia Chase)	1	2	3				
Charlie Weber (as character Ben)					5		
Chloe (Potential) (played by Lalaine)							7
Clara Bryant (as character Molly (Potential))							7
Clare Kramer (as character Glory)					5		7
Clea DuVall (played by Marcie Ross (invisible girl))	1						
Clem (played by James Charles Leary)						6	7
Collin (Anointed One) (played by Andrew J. Ferchland)	1	2					
Cordelia Chase (played by Charisma Carpenter)	1	2	3				
D.B. Woodside (as character Principal Robin Wood)							7
Dagney Kerr (as charcter roommate Kathy Newman)				4			
Danny Strong (as character Jonathan Levinson)		2	3	4		6	7
Darla (played by Julie Benz)	1	2			5		
David Boreanaz (as character Angel / Angelus / Liam)	1	2	3	4	5		7
David Fury (as character Mustard Man)						6	
Dawn Summers (played by Michelle Trachtenberg)					5	6	7
Dean Butler (as character Hank Summers (Buffy's father))	1	2			5	6	

Characters and Actors	1	2	3	4	5	6	7
Devon MacLeish (Dingoes lead singer) (played by Jason Hall)		2	3	4			
D'Hoffryn (played by Andy Umberger)			3	4		6	7
Doc (played by Joel Grey)					5		
Double Meat demon (played by Pat Crawford Brown)						6	
Dracula (played by Rudolf Martin)					5		
Drusilla (played by Juliet Landau)		2	3		5		
Eddie (lonely freshman) (played by Pedro Pascal)				4			
Eliza Dushku (as character Faith)			3	4			7
Elizabeth Anne Allen (as character Amy Madison)	1	2	3	4		6	7
Emma Caulfield (as character Anya / Anyanka / Aud)			3	4	5	6	7
Eric Balfour (as character Jesse)	1						
Ethan Erickson (as character Percy West)			3	4			
Ethan Rayne (played by Robin Sachs)		2	3	4			
Evil Willow (played by Alyson Hannigan)			3				
Fab Filippo (as character Scott Hope)			3				
Faith (played by Eliza Dushku)			3	4			7
Felicia Day (as character Vi (Potential))							7
First Slayer (played by Sharon Ferguson)				4	5		
Ford (Billy Fordham) (played by Jason Behr)		2					
Forrest Gates (Riley's friend) (played by Leonard Roberts)				4			
Gentleman from *Hush* (played by Camden Toy)				4			
George Hertzberg (as character Adam)				4			7
Giles, Rupert (played by Anthony Head)	1	2	3	4	5	6	7
Glory (played by Clare Kramer)					5		7
Gnarl (played by Camden Toy)				4			
Graham Miller (Riley's Initiative friend) (played by Bailey Chase)				4			
Halfrek (played by Kali Rocha)						6	7
Hank Summers (Buffy's father) (played by Dean Butler)	1	2			5	6	
Harmony Kendall (played by Mercedes McNab)	1	2	3	4	5		
Harris Yulin (as character Quentin Travers (Watcher's council))			3		5		7
Harry Groener (as character Mayor Richard Wilkins)			3	4			7
Hinton Battle (as character Sweet)						6	
Holden Webster (played by Jonathan M. Woodward)							7
Indigo (as character Rona (Potential))							7
Iyari Limon (as character Kennedy (Potential))							7
Jack O'Toole (played by Channon Roe)			3				
Jack Plotnick (as character Allan Finch (Deputy Mayor))			3				
Jack Stehlin (as character Dr. Angelman (of the Initiative))							7

Characters and Actors	Appear in Seasons:						
James Charles Leary (as character Clem)						6	7
James Marsters (as Spike / WIlliam the Bloody/Hostile 17)		2	3	4	5	6	7
Jason Behr (as character Ford (Billy Fordham))		2					
Jason Hall (as character Devon MacLeish (Dingoes lead singer))		2	3	4			
Jeff Kober (as character Rack (warlock) and Zach (vampire))			3			6	
Jenny Calendar (played by Robia LaMorte)	1	2	3				
Jeremy Foley (as character Billy Palmer)	1						
Jeremy Ratchford (as character vampire Lyle Gorch)		2	3				
Jesse (played by Eric Balfour)	1						
Jinx (Glory's minion) (played by Troy Blendell)					5		
Joel Grey (as character Doc)					5		
John Patrick White (as character Pete Clarner (abusive boyfriend))			3				
John Ritter (as character Ted Buchanan)		2					
Jonathan Levinson (played by Danny Strong)		2	3	4		6	7
Jonathan M. Woodward (as character Holden Webster)							7
Joyce Summers (Buffy's mother) (played by Kristine Sutherland)	1	2	3	4	5	6	7
Judge, The (played by Brian Thompson)		2					
Julia Lee (as character Chanterelle/Lily)		2	3				
Julie Benz (as character Darla)	1	2			5		
Juliet Landau (as character Drusilla)		2	3		5		
K. Todd Freeman (as character Mr. Trick)			3				
Kali Rocha (as characters Cecily)					5		
Kali Rocha (as character Halfrek)						6	7
Katharine Towne (as character Sunday)				4			
Kathy Newman (Buffy's roommate) (played by Dagney Kerr)				4			
Katrina (Warren's girlfriend) (played by Amelinda Smith)					5	6	
Ken Lerner (as character Principal Bob Flutie)	1						
Kendra (played by Bianca Lawson)		2					
Kennedy (Potential) (played by Iyari Limon)							7
Kristine Sutherland (as Joyce Summers (Buffy's mother))	1	2	3	4	5	6	7
Kristy Wu (as character Chao-Ahn (Potential))							7
Lalaine (as character Chloe (Potential))							7
Larry Bagby (as character Larry Blaisdell)		2	3				
Larry Blaisdell (played by Larry Bagby)		2	3				
Leonard Roberts (as character Forrest Gates (Riley's friend))				4			
Lily/Chanterelle (played by Julia Lee)		2	3				
Lindsay Crouse (as character Professor Maggie Walsh)				4			
Luke (played by Brian Thompson)	1						

Characters and Actors	1	2	3	4	5	6	7
Lyle Gorch (played by Jeremy Ratchford)		2	3				
Maggie Walsh (played by Lindsay Crouse)				4			
Marc Blucas (as character Riley Finn)				4	5	6	
Marcie Ross (invisible girl) (played by Clea DuVall)	1						
Mark Metcalf (as character The Master)	1	2	3		7		
Marti Noxon (as character Parking Ticket Woman)						6	
Mary Wilcher (as character Shannon (Potential))							7
Master, The (played by Mark Metcalf)	1	2	3		7		
Mayor Richard Wilkins (played by Harry Groener)			3	4			7
Megan Gray (as character Sandy)			3		5		
Mercedes McNab (as character Harmony Kendall)	1	2	3	4	5		
Michelle Trachtenberg (as character Dawn Summers)					5	6	7
Molly (Potential) (played by Clara Bryant)							7
Mr. Trick (played by K. Todd Freeman)			3				
Murk (Glory's minion) (played by Todd Duffey)					5		
Mustard Man (played by David Fury)						6	
Nancy Lenehan (as character Pat (Joyce's friend))			3				
Nathan Fillion (as character Caleb)							7
Nicholas Brendon (as Xander (Alexander) Lavelle Harris)	1	2	3	4	5	6	7
Olaf / Olaf the Troll (played by Abraham Benrubi)					5		7
Olivia (Giles' girlfriend) (played by Phina Oruche)				4			
O'Toole (played by Channon Roe)			3				
Owen Thurman (played by Christopher Wiehl)	1						
Oz (Daniel Osborne) (played by Seth Green)		2	3	4			
Paige Moss (as character Veruca)				4			
Parker Abrams (played by Adam Kaufman)				4			
Parking Ticket Woman (played by Marti Noxon)						6	
Pat Crawford Brown (as character Double Meat demon)						6	
Pat (Joyce's friend) (played by Nancy Lenehan)			3				
Pedro Pascal (as character Eddie (lonely freshman))				4			
Percy West (played by Ethan Erickson)			3	4			
Pete Clarner (abusive boyfriend) (played by John Patrick White)			3				
Phina Oruche (as character Olivia (Giles' girlfriend))				4			
Principal Bob Flutie (played by Ken Lerner)	1						
Principal Robin Wood (played by D.B. Woodside)							7
Principal Snyder (played by Armin Shimerman)	1	2	3	4			
Professor Maggie Walsh (played by Lindsay Crouse)				4			
Quentin Travers (Watcher's council) (played by Harris Yulin)			3		5		7

Characters and Actors	Appear in Seasons:						
	1	2	3	4	5	6	7
Rack (Warlock) (played by Jeff Kober)						6	
Riley Finn (played by Marc Blucas)				4	5	6	
R. J. Brooks (played by Thad Luckinbill)							7
Robia LaMorte (as character Jenny Calendar)	1	2	3				
Robin Sachs (as character Ethan Rayne)		2	3	4			
Rona (Potential) (played by Indigo)							7
Rudolf Martin (as character Dracula)					5		
Rupert Giles (played by Anthony Head)	1	2	3	4	5	6	7
Sandy (played by Megan Gray)			3		5		
Sarah Michelle Gellar (as character Buffy Summers)	1	2	3	4	5	6	7
Sarah Michelle Gellar (as character BuffyBot)					5	6	
Saverio Guerra (as character Willy the Snitch)			3	4			
Scott Hope (played by Fab Filippo)			3				
Seth Green (as character Oz (Daniel Osborne))		2	3	4			
Shannon (Potential) (played by Mary Wilcher)							7
Sharon Ferguson (as character First Slayer)				4	5		
Sheila Martini (played by Alexandra Johnes)		2					
Shonda Farr (as character April (the robot))					5		
Spike / WIlliam the Bloody / Hostile 17 (by James Marsters)		2	3	4	5	6	7
Sunday (played by Katharine Towne)				4			
Sweet (played by Hinton Battle)						6	
Tara Maclay (played by Amber Benson)				4	5	6	
Ted Buchanan (played by John Ritter)		2					
Thad Luckinbill (as character R.J. Brooks)							7
Todd Duffey (as character Murk (Glory's minion))					5		
Tom Lenk (as character Andrew Wells (Tucker's brother))						6	7
Trick (played by K. Todd Freeman)			3				
Troy Blendell (as character Jinx (Glory's minion))					5		
Tucker Wells (played by Brad Kane)			3				
Übervamp (Turaok-Han) (played by Camden Toy)							7
Veruca (played by Paige Moss)				4			
Vi (Potential) (played by Felicia Day)							7
Warren Meers (played by Adam Busch)					5	6	7
Wesley Wyndam-Pryce (played by Alexis Denisof)			3				
Willow Rosenberg (played by Alyson Hannigan)	1	2	3	4	5	6	7
Willy the Snitch (played by Saverio Guerra)			3	4			
Xander (Alexander) Lavelle Harris (played by Nicholas Brendon)	1	2	3	4	5	6	7
Zack (Vampire in *Helpless*) (played by Jeff Kober)			3				

Writers

This table shows all the writers who worked on episodes of *Buffy the Vampire Slayer*. The initials in the first column are those used in the episode reference tables starting on page 235. Note that some episodes were co-written by more than one writer.

For each season, the episode number is shown. The Total Eps column shows the total number of episodes this writer wrote. For example, Ashley Gable wrote episode 8 in season 1, for a total of just one episode written in the entire seven-season run of the show.

Following the table is a listing by the writer's last name that lists the episode names.

The episodes written in each season by each writer…

		SEASONS							Total Eps
		1	2	3	4	5	6	7	
AG	Ashley Gable	8							1
CE	Carl Ellsworth		6						1
DB	Dean Batali	5, 9	2, 15, 18						5
DF	David Fury		20	12, 19	4, 11, 13, 21	2, 8, 14	2, 5, 11, 22	8, 11, 17	17
DG	David Greenwalt	4, 7	3, 5, 11	3, 5					7
DiG	Diego Gutierrez						17		1
DP	Douglas Petrie			7, 14, 17	7, 15, 20	5, 7, 12, 21	4, 15, 21	2, 10, 15, 21	17
DR	Dana Reston	3							1
DrG	Drew Goddard							5, 7, 9, 17, 18	5
DV	Dan Vebber			8, 13					2
DZG	Drew Z. Greenberg						9, 14, 18	6, 13, 19	6
EH	Elin Hampton		20						1
HG	Howard Gordon		9						1
JE	Jane Espenson			6, 11, 18	3, 8, 11, 12, 17	3, 11, 12, 15, 18	3, 4, 5, 12, 13	3, 7, 8, 14, 16, 21	23
JR	Joe Reinkemeyer	6	4						2

The episodes written in each season by each writer...

		SEASONS							Total Eps
		1	**2**	**3**	**4**	**5**	**6**	**7**	
JW	Joss Whedon	1, 2, 10, 11, 12	1, 3, 7, 11, 14, 21, 22	1, 10, 16, 21, 22	1, 10, 16, 22	6, 16, 22	7, 17	1, 22	**27**
MK	Matt Kiene	6	4						**2**
MN	Marti Noxon		9, 10, 12, 13, 16, 19	2, 4, 9, 15, 20	2, 6, 11, 14, 19	1, 10, 17	1, 10, 20	10	**23**
RDH	Rob Des Hotel	5, 9	8, 15, 18						**5**
RRK	Rebecca Rand Kirshner					4, 9, 19	8, 16	4, 12, 20	**8**
SSD	Steven S. DeKnight					13, 20	6, 14, 19		**5**
TAS	Thomas A. Swyden	8							**1**
TF	Tracey Forbes				5, 9, 18				**3**
TK	Ty King		2, 17						**2**
TSJ	Thania St. John			11					**1**

Dean Batali

Steven S. DeKnight

Rob Des Hotel

Carl Ellsworth

Jane Espenson

Jane Espenson (continued)

Tracey Forbes

David Fury

Directors

This table shows all the directors who worked on episodes of *Buffy the Vampire Slayer*. The initials in the first column are those used in the episode reference tables starting on page 235.

For each season, the episode number is shown. The Total Eps column shows the total number of episodes directed. For example, Alan J. Levi directed episode 8 in season 7, for a total of just one episode directed in the entire seven-season run of the show.

Following the table is a listing by the director's last name that lists the episode names.

		The episodes directed in each season by each director...							
		SEASONS							Total Eps
		1	**2**	**3**	**4**	**5**	**6**	**7**	
AJL	Alan J. Levi							8	1
BLN	Bill L. Norton						21		1
BSG	Bruce Seth Green	4, 6, 10	2, 6, 8, 11, 15						8
CH	Christopher Hibler					11			1
CMS	Charles Martin Smith	1							1
DA	Dan Attias					8, 14			2
DF	David Fury						11	17	2
DG	David Greenwalt		5, 12	5, 9					4
DGr	David Grossman			17	2, 6, 17, 20	2, 4, 19	1, 2, 8	10, 14	13
DP	Douglas Petrie						4, 15	15	3
DSa	Deran Sarafian		18						1
DSe	David Semel	5	10, 20	8					4
DSo	David Solomon		9	20	5, 14, 18	1, 5, 9, 21	3, 6, 10, 16, 20	1, 5, 9, 13, 20	19
ESP	Ellen S. Pressman	9	4						2
JAC	James A. Contner		16	3, 7, 12, 19	3, 7, 11, 13, 19, 21	3, 15, 20	13, 18, 22	3, 12, 19	20

Directors

The episodes directed in each season by each director...

		SEASONS							Total Eps
		1	2	3	4	5	6	7	
JTK	John T. Kretchmer	2	3						2
JWJ	James Whitmore, Jr.		19	2, 4, 11,13					5
JW	Joss Whedon	12	1,7, 14, 21, 22	1,10, 16, 21, 22	1, 10, 16, 22	6, 16, 22	7	22	20
MGe	Michael Gershman		17	15	12, 15	13, 18	14, 19	6, 18	10
MGr	Marita Grabiak							16, 21	2
MGm	Michael Grossman							11	1
ML	Michael Lange		13	6, 14	8				4
MN	Marti Noxon					10, 17			2
NM	Nick Marck				9	7, 12	5, 12	2, 7	7
RB	Reza Badiyi	11							1
RK	Regis Kimble			18					1
RR	Rick Rosenthal						17	4	2
SB	Scott Brazil	7							1
SC	Stephen Cragg	3							1
SP	Stephen Posey	8							1
TG	Tucker Gates				4				1
TM	Turi Meyer						9		1

Dan Attias

Shadow (5-8) 157
Crush (5-14) 163

Reza Badiyi

Out of Mind, Out of Sight (1-11) 47

Scott Brazil

Angel (1-7) 42

James A. Contner

Bewitched, Bothered, and Bewildered (2-16) 72
Faith, Hope & Trick (3-3) 85
Revelations (3-7) 92
Helpless (3-12) 97
Choices (3-19) 106
The Harsh Light of Day (4-3) 118
The Initiative (4-7) 124
Doomed (4-11) 131
The I in Team (4-13) 133

David Solomon (continued)

Joss Whedon

James Whitmore, Jr.

References

The bulk of the information in this guide was collected through repeated, admittedly a tad obsessive viewings of *Buffy the Vampire Slayer*. I sometimes relied on closed captioning to get spellings right, but pretty much just rewound and rewatched.

Some tidbits came from the commentary and interviews on the *Buffy the Vampire Slayer* DVDs, and I also relied on the following online resources for information about the cast, writers, and directors of the show:

Buffyguide   There are quite a few websites out there devoted to *Buffy the Vampire Slayer,* but this is the one I consulted to check my matching of episodes with writers. This site has a wonderful reference to the episodes and has many images. Visit the site at www.buffyguide.com/

IMDB   This is the definitive reference for all things film and television and was a great way to look up names for the "Characters and Cast" table. Catch up on more details on the Internet Movie Database at www.imdb.com/title/tt0118276/

Wikipedia   The Wikipedia entry for *Buffy the Vampire Slayer* is available at en.wikipedia.org/wiki/Buffy_the_Vampire_Slayer_(TV_series). I also consulted Wikipedia for help identifying music, at en.wikipedia.org/wiki/Music_in_Buffy_the_Vampire_Slayer_and_Angel, in addition to the music reference below.

Music   Identifying the music was a serious challenge. I felt the information was important to include, but some of the music was obscure or I couldn't hear enough of a tune to identify it. I finally turned to online sources, including this archived website at http://offline.buffy.cd/outlink_en.php?module=/webserver/offline/www.buffyworld.com/buffy/music.htm

BuffyVerse Wiki

I found additional references to the Mutant Enemy story and the music references at BuffyVerse Wiki. This is a collaborative encyclopedia in "wiki" form for everything related to *Buffy the Vampire Slayer* and *Angel*. The wiki format allows any registered user to create or edit any article. Visit the site at buffy.wikia.com

Buffy-Angel Crossover Guide

I was able to polish the details of some of the crossovers between Buffy and Angel by consulting a wonderful table put together by Simon Hampnel at www.simonhampel.com/buffy.html

Fonts

There are several "Buffy" fonts available online. The best I've found so far and that I used in this book are "Rebuffed" (Rebuffed), and also "Kruella" (Kruella).

- Rebuffed www.urbanfonts.com/fonts/Rebuffed.htm
- Kruella www.ufonts.com/fonts/kruella.html

Other Great Online Resources

There are many other sites with great collections of information about *Buffy the Vampire Slayer*. Here are a few:

BuffyWorld

This site includes episode information, an index of slang, fan fiction, and more. www.buffyworld.com

Dark Horse Buffy Zone

This is your source for Buffy comics and books from Dark Horse. www.darkhorse.com/Zones/Buffy

Buffy Collector

This site provides links, information, and collectibles for Buffy the Vampire Slayer, Angel, and other Joss Whedon creations. These are also the fine folks behind the annual "Slay-a-thon," which raises money for the Make-A-Wish Foundation. www.buffycollector.com

Slayer Lit

This site celebrates the literary offshoots of Buffy the Vampire Slayer and similar literary works, including Buffy and Angel novels by talented horror and fantasy writers. www.slayerlit.us

Index of Episodes

Index of Episodes

Index of Cross References

This index lists the references to and from episodes throughout the show, including references to episodes in *Angel*. In some cases the references are indirect, or are in notes about the episode rather than in the actual episode.

Index of Trivia and Other Notes

Index of Film and Television

Index of Music Heard

This index lists the bands and songs heard in the episodes. See page 289 for an index of bands, musicians, and songs that are directly or indirectly referenced in the episodes.

Index of Music Referenced

This index lists bands, musicians, and songs that are directly or indirectly referenced in the episodes. See page 285 for an index of the bands and songs actually heard.

Index of Music Referenced

General Index

E

M

Q

R

Made in the USA
Lexington, KY
02 April 2017

Around
Maidenhead

IN OLD PHOTOGRAPHS

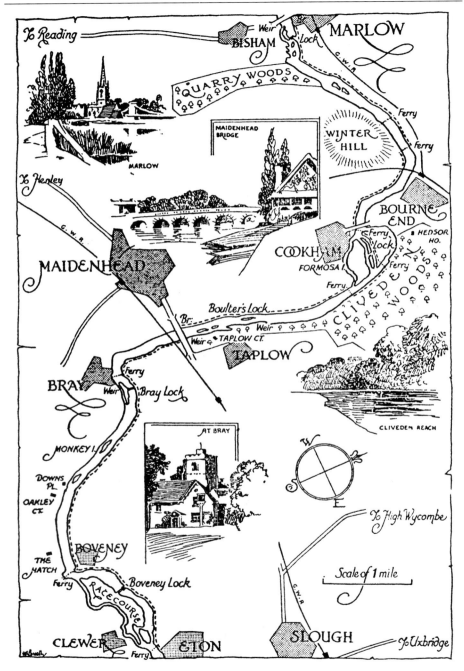

This map shows Maidenhead and the surrounding area.

Around Maidenhead

IN OLD PHOTOGRAPHS

MYRA HAYLES *and* BERYL HEDGES

A Budding Book

First published in 1994 by Alan Sutton
Publishing Limited

This edition published in 1998 by Budding Books,
an imprint of Sutton Publishing Limited
Phoenix Mill · Thrupp · Stroud · Gloucestershire
GL5 2BU

Copyright © Myra Hayles, Beryl Hedges, 1994

A catalogue record for this book is available from
the British Library

ISBN 1-84015-068-8

Typesetting and origination by
Sutton Publishing Limited.
Printed in Great Britain by
WBC Limited, Bridgend, Mid-Glamorgan.

This book is dedicated David Hedges
who inspired and shared our love of
the Thames Valley

Contents

Cookham Lock, *c.* 1885.

Introduction

This book not only extends the area, but also includes photographs not previously published in *Maidenhead in Old Photographs*. If it generates as much interest and feeling of nostalgia as that book, our efforts in the compilation will have been well rewarded.

The Thames forms a natural boundary and we have explored an area radiating about five miles from the town. Each place has its own identity yet all are closely linked with Maidenhead. The town was formerly shared by the parishes of Cookham and Bray, and it was not until 1451 that it came into being as a corporate body. Before this the site had many different names, with variations in spelling.

Throughout the ages the area has owed its importance to transport. The river was the first highway, and it was because of the construction of a bridge diverting the main road to the west from Cookham that the town gained in importance. William Camden, in *Britannia* (1586), stated that 'after they had built a wooden bridge upon piles Maidenhead began to have inns and to be so frequented as to outvie its neighbouring mother Bray, a much ancient place'. The main street was indeed lined with inns and posting-houses. Later the coming of the railway played an enormous part in its growth and prosperity. To the north, suburbs grew rapidly and the population quadrupled in the reign of Queen Victoria. Brunel's bridge, noteworthy for having two of the widest spans ever constructed in brick, also became one of the best known in the country when Turner painted *Rain, Steam and Speed*. In the 1920s and '30s the motor car brought in the socializing crowds and the river became packed with pleasure-craft.

On the south boundary lies Bray, which was once a royal manor and a Hundred. Its church and almshouses are of special interest and the village has many other notable buildings. Holyport, Oakley Green, Fifield and Ockwells Park all evoke the village atmosphere with their leafy lanes. White Waltham is dominated by the airfield, while Shottesbrook, Waltham St Lawrence and Littlewick Green also contribute to making this part of the countryside a pleasure to explore.

The old highway, the Bath Road, ran through Maidenhead Thicket which at one time was five miles wide. The thicket formed a barrier to the west of the town and had an evil reputation with travellers, who preferred to stay in the town overnight rather than attempt to pass through it in the dark. Burchetts Green is dominated by Hall Place with its wonderful surrounds. This was the home of the Clayton Easts but part of it was bought by Berkshire County Council and is now the Agricultural College. The route from Hurley to Bisham

The river and bridge were both very important to the formation of the town.

is a two-mile stretch of beautiful river and countryside leading to the grounds of Bisham Abbey. Bisham Church also stands by the river, and contains the historic tombs of the Hoby family.

Upstream from Maidenhead lies the manor of Cookham and some of its land is now owned by the National Trust. It includes Cockmarsh facing Bourne End, Cookham Dean Common, Cookham Rise and the Moor. Cookham, which once incorporated all of the town north of the Bath Road, is now a popular riverside village.

Many famous personalities have lived in the area and we have included some in the final chapter on popular events and celebrities. It is evident from this chapter in particular how the local residents have crafted the area around Maidenhead, and will continue to do so.

We hope this nostalgic trip is enjoyable. It is now up to us all to ensure that future generations will also be able to look back with happy memories.

Maidenhead – the Town

The High Street showing McIlroy's the draper at Nos 87 and 89. Their 'stocktaking sale [was] proceeding' – rather different from today's 'Sale now on!' Barclays Bank can be seen on the first floor with Mignon, a cake shop, next door.

An unusual view of King Street with the Bell Hotel on the left, 1939. Trains crossing the bridge would have seen the clock tower clearly. Cycling was very popular at the time, and there were several cycle shops in the town. These included Cox Bros, 63 Queen Street, Hildreth, 23 King Street, Timberlake's, 85 and 87 Queen Street, To and Fro Cycle Co., 2 Station Approach and Wilkins, 76 King Street.

gh Street, Maidenhead.

As the main thoroughfare from London to the west, the Bath Road had an abundance of inns. Here The White Horse can be seen at the west end of the High Street. The road was open for traffic which eventually became so heavy that there were numerous traffic jams.

The guildhall on the right was built in 1777 when the market house was demolished. When the council took it over in 1836 it soon became too small, but it wasn't until 1960 that work began on the new town hall.

St Ives Hotel (left) in Ives Place was demolished in 1956. It was a sixteenth-century property which once belonged to Bisham Abbey until ownership passed in 1540 to Queen Anne of Cleves. The library stands on the right. Next to it was the war memorial designed by a former borough surveyor, Lt. Col. Percy Jones. When the present library was built, the memorial was moved across the road.

Upson's the optician, chemist and druggist of 35 and 37 High Street.

Brock Lane, thought to have been called Brook Lane at one point, had a National School which was eventually used as a Sunday School and meeting-place. It was here that the Cottage Hospital Fund was launched in 1877. There was also an Oddfellows Hall in the Lane.

The parish church of St Mary Magdalene, built by local builders Jones and Sons, replaced the previous churches which were situated in the centre of the High Street in 1270 and rebuilt in the same position in 1724. In 1842 the church was built at the east end of the High Street.

Edwards and Co., the tailors of 56 Queen Street, had an interesting shop front.

In coaching days Castle Hill was called Folly Hill, then the top was developed for housing by J. Clark. The building on the left, built in 1891, is often called 'the Folly' because of its appearance, or perhaps as a memory of bygone days. The drive up to the Terrace, with its elegant homes, can be seen on the right.

Maidenhead College was founded by A. Millar Inglis and built in 1891. It later became the Convent of the Nativity but reverted to its original name in 1978.

All Saint's Church at Boyn Hill plus the official seal of the corporation, often called 'the lozenge'. It was the seal of John Godayne, canon of Thiers. The picture below shows the dedication of the church, after extensions were built in 1907.

A view of All Saints' Avenue, from the church. It is still lined with trees but the postbox and the police box have gone.

The Queen Anne Hotel used to stand at the bottom of Castle Hill. The architect was Charles Cooper but the designer and manufacturer of the bricks and tiles is believed to be J. Hardwell of Pinkney Green Kilns who supplied examples of every kind of moulding that they made for the building.

County Girls' School, Maidenhead
The Lawn

On 24 January 1905 Maidenhead Girls' School (for a long time known as the County Girls' School) was opened at the Technical Institute with eleven pupils. The school moved in May 1907 to a house on Castle Hill previously owned by the Nicholson family, while Queen Anne House was also used.

County Girls' School, Maidenhead
A Class Room.

County Girls' School, Maidenhead.
The Garden.

In 1959 the school moved to Farm Road and was officially opened by Princess Alexandra. It became Newlands Comprehensive in 1973. The headteachers have been: 1958–76, Miss Costello; 1976–90, Mrs Leighton; and since 1990, Mrs Brenton.

County Girls' School, Maidenhead.
A Class Room at Queen Anne House.

Maidenhead District Laundry Company Limited.

This Laundry has been inspected by His Majesty's Inspector and been found to be one of the best Sanitary Laundries in England—up-to-date in every respect.

Exterior and Interior views of the Maidenhead District Laundry, Furze Platt.

The laundry was opened in 1886 on the site of a poultry farm, and it provided employment for many of the local residents of Furze Platt. Here, a 1919 advertisement states: 'This laundry has been inspected by His Majesty's Inspector and been found to be one of the best sanitary laundries in England – up-to-date in every respect.'

The Golden Harp in Furze Platt still shows what its purpose was, besides providing liquid refreshment.

Crauford House was once the home of Mayor Pearce who was renowned for introducing electricity to Maidenhead. In 1890 he gave Kidwells Park to the town. At the time of this photograph, 1919, Crauford House was a school, and an advertisement declared that it 'imparts instruction on modern lines'.

Cordwalles School stood at the top of a hill, 1½ miles from the GWR station and was a high-class preparatory school for boys.

Spencer Farm gate, *c.* 1960, stood on land belonging to the medieval family of the Despencers. Aldebury Road and its surrounds has now taken its place.

In the earlier part of this century there was a boom in house building in this fashionable area owing to the proximity of the river. The Ray Lodge Estate was affected by the corporation when parts of it were bought to improve the entrance into Ray Park Avenue.

This picture shows the lovely Maidenhead Bridge and the Riviera Hotel with the rowing-club premises on the left bank. Judging by the number of spectators the event is probably a regatta.

Between the twelfth and eighteenth centuries there was a wharf on this site. The gardens were developed in 1945 after the Hungarian Club was pulled down.

The promenade became a meeting-place for people watching the boats at Boulters Lock. The road is named The Promenade in the top picture, and Raymead Road below, but it was also called Thames Road.

The Reitlinger Fine Art Museum exhibited local archaeological finds, prints, drawings, ceramics, carvings and paintings. It is hoped that the Heritage Centre will be able to continue to accommodate and display many of the area's 'treasures'.

The Guards Club, *c*. 1908. It attracted many of the socializing crowds. Its premises included the island in the centre of the river, and during the late nineteenth century Maidenhead became 'the most fashionable riverside resort'. Visitors included members of the royal family.

This scene by Edward John Nieman (1813–76) was painted in 1842. It shows Boulters Lock and Ray Mill House.

Raymead and Lock Island are up-river from Boulter's Lock. Many boats still moor here while waiting to go through the lock.

Though the Thames gave enjoyment and work, the menace of the river is shown here after flooding in 1894 and 1903. A flood relief scheme has now thankfully improved the situation.

SECTION TWO

Around Bray and Holyport

The Sounding Arch, Brunel's famous bridge, carries the GWR over the Thames. This view is from the Fisheries, an upmarket housing development.

In 1890 building began on the Fisheries opposite Orkney Cottage. Annie Smith's house was the first along Bray Reach. This 1908 postcard also sends a birthday greeting.

The original showboat in Oldfield Road was a popular nightclub. Oldfield was one of the common pastures of Bray parish – a place to practise archery at the butts and later to play cricket.

Monkey Island was made famous for fishing by Charles, 3rd Duke of Marlborough. The pavilion or banqueting hall is decorated with paintings on wall panels and ceilings representing waterside flowers and plants, and these surround hundreds of monkeys engaged in hunting, fishing and shooting. The gardens are reached by a bridge and the hunting-lodge, much extended, is now a popular hotel.

Braymead was built between 1901 and 1902 by F.I. Pitman. Bought in 1922 by a syndicate, it was then established as a hotel, and music and entertainment attracted many customers to its riverside terrace and ballroom.

HOTEL-DE-PARIS, BRAY, MAIDENHEAD.

The same hotel, which by 1928 had been renamed the Hotel de Paris, Bray. It was so called after the Café de Paris in London, which shared the same owner. The hotel went into decline after the Second World War and was demolished in 1964, to be replaced by Braybank.

The landing place in Bray is a short way from Monkey Island and Bray Lock, and visitors arriving by river have a most favourable first impression of the village. The original Waterside Inn was once on the other side of the road.

The ferry at Bray, *c.* 1904. Ferry Lane has many protected buildings, some of them dating back to the fifteenth century. Ferry Cottage by the landing place was built in 1883.

Bray village in 1907 is a peaceful scene.

The lychgate of St Michael's Church, with its rooms above, has carved on it the date 1448 in arabic numerals. The church itself was founded in 1293. The card below, which has a postmark dated 1905, is titled 'Bray vicarage' but other buildings in the village have also been used for this purpose.

Bray, *c.* 1890. It was a charming riverside village with its half-timbered buildings. St Michael's Church rises above the houses. It was once a royal manor and Hundred but is probably better known for its turncoat vicar!

Ferry End, or 'Mustard Row' as it was known locally, is a row of cottages that looks much the same as when it was first built.

Hind's Head Garage, Bray, Berks.
Open and Closed Cars, Day and Night.
Manager :— PERCY HALFACRE.

The Hind's Head Garage was formerly used as stables for the fashionable hotel, the Hind's Head.

Braywick Road, 1890s, was very much a leafy lane, though it was much altered by the sports development after the Second World War. Below, the Hare and Hounds at Braywick advertised good stabling, and there are records of its existence before 1845.

Maidenhead aerodrome was opened in June 1929 but only survived a few months. These pictures show an exhibition, and the planes used were from Brooklands School of Flying. Alderman Cox, at the age of 92, took a flight.

Boys Class. Spanish Children's Home, Bray Court.

The Spanish Children's Home, Bray Court, *c.* 1938. This was a Victorian mansion that used to be on the Windsor Road. It was built for John Haig and then became a centre for social occasions. During the First World War it was turned into a hospital and then in 1928 became a school. It was later used by the government during the Second World War, and prior to its demolition it was owned by Archers the stationers.

Oakley Court was used by its neighbour, Hammer Productions, for film settings. It was erected in 1859 on ground known as Water Oakley Wharf and has now been developed as a prestige hotel. Its lawns sweep down to the river so it is fitting that this picture shows the armorial ensign of the Conservators of the River Thames.

Shoppenhangers Manor is not as old as it would appear because it only dates from 1915. However, as far back as 1288 manors have been recorded bearing this name. Charles Pascoe Grenfell purchased a manor in 1861.

This postcard shows Holyport Green, Plummer. Originally there were two ponds on the green, one providing water for firemen's pumps. The ponds were also used to soak wooden wheels so that they would swell.

The George was one of many inns at Holyport. Others included The Cricketers which closed in 1967, the Belgian Arms and The Queen.

Above, the houses to the right of the man and child remain nearly the same. The transport here is a horse and cart. In the later picture, below, seen from a different angle, the house next to the car (centre) had replaced the two houses seen above left. The post office house still stands.

Behind Holyport Lodge, which faces the green, stands the building which houses the Royal County of Berkshire Real Tennis Club. This can still be seen bearing the date 1889.

The Belgian Arms used to be called The Eagle but the name was changed when German prisoners of war, who were billeted at Philberds, began saluting the sign. The inn is thought to have been a hat maker's and until 1835 housed a Wesleyan chapel.

The Old Cottage and Elm Cottages on the right are good examples of eighteenth-century architecture and are still easily identified. The road leads down to the site of the picture below.

The Philberds in Holyport was a large house replacing the manor of Philibert, which in 1208 belonged to Roger de St Phylybert and which was destroyed by fire towards the end of the eighteenth century. The later building was so badly used during the First World War, when prisoners of war were held there, that it was pulled down in 1919. The remains of the wall and moat can still be seen a short way down from Hamble Cottage.

The Army School was founded in 1905 by E.G. Beckwith. It prepared boys for an army career and was run on public-school lines.

Ockwells Manor was built by Sir John Norreys between 1446 and 1466, using a timber frame with brick infilling. It has some famous armorial glass in its east window, and it is a fine example of a manor house of the period.

SECTION THREE

Around White Waltham and Littlewick Green

Greenwold is one of the attractive residences at Littlewick Green.

Highfield Bridge, *c.* 1891. The bridge carried the Great Western Railway, bringing people and prosperity to the area. Charles Batting's foundry, Maidenhead, built the bridges which replaced the original brick structures, while Isambard Kingdom Brunel was the engineer responsible for the construction of the railway. The Great Western Railway had been named in 1833 and the royal assent was given two years later.

Waltham Signal Box helped to ensure that the Great Western Railway ran effectively from Paddington. As early as 1824 it was decided that a link was needed between London and Bristol, and Maidenhead was once the first terminus westwards.

Waltham St Lawrence Church. The oldest parts are the walls of the nave which may date to the eleventh century.

White Waltham Church is situated on rising ground on the east side of a branch road running from the Bath Road. Bray Court Farm, the old manor house, stands opposite.

The fair at White Waltham is an annual event held in the grounds of Shottesbrooke.

The post office at White Waltham. Other names for the village have been Bury Town or Waltham Abbots.

This hanger was built by J.M. Jones and Sons of Maidenhead (1919–68). This was the first of many contracts for the Jones Company from the de Havilland Aircraft Company Ltd. in the 1930s for work at White Waltham, Harefield and Edgware.

Mr Ewers, featured in this group, was one of the local men who, together with others from British Airways and de Havillands, formed the engineering section. A ground crew consisted of nine men.

Tea-time at the airfield with Commander d'Erlanger, early 1940s. The aerodrome was built at the bottom of Cherry Garden Lane. Below, the Air Transport Auxiliary was controlled from the commodore's room and the operations block.

This historic building was the original site of the ATA until it became too small. There was also a mobile control van, distinctively painted in chequers. The picture below shows a Hudson which was used as a trainer.

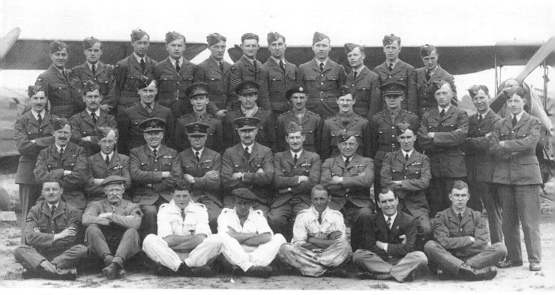

The flying instructors (second row from the front) included F.N. Scott, W.H. Maguire, H. Arnott, T.E. Wesson, B.P.A. Vallance, O.H. Lobley, A.C. Mills, W.M. Mackay, J.F. Schofield and T.D. Ainslie. In the front row, not in uniform, were the ground staff: Bill Hill, J. Ewers, M. Hutt, W. Evans and A.H. King.

An open-air service held at the airfield during the war.

Shottesbrook Church was built in 1337 by Sir William Tressel whose tomb lies in the north transept, and is situated in a manor that was owned by Alward the goldsmith in Rufus's time. Its magnificent spire is of the Decorated style of architecture and a rather unusual feature is that the nave is shorter than the chancel.

An aerial photograph of Woolley Hall, 1949. There are some noticeable features that no longer exist, such as the vegetable garden and hall chimney. The building on the bottom right became the Electricity Board's first canteen and rest-room, and an extension was built on the south-west corner at first-floor level.

Woolley Hall viewed from the south-west, 1880s.

The front gate and lodge of Woolley Hall, here shown in 1912, were replaced by William Cottingham in 1919. The gate opened on to the Bath Road.

Ivor Novello, born David Ivor Davies on 15 January 1893. The magic of his music, including 'The Dancing Years' and 'Kings Rhapsody', lives on. His home, Redroofs in Littlewick Green, was visited by many famous artists and it is said that 'We'll gather lilacs' was inspired by his love of the surrounding countryside. The house is now a stage school.

The annual Knowl Hill Steam Fair is one of the biggest of its kind in the south-east, although Appleford near Wallingford was the venue for the early steam rallies. This picture shows the impressive start to the chariot race. Enthusiasts travel many miles to

see these wonderful steam engines, and there are several other attractions, including veteran cars, farm machinery and animals. Craft skills are also demonstrated, and a good time is always had by all!

Here is a detail of a painting that was found in the stables of Woolley Hall. The picture was thought to be of a religious nature, but on cleaning it another picture was found painted underneath it. The original was by a fifteenth-century Italian artist. It was donated in 1963 to Littlewick Green and it now hangs in the Church of St John the Evangelist.

Sports Day at Littlewick, probably in the 1970s. The school, built in 1873, is still rather isolated despite its proximity to the busy A4.

SECTION FOUR

Around Burchetts Green, Hurley and Bisham

The Thicket at a tranquil stage in its history.

Now owned by the National Trust, Maidenhead Thicket once had a bad reputation as the haunt of highwaymen and robbers.

Burchetts Green took its name from the Saxon 'Byrechechurste', *hurste* meaning copse.

Burchetts Green. A small portion of this hamlet was in the parish of Hurley and the rest was in Bisham.

Burchetts Green
2715

A group of students pictured outside Hall Place when it became an agricultural college in 1948. The building still had a portico which had been added to the front entrance of the mansion but it has since been removed.

The Norman gate was demolished in 1967. It was positioned where the drive turned south towards the village of Burchetts Green.

This unusual beehouse has ten sides and is one of the finest examples of its type in England. It was restored in 1979 and is a listed building, standing in the grounds of Hall Place.

The Drawing Room, otherwise called the William East Room, has scagliola work of entwined dolphins topped by cupids, which is meant to symbolize an alliance between England and Holland. William, Prince of Orange, and his wife Anne are portrayed in stucco on the other wall.

Temple House. The hamlet of Temple took its name from the Knights Templars, who were granted the manor of Bisham during King Stephen's reign.

The Norman church at Bisham, photographed at the beginning of this century. The church has a fine tower, and the Thames flows by its graveyard.

The dining room at Bisham Abbey with its wood panelling and tapestries was built by the Knights Templars, *c.* 1150. The abbey was the seat of Sir Edward Hoby, Speaker of the Parliament of Elizabeth I. The last of the Hoby family died in 1766 and G. Vansittart bought it in 1781.

In 1947 Miss Vansittart-Neale loaned the abbey to the Council of Physical Recreation in memory of her nephews, Berkley and Guy Paget, who had been killed in the Second World War. In May 1901 Sir Henry Vansittart-Neale had discovered a tunnel leading down to the river, and another interesting feature is the 'marker stone' which dates back to neolithic times.

Bisham Church & school Children.

Schoolchildren from Bisham School stand outside the church gate, *c.* 1910. The school is one of the smallest in Berkshire and in the spring of 1893 was recorded as having ninety-seven pupils. Mr Henry Atlee was the headmaster at that time. School records go back to 1879 but there are indications that it is much older.

Bisham village has some interesting, pre-nineteenth-century buildings.

The Bull Inn 'has extended hospitality for over 650 years to royalty, nobility and commoners alike'. In the distance, the road turns sharply to the left, leading to the church and school.

The Gatehouse and church, Hurley, which remains a peaceful and lovely village, largely unspoiled by modern changes. Its position was at one time guarded by a toll cottage, situated immediately opposite the entrance to the village.

Ye Olde Bell is a gabled and timbered inn dating back to 1135. It was the original guesthouse of the monastery and remains on the same site. It was also a stopping-place for coaches, until 1890. The barn has been converted to a conference centre.

These cottages at Hurley have now been demolished. The entrance to the church hall is positioned just past the buildings on the left.

Lord Lovelace's mansion, Lady Place, was the meeting-place for Whig peers, who planned to overthrow James II and crown William of Orange in his place. The mansion was built in 1550 on the ruins of the priory and was later demolished in 1838. A secret tunnel ran to the cellars of Ye Olde Bell.

St Mary the Virgin was the church of the monastery. During Elizabeth I's reign its clergy were paid extra 'danger' money when passing through Maidenhead Thicket.

Hurley Church was consecrated in 1086 by Osmund the Good, Bishop of Sarum. The Lovelace Memorial in the church is nearly four centuries old.

The Cloisters, also called the Paradise, surrounded the original quadrangle. Hurley Priory was founded by Geoffrey de Mandeville in 1086 as a Benedictine monastery.

Two large barns and a circular dovecot, built in 1306, were formerly part of the monastic buildings.

Above, the bridge over Hurley Lock; below, the lock itself, built *c.* 1790 and called New Lock. There had been a weir in this position made from wickerwork traps. Attractive backwaters exist because the river is divided by many small islands.

Pinkneys Green post office.

St James the Less at Stubbings was erected in 1850. This postcard has the words 'Pinkney Green', and indicates that the church was formerly in this ecclesiastical parish.

Pinkneys Green is largely National Trust property. The brickworks there provided most of the materials for house-building in Maidenhead and they are believed to have existed as far back as Roman times. The Girl Guide movement was founded in Pinkneys Green by Miss Baden-Powell.

SECTION FIVE
Around Cookham

Cookham High Street.

One of the commons of Cookham parish, pictured above, is Cockmarsh which is situated between Winter Hill and Cookham village. Together with Widbrook it was designated common land by 1272 and later a grant of commons was made to the inhabitants of Cookham by Elizabeth I. In the picture below, the organ-grinder stops for a chat on Cookham Moor. Note the monkey on the top of the organ!

Above (looking east) and below (looking west) are views of Cookham High Street. Bicycles were a favourite form of transport between the wars and some fortunate people owned a motor car!

This postcard is earlier than those on the previous page. It illustrates Cookham High Street without traffic, only a solitary bicycle! There appears to be no footpath on the right, so that front doors would have opened straight on to the street. However, very little else has changed over the years.

Bel and the Dragon can be seen in the above picture. Parts of this building date from 1417 and it is one of the oldest inns to hold a licence. The restaurant is now a very popular venue.

The Tarry Stone originally marked the extent of lands owned by the Abbey of Cirencester and before it was moved it was the centre for many village activities.

The organizers of the Cookham festivities in 1911 are, standing, left to right: A.E. Flood, Col. T.J. Atherton, E. Cooper, W. Spencer (father of painter, Stanley!), C. Shergold. Seated are Col. F.C. Ricardo and the Revd A.W. Batchelor.

F. Chalfont had a cycle- and motor-sales shop on the Pound. This picture, *c.* 1910, shows three forms of transport – car, motorcycle and bicycle.

Cookham Dean Church

Cookham Dean Church and School were built on land which had been part of Cookham Dean Common. The land was given by Mrs Vansittart of Bisham Abbey who was Lord of the Manor of Cookham, and thanks to the great endeavour of Revd George Hodson the church was partly built by public subscription. The foundation stone of the church was laid on 24 June 1844, and the building was consecrated on 15 May 1845 and dedicated to St John the Baptist. The Revd Hodson became the first vicar, and he stayed in Cookham Dean until 1869. The school was built about fifty years after the church.

CKD.5   THE WAR MEMORIAL AND CRICKET PITCH, COOKHAM DEAN

The forge in Cookham Dean Bottom was worked by Harry Hunt from 1880, and this picture, *c.* 1889, shows the site before the pond was filled in. The old well was also slabbed over like those at Lea Farm and at the foot of Well Hill. Hunt was succeeded by James Howard and then Harry Crockford.

Behind the house on the right was Carmonta Bakery, which was very much in the centre of Cookham Dean, with Curell's Garage opposite and the church nearby. W.T. Deadman was the baker there until 1952, followed by his son Kenneth, but the bakery closed in 1957.

Cookham Dean School was opposite the bakery seen in the previous picture, and can still be found behind the present garage building. The Usher twins, Agnes and Marian, and Nellie Bishop are the small group seen here, *c.* 1902.

Cookham Dean Platoon (Maidenhead) Battn. Home Guard, September 1941. K. Deadman is seventh from the right, back row.

As with all riverside villages and towns, the water has played an important part in the life of Cookham. It has brought both disaster and good fortune. Flooding in the past has covered the commons and moor, but the River Thames has also provided work in the wharf at Hedsor, as well as good fishing. In 1840 the wooden bridge proved to be unsafe as the timbers were rotting and it was replaced by an iron toll-bridge within thirty years. In this picture the Revd Scott is seen with his son by the ferry.

A pleasant Sunday afternoon can still be spent watching the decorated pleasure-boats and their passengers passing through Cookham Lock. There are many more craft on the river now.

This picture of the toll-gate is dated 1946. The toll-gate was on the Buckinghamshire side of the river and all traffic passing through paid the toll to the man who lived in the small house next to the bridge.

Cookham Lock was opened in 1830, following many accidents on the river as a result of navigational difficulties of the barges.

As well as working barges, there have always been canoes and punts for hire and nowadays motor boats, too.

The ferryman rows passengers across the river. It looks as though it was a brilliant summer's day when this photograph was taken as the men are in their shirt sleeves.

Islands were formed by streams flowing from the River Thames near Cookham Bridge. They are said to be named after the Danish Odin, as in 1896 a Danish stone battleaxe was found near the millwheel of the stream which divides the two islands we know as Odney. The Odney Club now occupies the area, but during the Second World War the American Army used Lullebrook Manor. Its officers occupied the large house, while Red Cross workers were billeted in the village.

Formosa is the largest island on the Thames. Sir Graham Young had his home there, built with timbers from a ship, but unfortunately it was destroyed by fire.

Quarry Woods provided a passageway from the 'miracle' spring near Bisham through Wool Lane to Cookham, via Grubwood Lane and Kings Coppice Farm.

The royal manor of Cookham covered the same area as the old parish which originally extended from Bisham to the river at Maidenhead Bridge, including Cookham Dean and Cookham Rise. In 1818 George Bangley bought the manor from the Crown and at this time many large estates were divided and new houses built. Much later Odney Estates Ltd bought the lordship of the manor and in 1934 the National Trust took over the commons.

This scene today has changed little from this picture, *c.* 1930. Although the road is wider, the houses still stand and the Gatehouse can be seen in the distance at the road junction.

This photograph likewise shows how little altered is the pretty village of Cookham. A stroll can still be enjoyed from the High Street, through the churchyard and along the riverbank.

Personalities and Events

Ivor Novello at a garden party, thought to have been held in Elendene, Cookham Road, during the 1950s.

The *Maidenhead Advertiser*, spanning six reigns, contains the history and development of the town in its records. This unusual 'personality gallery' was printed in the centenary edition of the paper, 1969. Some of the people identified by present personnel are: Louis Baylis, Norman Baylis, Tom Middleton, Mike Colton, Don Seal, Gerald Baylis, Dick Easton, Colin Bowerman, Phyllis Neale, Cheryl Lump, Tony Anderson, Ron Cordon, George Stewart, Derek Gale, Florrie Attfield, Kath Hight, Sidney Horsham, Jim Brown, Bruce Powell, Pat Hill, Dennis Hill, Robin Maguire, Frank Stevens, Eric Addis, Ron Holmes, Harry Carter, 'Buzzer Bee' (Derek), George Lawrence, Terry Haines, John King, Les Hemmingway, Stan Woods, Harry Coleman, Garry Craythorne, Cecil Norman and Trevor Woodward.

Wesley Walker, who wrote *The History of Maidenhead*, 1909. He was the forerunner of others who have continued to research and record local history.

Tom Middleton was the editor of the *Maidenhead Advertiser* for twenty-six years. His books on Maidenhead give a pictorial history that has been difficult to match.

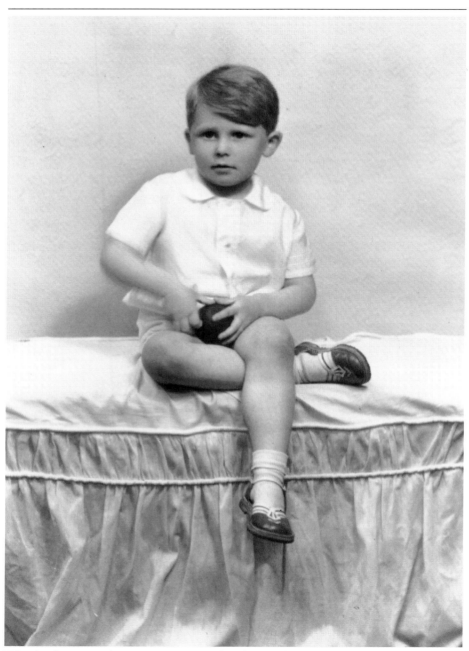

Who is this appealing young man? The clue is that he ranks with the previous gentlemen for his knowledge of the area. Everyone who is interested in local history should recognize the name – Luke Over.

Victorian Maidenhead can be seen in the many photographs taken by local photographers George Gude, Norman Greville and others. These, of the Bates family, are typical of the records that have come to light during the compilation of this book.

The 1891 Perambulation carried on the tradition of showing where the boundary of Maidenhead lay. Ancient stones and landmarks were checked and the boys beat them with flagged poles. Pictured below, 'Beating of the Bounds' in 1909 followed the same pattern. Mark Taylor is centre left in his town crier's uniform.

Lord Desborough inspects the 1st Battalion Berkshire Voluntary Defence Regiment, 1916. Many brave men from Maidenhead volunteered for this battalion, and some did not return from the Western Front.

Serving in the RAMC were members of the St John Ambulance Brigade from Maidenhead. Shown here are: (back row) W. Hare, W. Saunders, S. Hatch; (seated) A.W. Taylor, N. Moorcroft, T. Wetherall.

Lord Desborough hosted a reception for Maidenhead Corporation and neighbouring mayors, 30 July 1935. Those present included Alderman Cox, Councillor W. Thomas (Mayor), Alderman A. Upson, L.R.F. Oldershaw, W. Archer, E.B. Norris and H.H. Neve.

The Grenfell family, pictured in 1909. In the back row are Monica and Lord Desborough. In the front row, left to right, are Billy, Ivo, Lady Desborough, Julian and Imogen. Tragically, two sons died in the First World War and the third in a motoring accident. William Henry Grenfell inherited Taplow Court in 1867 at the age of eleven. He was actively involved in politics and sport, and was a generous benefactor, especially to Maidenhead. Pictured below, c. 1909, is the dining room where in later years his wife, Ettie, a renowned hostess, would entertain her guests.

Following the death of Queen Victoria in 1901 business was suspended throughout the country. Seen here is a gathering to celebrate the coronation of Edward VII. The *Maidenhead Advertiser* reported that the king adopted this title so that his real name, Albert, would be associated only with his father.

Maidenhead and District Sailors and Soldiers Recognition Day, 1919. A parade assembled at the moor, then marched through the town to Kidwells Park, accompanied by a military band. There, sports were played, followed by dinner at the cricket field. The day ended with a concert and a torchlight procession with fireworks.

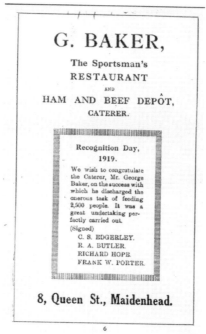

G. BAKER,

The Sportsman's
RESTAURANT
AND
HAM AND BEEF DEPÔT,
CATERER.

Recognition Day,
1919.

We wish to congratulate the Caterer, Mr. George Baker, on the success with which he discharged the onerous task of feeding 2,500 people. It was a great undertaking perfectly carried out.

(Signed)
C. S. EDGERLEY.
R. A. BUTLER.
RICHARD HOPE.
FRANK W. PORTER.

8, Queen St., Maidenhead.

6

A High Street celebration for Queen Victoria's Diamond Jubilee, 1897. The Falcon Inn at No. 92 (centre left) has been replaced by Barclays Bank.

In this picture, from 1966, the Bowling Club committee and officers were: J. Carter, E.F. Halfacre, M. Huckins, F. Green, L.S. Moore, H.C. Distin, A.W. Bennett, S.G. Potter, A.J. Hooper, S.H. Lovegrove, G.M. Thatcher, L.E. Arter, W.F.C. Mead and R. Mortimer. Missing from the line-up are W.F. Reid, H. Davenport and J.A. Kemp.

Here the officers were Sir Ernest Gardiner, MP, Captain Henry Hoare, N. Naylor and Mr Barley. The annual subscription then was 12s 6d.

The Berkshire District Folk Dance Group at Bisham Abbey in the 1950s. Among the group are John and Adeline Finch, Molly Claydon, Sam and Enid Vickers.

Here, Paddy O'Neill is raised in the air as the finale to a country dance.

Playing the 'fiddle' for the dancers is Sam Vickers.

Here Sir Stanley Spencer works on one of his treasured paintings. He supported many local functions in Cookham, and below, he is receiving a Christmas decoration from Grace Johnson. It was at a Christmas bazaar that he drew a self-portrait.

Tables in Cookham High Street are laid out with Union Jacks to celebrate the Silver Jubilee, 1977. Surely the whole of the village must have turned out for this event!

The Silver Jubilee celebrations at Holyport and Bisham. The twin towns of Bad Godesburg, Frascati and Saint Cloud all joined in.

At Littlewick Green the 1977 Silver Jubilee celebration for Elizabeth II closely followed the Queen Victoria Diamond Jubilee programme. Below, the Revd. Bruce Hartnell looks at the poster for 1897.

A float from a hospital pageant in the 1930s. These 'Bisto Kids' were members of the Wednesday Club who met in Brock Lane. They include Eva and Peggy Fuller, Enid Bullock and Alice Turk.

Cookham Arts Club selection committee from the late 1940s included Henry Trivick, Victor Clark, Bay Robinson, Bert Felstead, Thelma Carstenton and Frank Sherwin. Showing the painting is Mr Philips.

Odney pottery club in the late 1940s. John Bev (centre) ran the John Lewis's evening classes. Also pictured are Les Knight (left), Ray Davis (front), Mr Spindler and George Body (right).

Celebrations at Moor Hall for Gaumont British, which made cartoon films. David Hand, seen here cutting the cake, was involved in the making of *Snow White*. Also present were Mr Stringer, Bert Felstead, Pat Griffin and Ralph Ayres.

The cast of the pantomime *Jack and the Beanstalk*, performed in 1953 in Pinder Hall, Cookham. Some well-known names include Jean Felstead, Moyra and Ann Hutchinson, Peter and Jean Gigg, Sara and Elizabeth Smyth, Celia Wetherall, Charles Elly, Mary Ash and Dierdre Blaney. The pantomime was produced by Bert Felstead and Christine Millard. The first pantomime was performed in 1951 by the art club and the next in 1952 by the British Legion. Pinder Hall has been the venue of many first-class shows, with casts made up of local people.

For over five hundred years the sovereign's swan-master with the Vintners and Dyers Companies have rowed the river marking the swans and cygnets which belong to them.

Braywood Memorial Hall in 1973 with Mr Raymond 'Teasy Weasy'. Several villagers acted as models in the show. Mrs Mary Snow is seen here sitting between 'Teasy Weasy' and his wife Rosalie.

The turf cutting ceremony for Cox Green Community Hall in February 1976. Margaret Brill (member of the Cox Green Youth Club), Revd. D.J. Cawte (Priest Missioner of the Church of the Good Shepherd), and Mr Clive Bullock (Chairman of the Community Association) have been identified in this picture.

Acknowledgements

Although many of the postcards and photographs reproduced in this book are from our own collections we must acknowledge with thanks the help from local friends and organizations in its compilation – especially the following: Maidenhead Reference Library, in particular P. Dobby, J. Fox, S. Gogna and R. Thomas; the *Maidenhead Advertiser* – David Ranger, the editor and May Powell, the librarian; Margaret Smith of Reading Public Library; the sales manager of Berkshire Library and Information Service, N. Bond; B. Brinkley; E. Burden; Angela Bolger of SGI UK, Taplow Court; John Davidson of Miscellania; T. Deadman of the Thames and District Cycling Club; Miss Dickinson, Lord of the Manor of Bisham; Heather Evans and Mr and Mrs Baines of Hall Place, Berkshire College of Agriculture; Mr and Mrs Ewers; Mrs Jean Hedger; Luke Over; Mrs P. Knight; Mrs E. Vickers; Diana Cook of Richard Way, bookseller of Henley.

We have made every effort to establish copyright and have obtained permission to reproduce when required, but if we have inadvertently omitted to do so for any photograph we offer our sincere apologies.

Lastly, for their patience and support, we thank our respective families.